The Life of a Village Child
An Autobiography of a Medical Doctor

by

Francis Saa-Gandi

DORRANCE PUBLISHING CO., INC.
PITTSBURGH, PENNSYLVANIA 15222

Dorrance Publishing Co., Inc.
701 Smithfield Street
Pittsburgh, PA 15222
Visit our website at *www.dorrancebookstore.com*

ISBN: 978-1-4349-1247-3
eISBN: 978-1-4349-3961-6

Dedication

I dedicate this book to Bernadette, my wife;
George, my other father, Sumoe (died) my son; and Sia, my
daughter.

Acknowledgments

I wish to thank my second parents, particularly John O'Connor, Pa Harry Fillie, Mr. James Duke, and George Vellacott. I wish they could be paid in kindness as originally intended. They have, however, made it possible for me to help others.

I wish to thank my mentors: Alan Mearns, Peter Jones, and Georgina Turner-Pelling.

I would also like to thank Dr. Erdenetsetseg Gotov and her daughter, Otgontungalag Sainbayar, for helping me to design the cover page.

Contents

Part Three: Undergraduate Education

Part Four: Postgraduate Education

Part Five: Trinidad

Introduction

There is evidence in English literature to suggest that daily diaries have been written since the beginning of time. People who write, maintain, and keep daily diaries come in different forms—shape and size, race and gender. The reasons for doing so are just as varied—thinking aloud or recording a particular period in the diarist's life. However, are diaries written for public consumption or for the writer's "own eyes only"?

My interest in diary keeping coincided with my stamp collection, which I started when I was about eight years of age. I had no father or mother or a guardian at any one time with whom I could identify. I became fascinated with stamps and started collecting them. The collection became more varied when Sierra Leone (Sa Leone) became independent from Britain but remained as a member of the British Commonwealth in 1961. The stamps were colourful, mainly portraying the wildlife of Sa Leone. I glued the stamps in an exercise book with some information as to how they came to hand. This was the beginning of my diary writing.

The writing started purely as a record of people who gave me food from day to day. I had hoped that when "I grew up, I would repay all these people who were kind to me." However, by the time I arrived in Segbwema from Kayima via Fanema, Seidu, Yomandu, and Yengema, the style had changed; the jottings encompassed people and events. I maintained this approach until my entry to secondary school in Ireland. From thereon, the writings became heavily tinged with examination results—passes and failures.

I would have been handicapped, greatly handicapped, in writing this autobiography if I did not write these diaries. I read from somewhere that "It is our parents, normally, who not only teach us our family history but who set us straight on our own childhood recollections...." Therefore, I would like to be forgiven for any misconception I may have held about people and events, as they arose purely from observations rather than by instructions. My role models were numerous. This is more apparent in the chapter on "early years." This was probably what made me a child of two parents—biological and physical.

"By some miracle, you have managed to safeguard all these diaries. Why don't you put them together in the form of an autobiography?" my wife once commented to me. George, my physical father, echoed this independently. It was like a shot in the arm. An autobiography would be one way of remaking my life story and for me to tell it in my own way. I could not contact some of the people who were involved in the making of my life. I wanted their permission to be included in this book. Therefore, some of the names are fictitious and others not mentioned.

The ball is now in my court. According to William Bligh in *Mutiny on the Bounty,* you "set your goal; figure out what you must do to reach it; and get to work." This book is the result of these pieces of advice from my father, George; my wife, Bernadette; and from books.

Part One

The Early Years

Chapter 1

The Early Years

My mother ran away from home with my two brothers and me.
Tamba and Aiah died from childhood infection. Grandpa and
Grandma sent for me.

"Today is your seventh birthday," Grandma Feeyo told me one day.

Grandma Feeyo was the older sister of my mother. I grew up to call her so instead of Auntie. She was much older than my mother and looked like a grandma.

"But you cannot read or write. My date of birth is written in English. How do you know my age?"

We were both sitting under an overhanging rock, which sheltered us from the heavy rainfall. Before the interruption we had been picking peanuts since the break of dawn. The trees had begun casting their shadows in the southerly direction.

"Seven years today, your mother and I sat under this same rock, picking peanuts just as we are doing now," she continued. "Then she went into labour but your father wanted you to be delivered in a hospital. Yengema was the nearest hospital and luckily, there was a Land Rover collecting passengers outside Pa Bayoh's shop leaving for Sefadu. You grew up with me until three years of age, when your father came to take you away to Sefadu. However, within a year your mother came back with you and your two brothers."

I became curious and inpatient and interrupted, "But you still haven't told me how you know my age."

She took her time and went on, "Custom has it that one does not cultivate the same land within seven years. This is to allow the soil to mature and be ready for growing rice again. As you know, we have just completed harvesting rice at the end of the dry season. We planted the groundnut six weeks later. The nuts become matured in three months' time, when we eat them raw or dry them to produce oil or cook them with fish. This is how I knew you are seven years of age."

This is how I grew up to know about life in Kayima; grown-ups passed their knowledge by word of mouth but nothing documented. Important names and dates of births are remembered in relation to major events like the eclipse of the sun, flooding, and crowning of a chief. In the Kono tribe, the naming of new babies followed a simple formula. For instance, I was named Saa Wee at birth. "Saa" (same as Sahr) means "first boy-child." "Wee" is a "small clever bush fowl," which, as noted, was only caught by the most skillful trappers.

My mother left (or ran away from) home with me and my two younger brothers. I do remember my brothers (Tamba and Aiah), who died in their second and first years of life respectively. A week after arrival in Kayima, according to Grandma Feeyo, my brothers and I contracted high fevers accompanied by swollen glands from which my brothers died. "You survived but were left with a cough. Your mother did not think she could look after you and so your Uncle Tamba took you to your grandpa and grandma in Fanema."

I do remember vividly when Uncle Tamba came to collect me from Kayima. He arrived with a bag of rice just before darkness set in, but the night was shining bright with the full moon. Just at the crack of dawn, we were off to Fanema. We walked along the road that leads to Wordu, where vehicles stopped. From this point on he carried me on his shoulders seated behind his neck. He only let me down as we entered the next village. The sun was up but we were now on a dirt track and the big branches protected us from its rays. The noises produced by different creatures (frogs, crickets, bats) became displaced by a new set of noises (from monkeys, pigeons, doves, parrots). As the journey progressed, Uncle Tamba told me stories interrupted by singing. We finally arrived at our destination just when the moon was getting up on its round trip.

I have never met my new parents before. Grandma Fembawa (Femba) bore some semblance to my mother. She was a medium-sized lady and within a flash, she picked me up. She sat me on her laps and started counting my ribs. She remarked, "You are all bones, young man. No wonder they named you Saa Wee." She hugged and kissed me and continued, "You need to be washed, fed, and put to bed."

Grandpa was eagerly waiting for his turn. He smoked locally made tobacco in a clay pipe.

Grandpa Tachesumoe (a walker in Kono) was tall, muscular, and strong. His other name was Joemende but he was less often called by it. He let me stand by him while he sat in his chair, which was handmade from wood and cane. The "nails" used to assemble the chair were made from the palm tree.

With the fingers from his left hand running in my hair, he gently announced, "We are going to put some flesh on you and make a man of you."

Other family members asked me questions about Kayima and travel. Grandma washed me using a soap she had made herself. She gave me food served in a bowl of calabash (made from the shell of the fruit).

"This child has an ungrateful stomach," Grandma exclaimed. "He eats like his namesake, Wee," she continued.

I was tired and sleepy and so Grandma took me to my bed. The bed was a dried cow skin placed on the floor next to her bed. I was up early on the sound of the "clock bird" and out of the house to explore my new surroundings. Our compound formed the centre of the village. Grandpa and Grandma lived here with three of his wives. He also owned four more houses occupied by one or two of his wives.

At the time of my arrival in Fanema, I was the only child in the household. However, there were a lot of other children around about my age but from different families. All the children disappeared during the day with their parents to go to their respective farms. In the evening they reappeared. The village became alive again with us children playing hide-and-seek. As for the grown-ups, they sat and talked until bedtime.

Grandpa was the chief of the Kawama Section in the Sando Chiefdom. He succeeded his "older brother named N'Gandi, who had died years ago." He walked with a stick. The stick was not used to support him, but he carried it for many other reasons. He used the stick to make decisions in court cases, to scare away snakes and other unwanted creatures; he used it to maneuver a lit charcoal into his pipe to which he had become addicted.

The list went on. He was a born land surveyor. He was credited for the creation of majority of the roads between the villages in his section and those linking to others. His biggest achievement before his death was to define the road between Wordu and Fanema. This was partly realized when four-wheel drives were able to drive just within scores of miles from Fanema. I lived with them for two years and during this period, I was greatly influenced by Grandpa, Grandma, and Uncle Tamba.

Uncle Tamba was one of Grandpa's sons. He lived in one of the houses built for Grandma, his mother. He had no wife (an exception in my village) or children (again, an exception). He seemed to enjoy being alone and among other characteristics, he was highly respected by everybody in the village. He had a younger brother, Kai Joemende, who went to school in Kayima. Uncle Tamba resembled Grandma more than Grandpa. He was smaller than Grandpa in physique but equally strong. I rotated my time between his farms, Grandpa's short travels to the surrounding villages, and Grandma's feeding sessions.

Grandpa took me with him on his errands in the section under his domain. He was wealthy but not financially rich. He was never paid with money but rather supported by his subjects with food (including rice, fish, and meat). On his side of the bargain, he settled disputes between his subjects, coordinated the killing of animals that kill domestic animals or attacked humans. The most notorious of these maneating animals was the leopard. The chief also coordinated the rebuilding of houses, which may have been destroyed by fire or strong wind. He ensured that the head of each household paid taxes to the government. What used to hold almost all my attention was his ability to solve dispute between two parties. On listening to both sides of the story, he would make the final judgment with his pipe in his left hand and walking stick in the right. His decision was final and all parties seemed satisfied with it. My people had an explanation for everything that happened to people. One day a lady went to fetch water from the river in a big opened container. A few yards from home, she started trembling and shaking violently. Every drop of water spilled and they blamed the demon for the phenomenon. This was, in fact, Huntington's disease, a sudden onset of uncontrollable tremor.

For whatever reason, Uncle Tamba always wanted me to be with him. He would take me to his farm. He had cleared an area of swamp for the next crop of rice. A piece of swamp occupying a fraction of his main farm provided special rice sought after by the town people. For me, it was an excellent ground to play. It attracted all sorts of creatures, including insects like dragonflies, butterflies and wasps, snakes that chased frogs, and fast-moving red crabs. "The swamp was fed by a small pond, which in turn got its supply from an underground stream," according to Uncle Tamba. I would spend hours chasing and catching those crabs, trapping frogs that had been exposed from their hiding places by green and black snakes. Later in the day, we (or should I say he) stopped for lunch. During lunch, he told me stories in the middle of which he dropped to sleep.

Grandma's main preoccupation was "to get some flesh on my bones." She never allowed me to play with the other children before I had my belly filled with food. After a few hours of play, she would get me inside for more food. We stayed friends during feeding, while being cleaned and when she told me stories. However, hell broke loose when she decided to shave my head. All was fine until she got to the back of my head, the most painful part of my body. I will scream the whole village down. My screaming and kicking was no match to her strength. She pinned me down between her thighs.

We became friends at the end of it all. It was at my advantage in any case; no need to comb the hair and avoidance of the boiled leaves she used to get rid of my head lice. The concoction was painful and it always made me pee on my feet. Grandma enjoyed shaving my head. I concluded at the end that she did it to find out whether I was putting on weight or getting stronger. She could have asked my uncle or any of Grandpa's men to do it with no resistance from any of them. The other many things Grandma did for me was to dry out my wet bed (cow skin) in the sun. She was also an important person in the village because many people visited her from and outside the village. She was the folk tribal doctor. She anointed the girls during their initiation ceremonies.

Life continued to be a joy in Fanema around Grandpa, Grandma, and Uncle Tamba. After two years with them, Grandpa came back home one evening from Kayima with news from Uncle Sahr Joseph Wilson Gandi (SJW). He was going to send me to school. Within two weeks, Uncle Tamba and I were on the road again but in the opposite direction. It took us a day and a morning's walk to get back to Kayima. This time around, Uncle Tamba had to cope with a bag of rice. We arrived safely at our destination.

I met Uncle SJW, my two aunts, cousins, and more uncles. My mother was happy to see me but watched me most of the time from the distance. The main house was huge, which had a large box sitting in the corner of the parlour. From this box came voices and music. I learned later on that the box was called a radio.

Chapter 2

Primary Class 1 in Kayima

Uncle Samuel Gandi took N'Gundia, Joseph, and me to school. I gained double promotion to Standard 1, but that never materialized.

On the morning of school, I was well dressed up in my khaki shorts and blue shirt. The Evangelical United Brethren (EUB) School was less than ten minutes' walk from home. That morning, Uncle Samuel Gandi led us to school—N'Gundia on his left, Joseph to his right, and Yours Truly to the right of the latter. The trip took us down a hill, over a little bridge and a gentle incline up to the school. On each side of this lane was a row of tall mango trees at the foot of which were shallow gutters heading straight back to the stream we had just crossed. We spent the first two days of school making new friends and chasing each other. There were other girls other than N'Gundia. The whole journey must have taken us about fifteen minutes. My teacher was Mr. Sahr Yarjah.

There were three school buildings and a three-bedroom house for the headmaster and his family. There was no assembly hall or a headmaster's office. Each school building accommodated two classes, each class facing the opposite way. The boundaries of the school were blurred. In the easterly direction, it was bounded by a stream, which finally emptied into River Kaiso. This boundary was completed by a large swamp, which fed the stream. In the opposite direction was the Guava Mountain. The all-purpose Kaiso River occupied completely the northern boundary. Kayima got its name from this river, but some older people taught us that the town's name came from a much smaller river called Kayi, located some six miles away.

At home, there were many people. My mom was the only person I recognized. She arrived in the morning to clean and helped Auntie Kumba Lansana (N'Gundia's mom) to cook for everybody and then left in the evening. Komba and I were assigned a room while N'Gundia shared her mom's room. Mama Kumba, the senior wife, shared her husband's room. Our compound was a protected community. The main house was in front and a larger one at the back. This back house had many rooms, which accommodated many relatives, visitors, and a shop (not in use). The shop was similar, in usage, to a self-contained flat to be rented out at any time. They were joined to each other on the eastern side by a mud wall. A spacious kitchen occupied most of the northern part of the compound. Sitting next to the kitchen entrance was a huge cupboard kept topped up with rice brought by visitors. Next to this was a little house, which housed an electric generator (the only one in the village). The compound was completed by another small house with two latrines and two other rooms each for taking bucket baths.

In school we learned the English alphabet and numbers. We each had a black slate (breakable) onto which we copied what the teacher wrote on his blackboard. We used white chalk given to us by the teacher at the start of each class. He collected "all the remnants" at the end of each class. However, writings on walls all over the village were commonly seen.

I had done well at the end of Class 1 and was recommended for Double Promotion to Standard 1. This was not to be. Joseph failed his promotional examination and was kept in Class 1. N'Gundia passed to Class 2. This would have meant leaving my sister and brother behind. Therefore, I moved to Class 2 with N'Gundia.

Chapter 3
Primary Class 2 in Kayima

N'Gundia broke her arm. Uncle SJW and family left Kayima.

The new school year started after the long Christmas holidays. We did not celebrate Christmas in Kayima. The majority of the folks were animists who believed in the spirit of the dead. A good number of other people practised Islam, a much easier religion to practise. Grown-ups were Muslims and they did not have to go to school. Therefore, parents were either one or the other or both. Christianity was only for the educated; therefore, it was restricted to teachers and pupils. The Christians changed our names to Francis, Samuel, and Joseph, and so on after baptism in some cases. Others voluntarily adopted the names.

The month of December was a time of plenty and many activities. It was the time young boys and girls joined respective secret or rather initiation societies. Boys had circumcisions in their society but no one, at least in my age group, knew what happened to girls in their club. However, we knew that at the end of the initiation they could marry and have children. The girls' event was electrifying.

Kayima became alive, full of excitement. New faces appeared from nowhere. The community was mostly subsistent farmers whose main concern was with the season and what it brought with it. There was new rice steamed, partially pounded to remove the chaff and then dried. This with other goodies (dried fish, smoked meat) was displayed by the initiating girl's mat and guarded by a woman plaiting her hair. We, the little boys, would grab a handful of anything on offer. One of the women would halfheartedly chase us away and shout out our names after us. The air was full of sounds of skin and log drums and traditional songs.

After all of this excitement, one would have thought that starting in a new class would have been difficult. The motivation to learn was too strong. Almost all the children came from all over Sando Chiefdom of similar backgrounds and therefore similar goals: to learn the three R's (reading, writing, and arithmetic).

Unfortunately, Uncle SJW left Kayima with the rest of his family before the end of Class 2. The departure also coincided with N'Gundia breaking her arm after a fall. She had to leave for the hospital. During the time of my schooling, mom was the housekeeper at my uncle's home. Uncle SJW's transfer "marked the end of schooling for Joseph and me from next year." Joseph went to live with his family in Fanema. My mother brought me home to her sister, Feeyo, with whom we had lived before. We later moved to live with Uncle Aiah Monde, who eventually became my stepfather.

My father was a carpenter and literally lived from hand to mouth. His house had three bedrooms. One room, occupied by his youngest brother, Kai, opened into the living area (my room). Each of the other two rooms opened directly onto the veranda. He occupied one of the rooms with my mother. The third room, temporarily unoccupied, was for his older brother, Tamba, who occasionally visited Kayima from a small diamond town, Peyima.

My father was alphabetical, but he knew how to measure lengths because he was a carpenter, especially in putting on roofing of houses in Kayima and surrounding villages. He was not a rich man. His job, like most other "professionals, brought little financial gain but the rewards were by barter trade." We were never good friends but we did not hate each other.

Opposite our house lived the James' family. Mr. Komba James was a retired army officer from Freetown and now lived in Yormandu as a diamond miner. He was married to two of my father's sisters, Satta and Finda. He had one son and two surviving daughters with the older sister, Satta. He had no children with Auntie Finda. Living with them was my new grandmother, Femba, with a swelling in the neck. Uncle James never lived there but came occasionally to visit.

Uncle James, like all army officers, was a no-nonsense man. He was physically and mentally strong and a great disciplinarian. He built his house by himself. After school, I spent a lot of my spare time with him. He often asked me to help him do work on the building. He was pleasant but lost his temper quickly. One day while assisting him, he realized that I was not concentrating. He allowed one end of the wooden planks to roll onto my abdomen, sustaining a superficial wound above my navel. "You must always concentrate when you have dangerous objects in your hands," he rebutted.

I took to swimming and exploring the outskirts of Kayima, playing soccer and, above all, reading. I read everything I laid my hands on.

For all children, the question of "to swim or not to swim" never arose. All children, particularly those coming from the surrounding villages, swam. In the rainy season, it was not uncommon for a bridge to be washed away by a flood overnight, and we had to get to the other side of the river by swimming.

I visited Grandpa Joemende when he came down to Kayima to update PC Fasuluku about events in his section. During each visit, he stayed in his designated room at Uncle Kaimondo's house. I was very fond of him; he was calm and cool in his demeanour. Of course, I visited Grandma Feeyo often because she was always available for me. There was always something to eat by her. I was also her only child because her children had fully grown and all had left home.

It was towards the end of this year I became infatuated with postage stamps.

Mr. Komba Semba and I became instant friends. I also liked him because of the many stories picked up in his journeys between the two towns some hundred miles apart. He was responsible for collecting the mails from Sefadu (Koidu Town) and delivering them to Kayima. He could not read or write, but he knew that the stamps were responsible for his survival.

"A letter or parcel must have a stamp on it for delivery."

"Where do you get the stamps from?" I became curious.

"You buy them from the post office. They are no longer valuable once stamped by the clerk."

From henceforth, I decided to collect stamps. I had hoped that one day I would stumble on an unused stamp, which I would use to write overseas.

Chapter 4
Standard 1 in Kayima

Uncle James paid my school fees. Uncle Kai died.

On the last day of each school year, everybody gathered at the court hall. The gathering included students, teachers, parents and guardians, councillors/elders, PC Fasuluku, and other well wishers. The pupils and their teachers sat facing PC and other important people. The rest of the gathering sat behind the children and their teachers. The teachers announced the final year examination results for each class. It was a great occasion but not as exciting as the initiation ceremonies. The get-together ended with two sets of children. One group (the majority) full of joy and smiles passed for their next class. The second group (small number), who belonged to the "hold-back" group, failed to make the grade—50 percent. I passed for my next class.

The transition from Class 2 to Standard 1 was traumatic. Firstly, neither of my parents could read or write. The situation became further complicated by the loss of support from Uncle SJW, though scarce, and the sibling rivalry. N'Gundia, Komba, and I talked a lot about new things we learned from school. I was now on my own.

In the new class, they allowed us to write with pencil in a ruled exercise book. At the end of Class 2, we had washed our black slates and had them painted for the incoming class. My new class teacher was Mr. T W Johnny, who had just arrived from Wordu Primary School. The transfer to Kayima was a promotion for Mr. TWJ. He was not impressed with my handling of pencil and paper, but I was good with my slate and chalk. This was a dilemma for him and his solution was to demote me to Class 2. However, Mr. Sahr Yarjah, my previous teacher, did not agree. I heard him say to the headmaster that "he was one of my best students. Therefore, sending him back to me will be a waste of time for both of us." Henceforth, I stayed in Mr. TWJ's class but the relationship was never cordial.

He came in late one morning from the rains. He had his Wellingtons (rain boots, we call them) on. Prior to his appearing at the door, the class was quiet but some of us were not seated on our benches. Those of us out of our benches moved instantly to our respective seats. He pointed me to his desk.

He carefully laid his books and other teaching materials on the desk as I stood before him with my hands behind me. He ordered me to get under his table and started teaching. Just before the end of the period, I accidentally touched one of his feet. He bent over and asked, "Are you still here?" There were many other instances to follow. "Stand in the corner for making noise." I failed the comb test almost every morning.

To have the hair combed was one of the requirements to attend classes. As part of his health inspection (called hygiene), the teacher checked the hair, teeth, fingernails, and legs. He passed the sharpened end of a pencil through the student's hair and if he encountered no resistance, "you pass." I hated combing my hair, and this weakness haunted me throughout my school days.

My being in Standard 1 at all was a miracle or accidental. I had no one to pay my school fees following the transfer of Uncle SJW. As luck would have it, though, Mr. James was visiting his family a week or so before the start of the new school year. He heard about my situation and offered to pay my school fee. The amount was one pound and ten shillings. That was how I managed to get into my present class.

On the first day of school reopening, I went to school but this time with a difference. Like two years previously, when Uncle SWG took my cousins and me to school, I took Sahr James to school. He hung on to my left hand tightly as we approached the school. It took us about thirty minutes to reach the school.

Sahr had many characteristics similar to his father—strong and powerful. He played soccer with his left foot but did everything else with his right. Within a week of starting school, he won the wrestling tournament in his age group. He became very fond of me and tried to copy everything I did. Despite his efforts to emulate me, we remained poles apart. "I will forgive and forget." Sahr, on the other hand, "never let go once he got his teeth into something." He won every case against me.

On occasion, I would get into a quarrel with him or cheat him at his share of our lunch. Before the end of the school day, we were friends again, at least from my side of the relationship. A day or two later, we would be summoned by one of the grown-ups, often my father. Sahr had made a complaint. During the inquisition, Sahr listened carefully and quietly without interrupting my response. When he responded, it was with precision and, of course, I interrupted him many times but to no avail. The result was a scolding or beating for me.

I enjoyed going to school. I was never late for school and attended all the classes. Mom was home to cook and looked after my sister, Sia, who was now two years of age. After school, I roamed the town with my classmate Sahr Komba. In the evenings, I studied in one of the living rooms of Retired Major Sankor.

Pa Sankor was a powerful man in the chiefdom. He had at least three houses in his compound. He seemed to have great value in education as indicated by many of his children being in school. He had a big hurricane gas lamp placed in the middle of a huge table. One could see a fly in every corner of the room. Pa Sankor was a very generous man. He allowed all willing children (his and those of the neighbours) to study and do their homework in his house. Whenever the opportunity became available, I took it to study and do my homework.

Work at school remained above average. Mr. TWJ started to take more interest in me. He visited my home often to make sure I did my homework and wasn't involved in mischief. Unfortunately as time went on, I used home as an occasional sleeping spot and overnight at my friends' homes. Sahr Komba, Sahr M'Bawa, and I became good friends. Ironically, we spoke little about schoolwork. Sahr Komba (SK) lived with his grandmother in a big house. His father was a diamond miner living with his second wife in Yormandu. Like Mr. James, he came home occasionally to visit. Sahr M'Bawa (SM) was in a similar situation. He lived with his mother, grandma, a younger brother, and a sister. I did better in school than both of them, but we had one thing in common: outdoor activities.

At the end of classes on Friday, we disappeared into the bush. We came back home at sunset on Sunday. During the interval, we set traps to catch rodents, used our catapult to kill birds, and harvested wild yam and cassava. When adequate quantity of these products was gathered, they were cooked either above ground or in a hole lined by green banana leaves. We generated fire from two stones knocked against each other in a sliding manner over a heap of dry material made from the inside of dry branches of the palm tree. SK was the expert. At other times, he used one or two of "the borrowed matchsticks."

After the meal, we would set out to trace the source of the River Kaiso, continuing beyond the point we stopped at during our previous attempt. Before returning home, each of us would gather firewood and make a bundle. Along with this, depending on the catch, we brought back some meat. During one of these escapades, we discovered a beehive guarded by angry bees. I assured my friends that it was easy to get the honey. They should not have trusted me. It would have been an understatement to say that I got them angry; they chased us until we dove into the river. They were still waiting for us when we reemerged. We swarmed downstream and went home with swollen faces and arms. The next day I discussed our finding with Uncle Kai.

He was as excited as we were a day earlier about the prospect of harvesting honey. He was an expert. I did not know that he had harvested honey in the past. He demonstrated this by the way he did his preparation. We took him "to the site" the following Saturday morning. He had in his armamentarium of a cloth to wrap around his right hand, five bundles of special straw that generated a lot of smoke when lit, and two calabash containers to collect the honey and comb. Of course, he had his sharp cutlass, which he used, according to him, to shave his beard. The bees were still hovering around the hive. One group came in with their legs covered with white-and-yellow stockings (pollens). Others, with bare legs, flew out. Fortunately, the nest or hive was not visited or disturbed by other hunters (man and the mongoose/badger).

Before the start of his operation, he gave us strict instructions to follow. He handed each of us one of the bundles of straws. "Do not run away but hold the smoking stick in front of your face. Tolerate some stinging and no screaming."

He carefully approached the entrance of the hole. Almost all the bees that approached him dropped to the ground. The smoke or the horrible smell that came from the burning straws might have paralysed the insects. Within minutes, the whole process was over. It was a bumper harvest with minimum disturbance of the vegetation around the hive and few casualties to the bee population. He told us that by doing little damage to the entrance of the hive and allowing for the death of a few of the bees, "you are likely to have a new colony here in one year." The most important trick, however, he continued, "was leaving the big fat caterpillar undisturbed because it would kill you if you ate it." He understood and knew us well, "we ate anything that moved"—raw or roasted.

SK was stronger than the two of us and played football with both feet. SM, on the other hand, was highly protected by his mother and grandmother. He hardly played football but was not brilliant at schoolwork. I was smaller and skinnier than both of them. I was also faster, played more sports, and was more daring and ahead of them at school tests. Overall, we complemented each other in many ways and never fought. Sahr James had tried on many occasions to join us but was never accepted. We thought that he revealed a lot of our secrets. Instead, he stayed in the fringes and never gave up.

Sahr James' home and mine were the last two houses on the eastern side of the village. At the end of the street between the two homes was the rubbish dump. Beyond the dump, I planted many seeds (avocado pear, palm tree, mangoes, and guava) in a row, which had started growing into healthy plants with little or no attention from me. SJ was paying attention to them. In fact, he had started growing more plants in a second row beyond mine. Three years later, the plants had started bearing fruits but nobody touched them. The belief was that "they were poisonous because their feed came from the dump." Before the end of the school year, a major event occurred in my life.

Uncle Kai died. Two to three months prior to his demise, he lost considerable weight, the white of his eyes became yellow, and he looked pregnant. He was weak and frail. My father took him to the medicine man but came back after one week with no change in his appearance. He was no more after one month despite many visits from other medicine men and women. He was much older than me but we were friends. "Do not swear or shout at any creature of the night because they can see you. In anger the creature may attack you," was advice to me when I swore at annoying noises emanating from the nearby forest. I spent weekends with him in his farm, and those times were memorable. We sat under a big bushy tree to shade ourselves from the hot sun—a break from the rice ploughing. Not long after, we saw a snake, which to me was very big. I got up instantly to run away but he held me down.

"That snake is harmless; it is looking for rats," he said to me.

I had seen on other occasions that like a sword fighter, he would knock off the head of a snake with a single slice. "But last week, I saw Mom and other women killed a similar snake, already dead, to a pulp."

"This is the difference between men and women," he commented and then continued. "Men forgive and forget. Women, on the other hand, are like Rex [his dog]. They do not know how to let go once they get their teeth into something."

This remark explained why he never got married. He taught me how to set traps for birds and rodents, fish and, above all, "how to harvest wild honey."

The second event of my life was when Mr. Sahr Yarjah asked my father to allow me to live with him in one of Uncle SJW's houses. He was one of the clerks at the office (post office, treasury, and storage room for the chiefdom documents). He was one of the sons of the section chiefs. His father met with Grandpa quite often. I moved over to live with him with no resistance from my stepfather.

The end-of-year exams came and all three of us passed. Sahr James also made it to his new class. The end of year marked the long holidays. My team and I looked forward to the initiation ceremonies.

One day while visiting Grandma Feeyo, who also had left her husband, Uncle SJW appeared from nowhere. Grandma briefed him about life with me. I was all smiles but this was brief; he was off again in two days. However, prior to his departure, he left some money with Grandma to cover my school fees the following year.

Chapter 5

Standard 2 in Kayima

My mother and sister disappeared.

I did well on my end-of-year examination and gained promotion to Standard 2. For the first time, I started becoming aware of the presence of my mother, Sia. She was the first and only daughter of Grandma Femba. Her only brother was Uncle Tamba, suggesting they had lost the first boy. She was small in stature and walked with a limp. The left leg was shortened by a chronic leg ulcer sustained during a fishing expedition years before my birth. She always gave me the impression that she did not care very much for me but she did for my sister and other children.

"It is other children's parents who will look after you when I am dead and gone," she would response to my question, "Why do you give more food to so-and-so, name called?" She persuaded my father to get a second wife, Auntie Hawa. She was hardworking and resourceful. Often she had asked me to escort her to Uncle Kai's farm. We were able to bring back enough food to feed the family for at least one week. She quarrelled with me often, but I never saw her argued with anyone else.

Just as she was timid, my mother was just as hot tempered. I got home one afternoon after school to find her and my sister gone. The reason for her departure remained obscure to me, then and now. Her prediction, although I have my doubts as to whether she foresaw this, that I would be looked after by other children's parents when she was not around, became a reality.

On all accounts, I was on my own when my mom and Uncle SJW left Kayima and the passing of Uncle Kai. This marked the beginning of my writing down names in my exercise books and consequently diary keeping.

These jottings were aide memoir. My ultimate aim, on growing up, was "to repay all those people who gave me food."

Most times were, however, spent at Grandma Feeyo's home. Grandma Feeyo had two sons and two daughters. The older boy left home long time ago and was never seen again. Grandma knew "that he was alive and well." The younger son, Mbamba, had gone with Uncle SJW as a handyman. Sia Mointeh, the older sister, was married to Mr. Gborie, a primary school teacher. Both of them lived in Yengema. Her younger sister, Kumba, was married to a councillor in Sefadu.

Grandma Feeyo was really my aunt, my mother's half-sister. She was older than Mom but she looked and behaved like a granny; I was faultless from her point of view. Besides, in my community of extended families, the difference between a mother and an aunt was very, very blurred. When we first moved to Kayima from Sefadu, my two brothers and I lived with her. She was one of Alhaji S's many wives. She looked after me like one of her sons. Like all our women folks, she was kind, resourceful, and hardworking.

One morning during assembly, the headmaster announced that we were going to be visited by the District Commissioner (DC), a white man from Freetown. The DC's residence was on top of a hill overlooking Kayima. We were all to be dressed in our Sunday school uniform—"white and white." The girls wore white dresses and white shoes and the boys wore white shirts, white trousers, and white socks and shoes. The last two were optional. Actually, it was a question of whether you had or could afford them. That same evening, the town crier confirmed the great day.

The town crier had a trumpet made from an elephant tusk, which he blew as he walked along every street in the village. He would stop at each door and repeat the news. He was excellent as he always was on such occasions—accurate and clear. We called him Pa Moifa. He was a medium-built man who spoke with a different accent. He was also the praise singer. No sooner did an important dignitary came to town than he followed them everywhere for an hour or so, singing their praise.

Kayima became alive again. Every weed or grass on the streets was hoed out and every shrub brushed down. The houses, the majority of which were built of mud and thatched roof, were painted white. The paint was acquired from the banks of River Kaiso. This type of paint was applied to the walls using a broom. Cow dung mixed with mud offered another colour of paint. My father was a builder and our house was built from bricks made of mud and straw. He represented the slightly better-off. The more affluent ones built theirs in cement and sand (from River Kaiso) blocks. This last group of houses was painted with real paint.

To my group, the reason for the DC's visit was immaterial. For us it was another occasion when food was aplenty. Villagers came by their dozens and they brought food. Our white uniforms were washed and rinsed in blue solution, and those who had canvas (called crepe) shoes from BATA Shoe Company had them painted with white Blanco solution.

The villagers did not only bring food; they also had their drums. It was excitement all over Kayima. The nights became bright from pale dancing flames emitted from hurricane lamps with kerosene. The early-evening hours became filled with sounds from beating drums accompanied by traditional songs.

The DC finally arrived in a Land Rover, four-wheel drive, followed by three more filled with his dignitaries and their belongings. The teachers had lined us along the route the DC took to the court hall. At the end of the inspection and before he was led into the hall, we sang the National Anthem in English: "God Save the Queen." We knew the words because we sang it every morning during assembly. He shook hands with the teachers and said something to each of them, walked up the steps into the hall, and we were dispersed. It was worth standing in the hot sun. This was not the end of the day for some of the boys, including myself.

Late that afternoon we (my group and many other students) went up to the DC's residence. From this compound, one had a panoramic view of almost all of Kayima. It was a bungalow made of five rooms. It had an outside kitchen and toilets at the back. The house was blessed with rich, fertile land. Mangoes, guavas, bananas, and pineapples grew in abundance with minimal maintenance. Directly behind the kitchen was a huge cotton tree. Its flowers attracted hundreds of birds, which unfortunately could not be reached with slingshots. In the middle of the forecourt was a tall wooden pole and running from its top into the house was a makeshift radio antenna. The DC and his team were the actors and we the spectators. Unfortunately, this gathering was short-lived; an accident had happened.

To gain vantage points, some of the older boys climbed to the top of the mango trees. The sanitary inspector rode up on his bicycle. He started caning everybody within reach of his stick. Sahr Mani jumped from one of the branches but missed his target and landed on the ground, breaking his left leg. He was taken to the dispensary but transferred to Yengema Hospital in one of the DC's jeeps the following day. Two days later, the DC and his escort departed from Kayima. Kayima soon returned to normalcy.

I stayed with my stepfather, Aiah Monde. He was living with his second wife, my mother being the first. He was the third, as indicated by his forename, of five brothers and two sisters. The oldest brother, Sahr, died some "years ago." He was the local carpenter and probably one of the few men in Kayima who had nothing to do with farming. He could not read or write. He was never unkind to me "but never gave me anything"—money or advice. His house, made of mud and thatched roof, was situated with other houses on the western limit of Kayima. The house had four rooms, two of which opened directly onto the veranda, while the other two were connected to the living room. At the far corner to the left, as one entered the house through the front door, was a large cast-iron pot with drinking water. The pot sat in a carpet of sand and was surrounded by two tortoises. Floating on this pot of water was a "good-sized calabash cup." Everybody drank from this cup from which any remnant was thrown in the sand. The water was always cool and "it was attributed to the two tortoises that have refused to escape since their arrival over ten years ago."

The sources of cooked food were unpredictable but consistent. Uncle Tamba's wife, who was occupying one of the outside rooms, gave me food. Her husband was a miner and lived away. I also got food from Auntie Kumba, Sahr James' mother. She was one of my father's sisters and lived directly across the road.

Mr. James visited Kayima infrequently, and when he did I spent a lot of time with him. His house was much bigger than ours was; the roof was made of corrugated tin sheets, an outside kitchen (built with my assistance), and an outside washing room with a latrine. He was also an excellent shot. I came running to him when I saw wood pigeons feeding from heavily laden wild fruit trees. At other times, he would ask me to gather the boys under a huge cotton tree. "There were thousands of weevil birds nesting in the branches of this tall tree." He would then instruct us to form a circle some distance from the foot of the tree. He walked about three houses from the tree and took aim. On firing, tens of the birds came tumbling down to the ground. This was the start of the "great race." Each child kept what he (again, girls were not invited) captured. Apparently, he was once an army officer—fit, strong, and exact. One day while assisting him, a plank of wood supported by me dropped on my abdomen. I sustained a cut above my navel and he immediately said, "You must always concentrate when handling dangerous tools and building materials." I guessed then that this advice applied to all works of life.

The other consequence of Uncle SY's transfer was that Grandma Feeyo moved into the house some months later. One day, just by chance, SK, SM, and I were roasting a bird I killed with my catapult at the back of SK's home. Then Sister Mointeh (Cousin, actually) spotted, and ordered, me to come to her. After one look at me, she started screaming and crying with tears running down her cheeks. She remarked, "Your skin colour was like mine; you are dirty and you are all bones like a stray dog." Sister Mointeh was visiting her mom, Grandma Feeyo. She suggested I moved in with her mother. My stepfather offered no resistance to the move. Grandma Feeyo had again become my new parent.

It was one of the houses built to last forever during the colonial days. They were indestructible and were roofed by asbestos material. This house was probably the most elegant building in the village. It contained three rooms, a kitchen, and an indoor toilet. However, Pa Monde Kaminkundo and Uncle SJW always contested ownership. There was never an open war about it.

Chapter 6

Standard 3 in Kayima

Drinking water brought to Kayima through the long snake. We moved to the new school. A new hospital built on the outskirts of the town.

We did not have water through standpipes in Kayima. Women sourced water from River Kayi and the surrounding streams. Two years ago, a large water dam was created about half a morning's walk in the direction of sunrise. A rainforest surrounded the dam fed by a stream that never dried up, even in the dry season. The forest surrounding the dam carried the same rules as the secret societies—forbidden to everyone else except the security/maintenance men. This law was adhered to the letter by all—including boys and grown-ups. This year, PC Fasuluku, with financial support from SLST Company, central government, etc., undertook this wonderful project and the building of the school and hospital.

This project generated a special interest in me, particularly when "the big snake slowly crawled its way into town." It was heading straight for Uncle SJW's house. Prior to their union, the pipes lay loosely at their intended permanent positions. They provided us the means of racing through on all fours. Mr. Jai (called "Lofty") supervised the project. He was from Nigeria and employed by the SLST as a construction engineer based in Yengema. He was tall (tallest man I have ever seen), strong, and spoke little. The snake finally arrived but stopped short of our house by the main road. One day Lofty and his men arrived to test the effectiveness of their work. On opening the valve, a huge fountain of water headed straight for me as I sat in the veranda watching all the activities across the road. The water, however, continued to rise and landed on the tall coconut tree behind our compound. The fountain became a trickle when Lofty turned the steering wheel the opposite way. The anxiety on the faces of the little crowd that gathered turned into all smiles.

SK, SM, and I took a fascination to this new attraction—the track that carried this long snake. During one of our disappearing tricks, we decided to explore the course the snake took. The engineers and workers were determined to keep the pipeline straight and at a slight incline towards town. Whenever it came across a river, valley, or depression, the snake crawled across concrete pillars. The pillars were as tall as houses. These elevated portions became our main attractions. Without hesitation, SK and I walked across them. Neither of us saw the potential danger to our limbs and probably lives. SM, on the other hand, was happy to wait for us ahead.

Gathering of food often interrupted our journey. SK, our fireman, got the fire going under a tree we had earmarked to protect us from the sun and a possible shower. We added more sticks to the fire, which generated enough heat to cook our harvest.

Prior to setting the fire, we dug a hole in the ground and lined it with special leaves picked from plants similar to bananas. We placed three big sweet potatoes in this ground pot and then covered it with more leaves. We refilled the hole with soil and lit the fire over the pot.

The washed cassavas and yams were placed around the fire. As the cooking progressed, we plucked the birds and prepared any other moving creature we might have caught. Sahr Mbawa was the best storyteller in our group because he remembered everything the grown-ups had told him. The prepared birds, grasshoppers, etc., were stuffed with hot bird pepper and salt acquired from Grandma Feeyo. We left the food to cook and went for a swim. Sleep was not long coming after meal and the day's activities.

The clock birds woke us up as they made their mating calls. The following morning the buried food was ready for breakfast. We had breakfast. With renewed energy, the new day had started with the same enthusiasm as the previous day. We resumed our journey, which was full of exciting activities—picking wild fruits, walking on the big water pipes, setting traps to catch birds and rats. The sun was now directly overhead and so we set off for home. As on previous adventures, each of us had to carry back home a bunch of firewood and whatever moving food we might have caught in our traps. Next day we went to church and Sunday school dressed in white-white. All three of us were now in Standard 3.

This term was to reduce the frequency of such excursions. The authorities had decided that the school be moved to a new location, on the main road leading into town opposite Mr. SB Sonsiama's estate. Many reasons, none from the headmaster, were given for this move. The most branded one was that there were too many accidents at the present location—falls from mango trees or breaking of legs as we stepped or jumped down from the football pitch onto the road. They also proposed relocation of the dispensary on a piece of land diagonally opposite the cemetery along the main road leading out of

Kayima to Wordu. How very convenient—cemetery and hospital opposite each other.

The new school compound was built on a flat land with all four buildings facing the main and only road in and out of Kayima. Lying behind these buildings was a piece of land separating the school from Pa Sankor's rice farm. This lot also accommodated the outside toilets composing of pit latrines marked "MALES" and "FEMALES."

The whole front of the school was occupied by the football pitch and running track. Mr. Sonsiama's estate ran the whole length of the field; both of each was separated by the main road. Without malice, we envied Mr. Sonsiama's estate. As we chatted between ourselves, we would say, "When I grow up I am going to have the same farm in my village." It had every possible variety of mangoes, guavas, pineapples, and oranges.

The school garden occupied the western boundary. During Nature Study classes, we learned to grow vegetables and other plants. This marked the beginning of my interest in growing my own food up to now as I write this book.

The eastern boundary of the school was formed by another delightful estate owned by Komba Kayima. Mr. Kayima was an Englishman who fell in love with Kayima and changed his name to Komba Kayima. He donated money to the chiefdom and as a sign of gratitude, he was given this piece of land. The estate contained fewer fruit trees (mainly local) than that of Mr. SB. Instead, he specialized in animals. When I eventually read *Animal Farm* by George Orwell, I thought the book was set in this farm.

Fortunately, the land was cleared for farming some four years previously. Therefore, the vegetation here was mainly scrubs dotted by palm trees. These trees had to be dug out and the task was divided among the classes. Each class was grouped into small and big boys. A leader appointed from Standard 4 coordinated work each weekday after school. It was fun. During the construction of this new school compound, another major project was being undertaken at the opposite end of town. This was the hospital.

The present dispensary was located exactly opposite Uncle SJW's house. Unfortunately, they gave us no history lessons on those buildings (the dispensary and its accommodation, the community hall, PC Fasuluku's one-storey house, etc.). They were built of material that seemed to last forever. The dispensary occupied a compound of a three-roomed house, an outdoor kitchen, an outdoor latrine, a shower room, and a storeroom adjoining a repair room.

The lawns were evenly laid out with well-trimmed savannah grass. The front part of the compound facing Uncle SJW's house was lined by a row of mango trees. The back and southern boundaries had orchards of mangoes and guava intermingled with cocoa and coffee plants. Between the buildings were rows of citrus plants such as orange, tangerine, lemon, and lime, and what fascinated me most was one plant composing of sour lemon and orange. The lemon portion bore fruits all the year around but more profused in the raining seasons. It was also in abundance because very few boys cared for it—too sour.

My fascination for it was because of its uniqueness of being one plant that produced two different fruits.

My other attraction to this compound was that I was able to obtain discarded scalpel blades. Instead of getting rid of house rats caught in my traps, I skinned them. I dried the dissected skins out in the sun as Grandma Femba did with my cow skin. The majority got lost during the drying process to vultures, cats, and the rain. I joined the rest together to make a mat.

The new hospital, on the other hand, had a different attraction to me. For its foundations, the workers dug a maze of trenches. I was able to stand in the trenches without anybody seeing me from around. I regularly roamed in them. Heavy rainfalls filled the trenches and next came edible frogs to spawn. I lost all this when they completed the building a year later. Immediately behind the dispensary compound was Pa Mondewa's estate. Most of this southern boundary became over grown by cocoa plants, which became the home of the Sande Society, the female equivalence of the men's (Poro) society.

The school year was coming to an end, and it marked our moving over to the new school. Each pair of students carried their own table and bench to the new school. Where necessary, the older boys helped. We had only three girls in my class because it was not common that girl children went to school. The benches were made of hard wood with two legs, a plank to sit on, and a back support. The accompanying desk had a top, which sloped towards the students and held by two hinges. Few inches from the hinges and along the whole length of the top was a depression designed to hold pencils and nib pens. At the end of each pen or pencil holder was an inkwell. The pens and inkwells were never disturbed when one opened the top. Underneath this was a common draw for storage of our notebooks.

I was chosen by the drama teacher to act in the end-of-the-year school play, "Songolongobangolasay." I acted the part of the dog, one of Motilewa's animal friends. The cast travelled to Yormandu for fundraising.

Yormandu was probably the biggest town in Sando Chiefdom. It was a mining town. Having arrived in Yormandu, we set about preparing the court/community hall. Like the one in all the villages and towns in Sando Chiefdom, the walls formed part of the sitting area of the hall. Therefore, during meetings or court sessions, more people would be involved directly. But during an occasion such as ours, the space was enclosed by walls of palm leaves, except for the entrance guarded by the collectors of the entrance fee. Bright lights came from pressure lamps similar to the one owned by Pa Sankor. To own one meant that the owner had arrived. He was rich. This lamp had a velvety glowing bulb supported by metal tubing in its centre. The lit bulb was maintained by an aerosol of blue mentholated spirit in a reservoir forming the base of the lamp. It emitted no smoke or smell but generated intense heat. It also attracted insects and in particular winged termites, which provided an excellent snack.

Emmanuel Carram, acting the role of a chicken, was the crowd favourite. They poured currency notes on him each time he opened his mouth to say his lines. The next crowd puller was a beautiful girl called Sia Sonsiama, the main actress. We were arranged according to the order of appearance. Each actor stood up to say his/her lines and then sat back down again. It was a bumper harvest. The play was staged for two nights, and on Sunday we traced our way back to school in Kayima.

The school soccer (sport) field, still incomplete, required surfacing with savannah grass. The pitch ran the full length of the school, separating it from the road. The fundraiser concert also provided us with a new football made of leather and a handheld air pump. There might have been other benefits gained from the venture, but for us boys these two improvements were worth the experience.

We completed the transfer of everything to the new school within a week. Assembly was called a week later at the court hall for the usual school report. SK, SM, and I passed for Standard 4. It also marked our turn to join the Secret Society. Grandpa Joemende and my friends' parents were all for it. We enjoyed the experience.

Chapter 7

Standard 4 (Final Year) in Kayima

Weaverbirds were enemies to the palm tree. Faced with another end-of-year examination in Fanema. Went to live with Uncle SJW and wife.

My friends and I arrived at our final year of school in Kayima. After Standard 4, students move to Yengema or Jaiama Nimikoro School to prepare for the Common Entrance Examination (CEE) to secondary school. Jaiama was the prestigious school to which we all aspired. Students from there came back as teachers, chiefdom clerks, etc. Of course, there were other schools offering CEE curriculum but were limited to students whose relatives lived in those places. This was one of the best sides of the extended family.

Grandma Feeyo was able to feed me but could not pay for my school fees. Grandpa Joemende was again in town before the start of the school year. During those visits, he stayed with Uncle Kaimondo (K) and family.

Uncle Kaimondo and wives came to my rescue. Uncle K was a true farmer. He was only seen in town when there was an event—court cases, ceremonies, meetings. I made no effort to find out why they wanted me to live with them. They had four children, two from the first wife and two from the second, and two nephews from his village that took over a day's walking. He had two houses both covered with corrugated tin roofing. He "lived separately" in an outside room of the first house shared with his first wife and children. The front building housed the second wife and her two children. Uncle K, although not related to but may have been influenced by Grandpa J, looked after me. They provided us adequate accommodation. The junior wife prepared food, which was just about adequate to fill the belly once a day. For me this was an improvement on my life—now a place to roost after school activities and roaming the village.

Uncle Kaimondo did not take me in purely as an orphan but he had two other reasons. Firstly, he wanted me to teach his two children how to read and write. He acted as the supervisor, and the two mothers in their respective rooms listened and most probably pulled at their hairs. The two children were in Standard 1. I caned them if they could not recall what I had taught them an hour or so earlier. They made progress but the mothers were not pleased, and this was conveyed to me clearly. "You and your uncle are wicked." I did not consider myself then as street-wise, but I came to learn that you do not bite the hand that feeds you. The women did the cooking.

His second other motive was for me to visit him in his farm. He always farmed at the foot of Mountain Boana. One could see this mountain from anywhere in the village. There were many stories and myths about it.

I gladly accepted the offer. It took us almost a day to get to the farm, thus emphasizing that the eyes could be deceiving. Another example of this was that my two friends and I were still trying to get to the source of River Kaiso! We walked along a dirt track that took us through Old Town Kayima, other farm settlements in the middle of nowhere, and streams that we waddled through (others had bridges made of that versatile palm tree). The wild life was just abundant—colourful birds flying off, animals crossing the road in a hurry, long snakes climbing trees in search of food, and noisy insects that tried to enter our ears. We finally arrived when the sun was just directly overhead, no shadows. The first thing I noticed was a colony of weaver birds occupying a tall cotton tree standing right in the middle of the man's farm. This crowd found it difficult to fly into town, underpinning that they were sedentary birds.

He took me in as a lodger/tutor. As the year progressed, I learned that my invitation to join Uncle K was through the influence of his first wife. I could not have done better. Despite the extended family life in my society, the way one was treated was dependent on the attitude of the wife towards you. Auntie Finda was my mother's friend. In fact, my mother had secretly sold some of her belongings to her. It was one way my mother raised funds to pay her transport to leave my stepfather and took my sister, Sia N'Gundia, with her. My mother and her mother-in-law, Grandma Femba, never got on well. Femba was indeed an unusual grandmother; she was always in a bad mood and was at war with every family member except her sons. She had a huge goitre. Retrospectively, it was possible that she might have suffered from thyroid over-activity.

Uncle K had made the clearing near a river running from the mountain; I fell in love with it. I was reminded of my days in Fanema. Fresh food was easily available and in abundance. I had an opportunity again to apply what Uncle Tamba had taught me in Fanema. I was able to set traps to catch wild animals of small and medium sizes. I also learned to make cooking oil from palm trees: red when made from the skin and black when made from the kernel. The palm tree was probably the most versatile plant in the whole of the Sando Chiefdom. The palm tree provided leaves for roofing and broom from its straws, the heart provided wine, the trunk for making bridges, the fruits used for cooking oil, and the young nuts as a snack. Finally when the tree fell down (naturally or artificially) and was allowed to rot, it provided an excellent source of protein from caterpillars of the palm weevils. The adult weevils were also used as toys and food. The insect was mounted on a straw (again from the palm tree) inserted into one of the hind legs and allowed to fly away but only succeeded in producing a pleasant musical sound from its wings. When the food stopped flying, it was then roasted and eaten. The palm leaves also provided building material for the weaverbirds.

The other attraction I had for that part of the bush was being able to do a lot of other manual work rather than scaring the weaver and other seed-eating birds from the nearly matured rice. I learned to catch crabs, fish with a line attached to self-made hooks and a floater, watch creatures looking for food and mates, and my friend and enemy, the weaverbird. This particular group was too lazy to fly back to Kayima; instead they formed a temporary home here. This was rather unusual because they loved human habitats. They were annoying in every way; they were noisy, had an avid appetite for rice grain, and would strip a whole palm tree of its leaves, leading to death.

Uncle Kaimondo recognized my deep interest in this type of lifestyle and was also appreciative of the extra pair of hands I provided. However, he made sure I returned to Kayima every Sunday afternoon whenever I visited him. Uncle K came back home infrequently, particularly when there was something big in town. At most times he stayed in this world of his with his first wife, his first son, and a mixed-breed dog called Boa.

"Nobody travelling alone ever made it back to Kayima," so we were told. Those who made it back had a dog with them or another person as company. To get to these farms one walked along a narrow footpath. There were stories, real stories, that farmers had been attacked and killed by leopards or snakes or by drowning in rivers. Therefore, families move to and from their respective farms in groups—better defence in numbers.

In comparison Uncle K's family was small. Most families may be composed of six or more members. A large family brings wealth and power to the head. This position of power must have been the one most important reason why men in my society married more than one wife and had as many children as possible. The wives and children provided an excellent labour force. The practice worked. However, in Sunday schools, we were taught against polygamy and having too many children when we became adults.

The school year was fast coming to its end. The drama teacher, Mr. Foday Mani, selected a few boys and girls to rehearse for a play. Mr. SS Pittiquie, the music teacher, invited all those students with flutes to his home. A metal flute formed part of my worldly possession of a catapult, exercise books, and an "HB lead pencil." Therefore, possessing a flute qualified me to join the group of six. At the end of one month, Mr. P made a choir out of us. On the evening of the concert at the court hall, dressed up in white and white, my group was lined in front of the audience. We played the National Anthem, "God Save the Queen." It was warmly appreciated, although the majority of the parents could have hardly understood it because they could not read or write. The play was even more exciting.

The play was an adaptation of Edward Lear's *The Owl and the Pussycat*. The two main actors became instant stars and for the subsequent years that followed, "Master Komba Finoh and Miss Kumba Mei were considered as husband and wife in our eyes." The author would have winched in his grave to hear every student child in Kayima going about his/her business singing, "The owl and the pussy cat went to sea in a little pilgrim boat" instead of "in a beautiful pea-green boat." The drama teacher matched them well. It was exciting—the students felt good and the children were proud of them. Now that the excitement was over, the reality was here.

A week later, we had another gathering at the courthouse, this time for the announcement of the school report. As in previous years, each teacher stood in front of the audience (students, teachers, parents, guardians, and well-wishers) and read out the report of each student under his care.

I passed for Standard 5, the class for CEE, but my two pals were held back. Yes, I had completed my schooling in Kayima, but where was I to go next? Yet again I was stoked; who was to pay my fees to my next big school? Grandpa Joemende came to my rescue, but it turned out to be for a different reason.

I travelled back with him and his entourage to Fanema. In Fanema, I started my exploration as I did six years previously. This time around, however, I could read, write, and do arithmetic, the three R's. My former playmates had grown up and seemed to have more responsibilities than I and other boys my age did in Kayima. For instance, some of them ran the affairs of their father's farm. I had now become an outsider. I was also an outsider because I had not been initiated into the Sumoe Society, the start of manhood.

I met with Joseph again, who came back here after the transfer of Uncle SJW. Although we were about the same age, he was actually my uncle. He was the fourth boy, Komba, from one of Grandpa's wives. We saw little of each other, however, because, like boys of our age, Komba had his own farm. The other reason was that Grandpa always wanted me to be with him.

Fanema had changed but little. There were now four houses all covered with zinc roofing in Grandpa's compound. All the various families were alive but some not well. Grandma Femba occupied the first house with her family, which consisted of two sons (Uncles Tamba and Kai), their wives, and a grown-up sister in transit. The second and main building was occupied by Grandpa and his three younger wives, two of whom were twins. The house had two extra rooms equipped with a handmade bed. The third building was occupied by Grandpa's second wife and family.

Grandpa hardly went to that house, the home of his second wife. But I was there almost every day. In one of the outside rooms was an old man, the town crier, sorcerer, and witch doctor all rolled into one. He had come originally from another tribe but spoke Kono perfectly well. I wanted to learn from the doctor, but my visits to him were always short-lived. At the end of my stay, I learned little or nothing from him.

The fourth house, located directly across the main house, was occupied by Joseph and his family—mother, a brother and wife, and a sister. Here again Grandpa made little or no visit. The general pattern was that Grandpa provided accommodation for his four most senior wives and left them on their own devices. Each roof was covered with corrugated tin materials.

The rest of the houses in the village remained the same except renewed thatched roofs. The roofs were conical in shape supported by circular mud walls with no windows but one door. The inhabitants were safe from the elements and wild animals but not from fire. Ironically, though, I was never told or had seen a single house that caught fire in this village. House fires were quite common in Kayima. The majority of the houses (almost all rectangular in shape) in Kayima had two doors (one at the front and the other at the back) but the inhabitants used kerosene lamps, a sign of prosperity.

When Grandma Femba recognized me, the smile on her face extended from ear to ear. She picked me up and sat me on her lap, felt my bones rather than fat, passed her fingers in my hair, and squeezed me tightly against her breasts. Unlike my first time living with her before going to school, I was now a grown-up—heavier and taller than she was. None of these changes made any difference to her; I was "the same Saa Wee with the same ungrateful stomach."

News spread like wildfire in Kawama Section. A few days after my arrival at Fanema, Grandpa ordered a sheep to be killed for me. On such occasions, Pa Bangali, the town crier, a man of many talents, would pray in Arabic (supposedly from the Holy Quran) before the animal was killed and the meat distributed to everybody in attendance. This recitation would last for about ten minutes, but for the little boys it lasted forever; they started scratching the back of each other's knees. The affected boy would jump uncontrollably with a yell, thus reminding the doctor that it was time to proceed. At the end of his prayer, nobody in the village understood the words, including the doctor himself. At the end of his recitation, I volunteered to say something I learned from school.

I recited the twelve books of the New Testament in about three breaths. Thereafter, the impact was dramatic and instant. "Chief JM's grandson can read book." Two days later Grandpa decided to tour the section under his domain to settle cases/palavers between his subjects. Ahead of us in each village, news had arrived with regards to my learning. I was faced with an end-of-year examination, again this time in spelling and reading.

I was asked to assign documents to their respective owners. These came in three groups. One set of examiners deliberately mixed their papers and pretended not to know the owners. I said "pretended" because on careful examination I could see that one corner had been marked with palm oil, kola nut juice, ground tobacco, or any other permanent stain. The second set of examiners was genuine in that they had mistakenly mixed their documents. This group was thankful and smiled with joy. The final group of examiners was a mixture of the other two. The main aim of this last group was to demonstrate to the rest of the villagers, the chief and his advisers, who had paid their respective hut taxes. I passed with flying colours!

I was indoctrinated into the Sumoe Society and given the name Sumowa. It was the most secretive and highly respected society in Kono District. The Sumoe Society had two versions in terms of the length of time spent away from one's family. I was enrolled into the shorter version (three months) because I was still a student. For the longer version (twelve months or more), the boys learned everything about life as an adult. That group also learned to dance to the beat and communicate with each other by the notes of hollow wooden drums. They lived like army recruits (without guns but with bows and arrows to kill animals for food), messengers, and news carriers. Everybody (particularly Grandpa) wanted me to stay forever, and I was too happy to do so. One morning, however, I woke up crying to myself, and this continued for a few more days. Grandma became aware of the sudden change in me and was determined to find out why.

I finally broke down and told her, "I want to go back to school." She managed to get me to discuss it with Grandpa. Grandpa did not want to hear of it but with my daily crying, he acceded to my nagging. He ordered Grandma Femba to prepare a bag of rice. Uncle Tamba again accompanied me to Uncle SJW in Seidu. The trip was longer but more relaxing, as most of it was out of the sun. We travelled two days, stopping at the end of the first day at a family's home. At the end of the second day, we spent the night in Yormandu with Uncle James Gandi. The following morning we crossed the Baffin River in a canoe hollowed out of a tree trunk. By mid-morning, we arrived at Uncle SJW's home in Seidu, Nimikoro Chiefdom. He was alone home, as his wife had taken the children back to school in Freetown. Uncle SJW had married his third wife, Mama Marie. She was of an African mother and a Lebanese father. She spoke fluent Temene and Creole and understood Kono well. She was the "businessman" of the family. She brought with her two sons and three daughters from her previous marriage. His other two wives had left.

Living with SJW and family was Kai M'Bamba (M), whom I remembered vaguely from Kayima. He was one of Grandma Feeyo's sons. He stammered very badly and he could not read or write. Also in this pool of domestics were Aminata Conteh (a girl) and Aiah Gandorhun (a boy), both from Mama Marie's side, and neither could read or write. Except for Kai, who was much older; we were all about the same age. All four of us had our respective roles to perform in this family unit.

M'Bamba was excellent with his hands—you could see your face through the linoleum covering the floor when he finished polishing it, he washed and did the ironing, cleaned and maintained the kerosene refrigerator, and he lit the pressurized hurricane lamps. He came to live with SJW on the understanding that he would learn to drive. Apparently, after many tries, the teacher gave up on him. He had a wonderful appetite. Aminata helped Mama to cook and attended to her personal needs. She had been living with them for almost as long as M. We, the two new recruits, Aiah and I, filled the two tanks (each holding four hundred and fifty gallons of water) with drinking water from a public well about a mile away. When night came, we were on our own.

Seidu was a small mining town. The layout was completely different from what I had been accustomed to. There were hardly any tall trees except elephant grasses surrounding abandoned mine holes filled with rainwater. There was no river to fish or swim in. I spent most of my spare time reading books, papers, etc., left lying around by the children.

Two months after the return of Mama Marie from Freetown, the family started making plans for moving to Yormandu. Yormandu was on the other side of Baffin in Sando, my chiefdom. We were to live with Uncle James Gandi, one of Grandpa's sons who had owned a few properties around the town. He acquired his money not by mining himself but "acting as the town judge."

Uncle James was completely blind in his left eye. He reminded me of Grandpa JM in physique, walk, and talk. He feared nobody and was always ready to fight. Years ago, I was told, he picked up a fight with Uncle Tamba, who pinned him down on the ground. He reached out to Uncle Tamba's left ear and bit it off. The designated town chief was Pa Sumana but in view of Uncle James' charismatic mannerism, he was considered the judge by everybody. He sat over cases in his big living room, which was to become my bedroom. He was accorded the respect due to a properly ordained chief. Like Uncle SJW and Grandpa, his sentences were final. This was one of the ways he became a wealthy man in Yormandu. The court fees were paid directly to him and he paid the jury members.

Prior to our moving to Yormandu, Mama Marie had already opened a variety shop just opposite the town market. I recognized the town hall, in which we staged a fundraising play from Kayima some years back. I learned from M how to polish the floor covered by linoleum, to make charcoal for ironing, and to paddle the canoe across the river, among other things.

One morning, Mama Marie assigned seven lapels to each of us. We were supposed to sell each lapel in town and its environs. I sold everything and brought back the exact amount. Aiah and M "failed the test." This was the beginning of yet another responsibility for me in the family.

During those rounds, I explored every corner of Yormandu. The discovery of diamonds in the 1930s was supposedly a step towards a better life but was actually a milestone for the worse. Growing up in the fifties, almost all boys were sent to school but only to drop out after a year or two because of lack of financial support. These young people became magnetized to the diamond mines, the start of family breakdowns and beginning of the end of agriculture. Thus, the arrival or discovery of diamond in Yormandu represented a mixed blessing, a point halfway between prosperity (roads, electric generators) and degeneration (violence, disrespect to elders and environmental destruction). I fit in well.

One day I went to launder by the jetty on the Yormandu side of the Baffin River. I completed my washing and neatly packed it in a large cane basket. I then decided to go for a swim and dive. For no apparent reason, I came up with a handful of silt. It was all coins but they were muddy. Further dives had the same result. That evening I told Sahr Kabba my discovery. The coins had dropped out of travellers' hands during boarding of the ferry or canoes. Sahr was in class with me in Kayima until the end of Standard 1. He was now living in Yormandu with an uncle and had become street-wise. We became friends again. Unfortunately, he was a bragger and soon everybody knew about my discovery before we became "rich." Within days the whole treasure was plundered. Unlike the people back in Fanema and Kayima, everybody here spoke with a different tongue, had a different skin complexion, and came from different backgrounds. The only sharing characteristic they had between them was hunger, either for food or for diamonds.

I continued on with my routine responsibilities, and Mama Marie was becoming comfortable with me. Regarding Uncle SJW, we spoke little and he was quick to punish me for any wrongdoing. Between the two of them, it was decided that I went with Mama to Freetown. I was told this the night before the journey. "If you don't get up now, they are going to leave you behind," shouted Uncle SJW as he shook me up from my sleep.

Staying at the same accommodation in Freetown, I met with my uncle's children, N'Gundia, Daniel, and Emmanuel, and four of his five stepchildren. One week later, Mama Marie had arrangements for me to go back to Sefadu. She had acquired a Bedford truck and loaded it with bonga, a dried seawater fish, which was universally eaten in every SL household. The driver and his conductor, both almost three times my age, and a truck full of precious fish were placed in my care. I delivered all to a Mr. Jareed, a shop owner in the heart of Sefadu. I made other trips between Sefadu and Yormandu but on much smaller scales.

I made some of these trips with Adip, Mama's oldest son (in his thirties). He was a chain smoker and drank cool Coca Cola by the gallons. He became friendly and kind to me. I was the fastest little boy to replenish his supply of Coca Cola and cigarettes. At the end of each trip, he would ask me to "keep the change." In Yormandu, "keep the change" was a language of prosperous people and those not so rich would say, "Put it in the back pocket." For the latter group, one decided what to put in the back pocket and what to put in one's front pocket.

Just out of the blue one day, Adip asked his mother to send me back to school. I found this baffling. It was almost two years now since I left Kayima. I spoke to nobody about schooling; I dared not. To let me go was like "slapping your own face." He must have seen something in me that no one else did in the family. He probably realized that I loved books. I read everything I could lay my hands on as I accompanied him to and from his business dealings. Mama Mary and Uncle SJW agreed, and I was sent to Yengema to live with my cousin, Mointeh, and family.

Chapter 8

Standard 3 in Yengema

I came to live with Cousin Mointeh and family. My sister and I reunited. I started school again but this time in Yengema.

On March 23,1962, Adip gave me a lift to Yengema on his way to Sefadu. He dropped me outside the school, which was situated on the main road. With all my worldly possessions in a cardboard box on my head, I set about locating the home of my cousin and family. They were living about one mile from the school. One had to cross a slow-flowing stream on a palm tree trunk.

Surprise, surprise! I met my half-sister for the first time after the disappearance of our mother. Apparently she was dropped here temporarily on the understanding that our mom would come back to collect. She never came back. It was a reasonably large building that housed three different families. Sister Mointeh, her husband, two children, a male cousin of mine, and I made one unit. The first unit composed of the landlord, his wife, and their two children. The third and the largest unit was that of Mr. Turay, assistant headmaster of my new school. His family consisted of his wife, one son, three schoolboys, and his younger brother (Mr. Sidiqque), who taught music at the same school. There were four rooms each of which opened directly onto the sitting room and none opened directly into the verandah. Each room had a window. This was going to be my home for the next one and a half years or so.

A typical day started by sweeping the yard, filling the drum with drinking water, and then going off to school. Having lost over two years of schooling, I resumed in Standard Three. I was not completely removed from the books, and so catching up was not difficult.

The school was one of the oldest schools in the district built by the EUB Mission. It was a coeducational school headed by Mr. Kassegbama.

Sister Mointeh was married to Mr. G'Borie, a schoolteacher. She was the older daughter of Grandma Feeyo. She was alphabetical like most of my women folks from Kono District. She was authoritative and ran our unit with an iron fist. She had two boys who were not of school-going age yet. They were looked after by my sister, who was four or five years older than Tamba, the older of the two boys. Sister Mointeh was resourceful and did everything to supplement her husband's salary to feed all of us. Mr. G'Borie was tall, handsome, and bright. Apparently he was a beautiful dancer and lived a free life.

After a few months in school, things started looking bright. I started topping my class in most subjects, particularly spelling, religious knowledge, arithmetic, and writing. Sahr G'Borie, Joseph Fefegula, Sahr Bockerie, and I became instant friends. They were living under similar circumstances to mine but marginally better. They lived with a relative and spouse with one or no children. We spent a lot of time together in school but went our different ways at the end of classes.

The Sierra Leone Selection Trust was a diamond company with its offices located at the edge of the town. The town benefited from asphalt-coated streets, water wells for the inhabitants, a hospital, two football pitches, and a cinema. The company itself had a huge estate separated from the town by a meandering stream. It was a self-sufficient town separated in two halves by a road led from Sefadu to Seidu. On one side of the road were the offices and accommodation for the expatriates and senior African administrators. On this same side were the hospital and a cinema. The estate then spread across the road to form a mirror image of the senior officers' quarters. The houses here were designed for the workers (miners, machine operators, security personnel, etc.) and their families. My new friends came from these working families.

Each side of the divide had a nightclub fully equipped with a bar that had table tennis boards, a billiard table, and a lawn tennis court. Neither club allowed school children to enter. The boys talked about them but none bothered about their existence. The company also had an airstrip, which was able to accommodate big planes. For me Yengema was a very big town with two schools (one controlled by the Catholic Church and mine by the EUB Mission), many big shops that sold everything, and two football fields, and all homes had hurricane lamps and torch lights. Despite all this apparent wealth, Yengema did not lend itself for exploration.

This, as I saw it then, was due to two main factors. Firstly, it was almost impossible for any group of boys to organize themselves in groups. This was easy in villages beyond the Baffin River. Almost all of us children lived with relatives and we had to work for our keeps. Therefore, when classes ended at about 3 P.M., we went home soon after. We had to go home immediately after school, as it was the only time one had a cooked meal. The exception to this was on Friday afternoons when we had inter-class soccer challenges.

My situation was, however, unique in that I was a tradesman in addition to my daily house chores. Prior to my arrival, Sister Mointeh had become aware of my ability "to sell things." She assigned me to selling kerosene in beer bottles from door to door in the evenings. On Saturdays, I sold balls of starch and akra to the miners.

During the week Sister Mointeh would acquire the necessary ingredients for making the akra, starch, and peanut cakes. At about 2 A.M. on Saturday, she and I would wake up to fry the akra and pack my tray. I enjoyed my trade-man ship. It gave me the opportunity to explore Yengema more. Also interesting was the eagerness of people to buy from me. Some thought I was polite while others labeled me as being bright. I enjoyed this added task to my daily routines and Sister Mointeh was never short of money.

With regards to my sister, Sia N'Gundia, there was no suggestion in my diary that we ever discussed the whereabouts of our mother. Maybe we never missed her or we were too young to understand. We were surviving with one of our second parents. She was not left unemployed. She took care of the peanut-rice delicacy. While we are away in school, she would assist sSster Mointeh to ground rice, sugar, and roasted peanut together to a paste. Pieces of this paste was rolled into balls and stacked on top of each other on a tray. The cost of each of the ball was one pence. She did not have to pry her trade as I did; she just sat beside the tray, collected the pennies, and ate none of it.

The second reason that made Yengema not amenable to exploration was that one got arrested or shot at by the security men if caught loitering in and around SLST properties. They virtually owned every important spot in and around the town. None of these potential threats were ever carried out on school children, but the fear was enough not to dare breach the boundaries.

My two friends and I did manage to get together most often during school hours. These times included the absence of the teacher, half-day holiday, escaping general cleaning periods, etc. We found ourselves breaching the security to the expatriate side of the SLST compound. We just wandered around in the bushes, helping ourselves to ripe bananas and other fruits. We got greedy. Each of us picked two grapefruits to take home. The security men spotted us and a chase had begun. We escaped minus the fruits. We were very fortunate to escape because we would have been given a good beaten by the men and then canned before the school gathering.

I was really enjoying life in Yengema. I did well not only in my subjects but I made the first team for the school soccer. I sold kerosene in the evenings after which I would study until midnight. Twice a week the teachers would play a game of Monopoly, which they made very exciting. Apparently they played the game from home to home throughout each term. One got the impression that this was all the teachers, all men, did in the evenings. Mr. Turay was an exception. He acquired a spot of land close to school and decided to build a house on it. Every day after school his family would spend their spare time on the land making cement bricks, clearing the land, etc.

I admired Mr. Turay and wanted to be like him. In addition to his teaching, he was the soccer coach and a director of plays. He starred in the *Tragedy of Patrice Lumumba*, a play he directed for the end of the school year. Mr. G'Borie was considered the brightest of all the teachers. He was awarded a commonwealth scholarship for a year in England. What I found odd with Mr. G'Borie was the desire to whip me for coming to school late—late when not in line when the school bell rang. He had left me half an hour earlier cleaning the yard and filling the water tanks. He succeeded in getting me to be on time for school.

The school year ended abruptly and sweetly for me. Mr. Turay's production was a success. It attracted dignitaries from the SLST, near and far. On the last day of school, teachers and pupils gathered on the lawn in front of the administrative building, which housed the headmaster's office. Mr. Kassegbama, the headmaster, was an imposing man. He announced each class report with special praise to the first three students in each class. I topped my class and my class teacher recommended double promotion. However, Mr. K announced that "double promotions are not allowed this year." Mr. G'Borie, for the first time since I started living with him and his family, said to me, "It is a pity because you were the best." He was really disappointed but somehow I was not. He was probably disappointed because I had already lost over two years of schooling.

I came back to Yormandu for the long holiday. Uncle SJW was a Christian, but there were no churches in this town. There was something resembling a mosque, which was flocked on Fridays mainly by the miners. However, Mama Mary gave each of us a little something for Christmas. I received a pair of shoes for school.

Chapter 9
Standard 4 in Yengema

Kadiatu's mother was not impressed by me. I continued to sell kerosene, starch, and akra. I went to live with Uncle Paul Gandi in Segbwema.

I was now in a new class and found myself sitting behind Kadiatu M'Bayoh. She was one of two girls in my class. The other was Aminata Barker. Aminata and I were friends. Last year while playing with my friends during a break, she sent me a present through a friend of hers. I accepted the friendship but I had no idea what it meant. Up to now, I thought that boys stayed with boys and girls stayed with girls. As time went by, Joseph Fefegula (JF) gave us the impression that this was not so.

One morning, Mr. Kassegbwama, the headmaster, walked into our class in the middle of a lesson. Of course, all of us stood at attention. "I have come to weed out unwanted students," he announced. "Firstly, is there any student here from another school?"

Three students stood, one of whom was Sahr Komba, my Three Musketeer complements in Kayima. They had a verbal test and when they failed they were instantly demoted to Standard 3. Three other students failed and they had the same fate, demotion.

I wanted to know more about SK, particularly what happened to him when "we all scattered after Standard 4 in Kayima." Unfortunately at the end of the class, SK was nowhere to be found. He was gone. He always had the trait in him to be rebellious of authorities. He too obviously lost some years because he was in my class in Kayima.

One day I wrote a love letter to Kadiatu, not knowing what it meant and what the implications were. She took the letter to her mother. The following day I was summoned to appear before Mama Baryoh. I disowned the letter but it did not matter. She was alphabetical. "I did not send my daughter to school to get married to a poor schoolboy." She was so threatening to me that I started peeing on myself. That confirmed my belief that boys and girls should not mix. This I called an irony, but JF reassured me that "it is a common occurrence with women—the one you want does not want you, but the one you don't want wants you."

The term was now in full swing, and I continued to do well. Sahr Bockerie was competitive and he had decided to be the expert in Division. He spent hours practicing to solve problems in division. He did not, however, appreciate the concept of recurring decimal and that there was a word called "infinity." I still beat him in the overall score. Sahr Gborie won a trophy in almost all the events he entered during the annual sport day. He was best at long-distance running. He was born and bred in Yengema and therefore knew every corner of the town. JF, on the other hand, had a bit of our attributes (bright, athletic, and resourceful), and above all he knew about girls. He came from a different tribe, Mende, which was never held against him. At the end of every weekend, he brought with him to school fruits, particularly avocados and sour sharp. He knew how to get into the garden on the expatriates' side without being spotted.

I resumed my trading after school and on weekends. During the week I sold kerosene every night. One evening I got called, from a distance, "Kerosene Boy," and I ran towards the sound. The buyer was Mr. Komba Kamanda (KK), my tailor friend from Yormandu. I spent a lot of time with Mr. KK then, and we just hit it off again. I always dropped in to see him on the way home after my errands, and he would buy at least two bottles from me. He was a bachelor and always had food. Although much older than me, we enjoyed each other's company.

At the end of the first term, I was allowed to go back to Yormandu. My arrival was a welcome relief for both Kai M'Bamba and Sahr Gandorhun, as they now had an extra pair of hands to do the housework and fetch drinking water from the well. During one of my trips to the well, three girls were already there giggling. One of them was Aminata Barker from Yengema. Their bucket disappeared at the bottom of the well when the rope broke. Without hesitation, I climbed down the well and after two dives, I retrieved the bucket. They thanked me and I never saw them again until three days later.

As I went passed a door, "Kerosene Boy, kerosene Boy" came rushing to me. It was the voice of Aminata. She invited me inside their house and introduced me to her mother and father. "Not all mothers of girls are terrible," she said, which proved my theory completely wrong.

Three weeks into the holidays, Uncle Paul Gandi came along. I remembered him vaguely when I was a little boy in Kayima. He graduated from the Methodist Secondary School in Freetown. He was the manager of the

Segbwema branch of MOBIL Oil Company. He distributed the petrol that arrived by train to the rest of the country. He was good at his job and looked prosperous. He wanted a boy to do housework and attend school. The choice was between a cousin, Tamba James Gandi, and I. Neither of us were aware of this at the time.

Christmas arrived while I was with Uncle SJW and Mama Mary in Yormandu. All the cousins were back from school, and they came to enjoy themselves. It was extremely boring for them. There were no cinemas or restaurants or organized soccer to watch. Aminata helped Mama to cook, M'Bamba did the cleaning, and I did the laundry in the river. At other times I went to do what I enjoyed most, selling clothes. Their arrival brought its advantages.

They had a lot of reading materials but none of them liked reading. I read all their schoolbooks. I did this secretly because the girls despised me for whatever reason. One day while assisting Mama to do some frying, a splash of hot oil spilled onto my left forearm. The skin pilled off instantly, exposing the underlying pale skin. One of the girls commented, "I never thought that the black man had a white skin underneath the black skin." There were other instances that were equally unpleasant, but I just brushed them aside. They left for Freetown after one month with us. Life again returned to normality for me. "They were a handful but I am missing them already" was Uncle SJW's comment afterwards.

I knew little about Tamba except that he ran errands for Uncle James. He was tall and athletic but not particularly bright. Uncle Paul returned to his work and life with me went on as usual.

I spent a lot of time with Adip with a bit of annoyance to his mother. More time spent with him meant no selling of lapels. But suddenly Adip's countenance towards me changed. A few days later, Uncle SJW asked me to pack my belongings, which included a pair of school uniforms, old exercise books and a self-made dictionary, and a pair of sandals, which I had on. I had no difficulty encasing them in a cardboard box. That evening Adip gave Bobor, his younger brother, and me a lift to Sefadu. The following morning he told me to "find your own way to your educated uncle in Segbwema." This was the first time I became aware that Uncle Paul had opted to have me instead of Tamba.

I have never been in Sefadu on my own before and worse still, I had no money to my name. I traced my way to the lorry terminal and got a driver who was willing to take me to Segbwema with the hope that he would be paid by Uncle Paul.

Chapter 10

Standard 4 in Segbwema

The aftermath of Uncle Paul's visit to Yormandu. Adip was extremely unhappy about my leaving for Segbwema. Joseph Kallay and I became friends.

Just over four hours later, we arrived in Segbwema. The drive in the back of a Bedford truck was bumpy, dusty, and at times, the heart moved towards my throat. Yet I enjoyed it, the cool air blowing into my face and the thought of a better life that lay ahead of me. It was easy to locate Uncle Paul; in Segbwema, everyone knows anybody of any substance. He was excited to see me and I was probably more so. Uncle Paul paid the driver and gave him a tip.

He lived in a three-bedroom house with his girlfriend. I was assigned to a room, my second bedroom so far. The house was bounded on one side by Nixon Memorial Hospital separated by a strip of bush; the other side was bounded by the police quarters, which had a football pitch, and the front opened into the rest of the town. Attached to it was a shed made of two rooms, one for a pit latrine and the other for taking bucket baths. I had met Uncle Paul's girlfriend in Yormandu but very briefly. I was not aware of their relationship then. Aunty Finda and I became great friends.

Aunty Finda was an excellent cook. She was a few years older than Uncle Paul and neither of them have had children of their own. The hospital had a standing pipe outside the power-generating house from which the locals were allowed to collect water in the evenings. To fill the water drum for the three of us was child's play for me. The town itself was split in the middle by a tarred street running from east to west. It started from on top of a hill, down a gentle slope for two miles, and then up again for another mile. By all accounts, I was going to enjoy myself in this town.

The following Monday, three days after my arrival, Uncle Paul took me to school, Methodist Primary. I was interviewed by Mr. Y'Nenge, the headmaster. He agreed to let me continue in Standard 4. How very interesting; I left Kayima at the end of Standard 4, I left Yengema in the middle of Standard 4, and now I was starting in the second half of Standard 4. During the break, I was surrounded by a few of my classmates. The majority of them were curious to know where I came from, and others want to know why I knew most of the answers to the teacher's questions. At the end of school, I was joined by two boys, Joseph Kallay and Mohammed Mansary, both going in the same direction. Joseph's father was the grounds supervisor of the hospital, and Mohammed's parents lived in Liberia and he lived with his grandma and two of his siblings.

Segbwema was heading to being heaven for me. At the end of each week, every class had their respective tests. The student who came first in his or her respective class was crowned king. The reward was twice the amount of cake made of corn flour the following week. I won this prestigious trophy every week, and with it one of the junior boys assigned to me to carry my bag home. My followings increased as the months passed by. The classes went up Class 6, which was created for students who failed the CEE one or more times.

The end of the year was already on us. My class teacher entered me into the school play. I was the incorruptible judge by the same title, *The Incorruptible Judge,* set in Nigeria. Unfortunately, the play never made it because the organizing teacher was delinquent. This was a rare occurrence. Until now, all my teachers attended school every day. In the final examination, I came in second, overall beaten by Foday Bayah, the vice headmaster's nephew. Uncle Paul was disappointed but I was not; I was finally out of Form 4.

Just as I had anticipated, Segbwema was just ideal. The railway station was a centre of focus. The trains carried passengers and goods from Freetown to its final stop at Kailahun. The station attracted people for various reasons: passengers boarding and alighting, the joy of waving; and the detachment of caravans from the passenger coaches. Near the station were old warehouses, which have had their days and are now locked up. In the good old days they had thriving trades in palm oil and kernel and groundnut, and holding receptacles for goods destined for Kono and its environs. Segbwema also had a second coeducational school, run by the Roman Catholic Church. My school had a sister secondary school, which was unique as well. It had an extra class specifically designed to coach students to enter secondary school. It was a clever move by the Wesleyan missionaries to keep their flock together.

In school we spoke English outside of which people spoke mainly Mende and then Creole. People here were less in a hurry and did not look so hungry for money. Above all, the majority of the children lived with their parents and did not have the know-how to venture into the bush for food. This meant that the river we crossed every day to school, the surrounding forests, and the railway track would be left unexplored. I no longer had to sell to supplement my parents'/guardians' earning. There were other excellent ways to dispense with our energies.

Each school had its own soccer pitch and ping-pong table(s). The hospital had a lawn tennis court lawn and a table tennis table at the nurses' recreation room. The town itself had a community centre and a soccer pitch and next to which was a weed-covered lawn tennis court. We the children exploited all these facilities, except the tennis courts, which were covered by savannah grass. Life at home was good. Aunty Finda was an excellent cook, kind to me, and very supportive of Uncle Paul.

After six months things start changing, probably for the worst. Uncle Paul was well known in Segbwema. He entertained all the men in the evenings by buying drinks in the local rum shop and at home. At each location I collected the empty bottles and sold them to the proprietor of the grocery shop. I used the money to buy white canvas shoes and books from the CMS Mobile Bookshop.

Uncle Paul started drinking, which he never did before. He started dating Juliet, a mature grown-up Form Two student from the secondary school. This created friction between Uncle Paul and Aunty Finda, and I was caught in the middle of it. To further complicate matters, Uncle Samuel and two other relatives, secondary school students, arrived on the scene. They were with us for three weeks. They drank all night and slept all day.

During class we all stood in a line. The first in line was asked to recall the passage. If correct he would be asked to return to his/her seat. Should he fail to reproduce the passage, he would be asked to remain standing and the next student was asked to continue. If the next student was successful, he would be asked to slap the "failed candidate" on the face. These practices were common in all the classes and accepted as normal. In Yengema, "the failed student" was told to sit down. Now in Segbwema, the successful student used his belt to beat the unsuccessful student in his/her open hand. The teachers involved must have enjoyed the practice. I therefore found it difficult to understand that the students enjoyed it, especially one's "secret lover."

Unlike Kayima, the final school reports were read before the school assembly without the parents. My group was a bright class on the whole. We all passed to Class 5, the CEE class.

Chapter 11

Standard 5 (Final Year) in Segbwema

I was now living with the Gbondos at Nixon Memorial Hospital. Somebody assassinated President John F. Kennedy of USA. I passed the CEE for CSS.

Uncle Paul left Segbwema for Sefadu. He moved there on the request of Mr. TR Yamba, a wealthy diamond miner and dealer. He originally came from Kayima, our hometown. He owned the only MOBIL Oil Filling Station in Sefadu. Mr. Yamba was a rich diamond miner with businesses in Sefadu, Yormandu, and Kayima. His illicit mining was ignored by the SLST authorities because he "was considered as one of the local boys." Uncle Paul took the offer because the pay was better and he was going to be among his own people, the Kono tribe.

For me it was the start of the Common Entrance Examination year.

While in Segbwema, Uncle Paul had made many good friends, including a qualified male nurse, Mr. Sahr G'Bondo. Mr. G'Bondo was too happy to look after me while preparing for the Common Entrance Examination. He was married to another nurse but they had no children of their own. However, they were already looking after two other children. Komba, the boy, was in my class and Anna was three years our junior. These new parents of mine, like other grown-ups, liked "bright children." They knew I always came first on all the tests and I was on the school's table tennis, second eleven, and athletic teams.

I did the cooking and ironing when Mrs. G'Bondo was unavailable. This skill of ironing acquired from Cousin M'Bamba was to earn me enough pocket money from the male nurses. I made perfect corners in their gray khaki uniforms using starch made of cassava. These were happy times for me, though I was away from home and had no relatives.

The Gbondos were both qualified general nurses, and therefore each was entitled to an accommodation, one room and a living area. Each accommodation had a kitchen and communal toilets and showers. Komba and I had the house to ourselves with occasional sleepovers by Mr. G'Bondo. Nixon Memorial Hospital was a general hospital providing health to Segbwema and its environs and as far away as Kono and Kailahun districts. The hospital trained its own staff and the doctors came from the USA for a period of time. It was an organized and well-run institution. It attracted trainees from all over Sierra Leone and other West African countries. The support members of staff were, however, from Segbwema and its surrounding villages. These latter employees cut the lawns, cooked food for the patients, and cleaned the wards.

The hospital turned out to be an ideal place for me. According to Komba, "grown-ups like to look after bright children. You always come first in all the tests, and that's why my uncle and aunt like you. Even the foreigners like you," he continued. My friendship with Joseph Kallay became stronger. He lived with his family just outside the hospital. His father was head gardener who had four children, including Joseph, the only boy. Joe was not a book person but strong and athletic. He was good at boxing and table tennis but mainly soccer. At the end of the first term, I went to Sefadu for my holidays. Joe went to Monrovia in Liberia to stay with a relative.

Joseph also knew about girls. One day during a school break, I twisted my right ankle while playing football in the school yard. Joseph took me on his back to a medicine woman just outside the school compound. She manipulated the foot and to me she made it worse. The foot became bigger and the pain worsened. We dared not skip classes; Joe took me back to school on his back. I could not make it to school the following day, as I was unable to weight-bear. On the third day absent from school, I received two handkerchiefs from Alice Kuyembe. The edges of the handkerchiefs were embroiled by hand and a note to say, "I wish you a speedy recovery."

I could not resist showing my present and note to Joe.

"I knew that girl was in love with you. She enjoys you beating her in the hand in the spelling classes. I always see her smiling at you." He was probably right because I was as ignorant as ever.

The second term came to an end, and I went back to Sefadu for the holidays. I ran into a former mate of mine from Kayima and Yormandu (where he revealed the secret of my treasure). Sahr Semba had dropped out of school and became a miner. Unfortunately he was also a thief. He took me to the Hollywood cinemas almost every evening.

During one of my trespasses in the neighborhood, I ran into Auntie Finda. She remarried and had a child. She encouraged me to visit her often to eat and keep her company. Across the road from us was a huge artificial pond left behind by open mining. It was dirty because you never saw your feet, but boys my age spent hours in it swimming. On the banks one saw women washing clothes and wares. The holidays ended abruptly, and I was back in school at Segbwema for the last term.

Through the encouragement of Joe, I became friendlier with Alice. Alice was really a beautiful girl; she had a fair complexion, and she was slim and gentle. She was not very bright but hardworking, particularly at home. She and two other girls lived with a relative. We often visited them on our way to play football after school. She and another girl came to see us at the hospital. Most of the time we discussed schoolwork and talked about other students and teachers. Probably because of the strict teaching of our churches, we never spoke about or practiced sex. We held hands but only when alone.

The date November 22, 1963, was a day to remember. Joseph and I almost got killed by a driver who had suddenly gone berserk. On this day while walking home from school, an American Peace Corps lost control of his jeep. Joseph saw the van coming in our direction. By some miracle, he managed to pull me with him into a ditch just in time for the van to fly over us into a house. The driver apparently lost control of his vehicle on hearing over the radio the assassination of John F. Kennedy, President of the United States of America.

This term marked the final preparation for the Common Entrance Examination to enter secondary school. Entry to secondary school was the results of the teachers' and students' effort. Most, if not all, had no relative or guardian to help us through our revision, and there were no extra classes.

The day finally came. I had ironed my uniform the day before and with my pencil and sharpener in my chest pocket, I set off to school. For breakfast I had cassava and banana. I completed the papers well before the allotted time and sat down, fidgeting afterwards. I was approached by an examiner with a worried face. He flipped through the papers and with a smile he asked me to follow him. He asked me whether I was happy with what I had done and I said yes. He let me through the door. The next day we were all back in school as if nothing had happened the day before.

A month later my result came to the headmaster by telegraph that I passed for CSS and was placed first. The headmaster was not pleased about this, as it never happened before. News broke out that I passed the "common entrance." He normally received the whole school results as a bulk. The rest of the results eventually arrived, and he was to have the last laugh.

As usual the school assembled in front of his office but with a difference. The CEE students stood in the first row. All the successful students were called individually to stand behind him. Each time a student was called, everybody turned in my direction as if to say, "Your telegraph result was bogus." When he finally called my name, the complete silence broke into joy. On the whole, the school did very well.

Part Two

Secondary School Education

Chapter 12
Form 1 in Mattru Jong, 1965

I started at Centennial Secondary School. Latin was no longer taught. Walter Tucker and me became friends over the holidays. I topped my class at the end-of-year exam.

I went to stay with Uncle Paul in Sefadu after the CEE result. He showed no emotion, as he was under the influence of alcohol. As expected, he lost his job. He was to be blamed partly for this. I assigned the other part of the blame squarely at Mr. Yamba's feet, but he too was looking for the best man for his business. He got carried away with his success in Segbwema, but Sefadu was a different world.

In Sefadu, friendship was not for caring but survival. He attended many parties, smoked by the pack, drank alcohol heavily, and had a new girlfriend every week. All of these (which he admitted to me years later) contributed to his downfall. Fortunately for me, I was able to assess the situation and soon after I moved on to Kayima. This was an excellent decision.

Uncle SJW, in the company of Uncle Samuel and NGundia, arrived two weeks later. Uncle SJW had been reappointed as chiefdom clerk, bringing back into memory the good old days. He had been in office for the past year. All three of us were there to collect school fees. At this stage of his life, Uncle SJW had wealth but not enough liquid money. This was my other resolution I made early in my life, that I would "never go without money to do what I want—cut your coat according to your size."

I became the go-between for N'Gundia and Sama Monde. Sama was one of the many children of Pa Monde Kaimankondu. Our only house was situated on an island of Pa Monde's estate. There was an ongoing feud between Uncle

SJW and Pa Monde, but it never directly affected us, the children. We the children happily mixed together with not a care in the world. Besides being the go-between, I adored Sama. He was two years in Jaiama Secondary School and topped the class at the end of each year. The other thing I admired about him and the rest of his brothers and sisters was that they each had a room. He called his "my den."

As usual, Kayima attracted students to itself like a honey hive. Majority was here to illicit school fees and the others came to be part of that group of "I was away, too." The first two months of the holidays were exciting—football matches, occasional discotheques, folk dancers, and storytelling. Boys and girls mixed freely, but there were no pregnancies and nobody smoked. The last month of the holidays took a completely contrasting outlook. It was the month of "break or make." Those children whose parents were able to pay their school fees made the final arrangements to go back to school. The rest either went back to their respective villages to do subsistence farming and the rest "the mining industry." This time around, I fell into the first category.

Centennial Secondary School was a coeducational school located in a quiet town of Mattru Jong. The town, like most towns in Sierra Leone, was named after a river by the same name, Jong. It also had a primary school and a general hospital, both run by the United Brethren in Christ (UBC) Mission from United States of America. There was also a church in town overlooking the jetty to Bonthe Island and a well-stocked library. The town itself was crisscrossed by clean little streams. The streets were not paved with tarmac but covered with dirt and there were no potholes. In many ways the layout of MJ and Segbwema was strikingly similar and so too the social life and tribal language spoken. They were both designed for student life—study and play hard.

Uncle SJW and N'Gundia left for Freetown a week before the start of classes. Mr. Samuel Wilfred Gandi (SWG) and I travelled to MJ two days before the start of school. He lived in the boarding school but managed to get me to share a room literally across the road from the school with another student. SWG was "one of the mature students in Form 4." This group was self-sufficient, older than their classmates, and some of them lived with permanent girlfriends. Unfortunately they never came top of the class.

All the new students gathered before the administration block. We were then marched into the principal's office one at a time by one of the school prefects. It was more or less an interview but more importantly, we all got assigned an admission number. That number (656 was mine) was to become like a birthmark as it was to be used in all documentations. The principal, Mr. Jones, was an English man who majored in history. He was a great disciplinarian, firm and fair. He dressed in all white except black leather shoes. He wore his socks above his calves. He reminded me of Mr. White in Yengema. It was said that Mr. White went to England for one year on scholarship and on returning home, he could not tolerate the heat anymore and started wearing white long trousers and white long-sleeved shirts. Mr. Jones' mannerisms were similar to those of SWG. I later learned that SWG did his washing, ironing, and shoe polishing for a pay.

The first term went by quite fast and probably very well. I was, however, greatly disappointed that Latin was no longer offered by the school. The teacher had finished his assignment and returned home to England. They could not get his replacement. I really wanted to learn Latin because the most respected students returning to Kayima for holidays were those who said a few words in Latin. Those students were considered as "the crème of the crème." However, all was not lost; Miss Tucker from the United States of America taught French. I made no friends this term but came first in all the subjects except geography.

The school offered a wide range of subjects taught by well-trained teachers mostly from United Kingdom as missionaries, from USA as Peace Corps volunteers, and a few Sierra Leoneans trained in one of the teachers' colleges, Fourah Bay College (FBC) or Njala University College (NUC). I enjoyed all the subjects but consistently did well in biology and French.

Sports played a major part in our lives, but we were trained to enjoy them rather than compete to win. Mr. O'Connor taught history and also taught physical education. He was known for phrases like "Take a lap," "Siaki [his chimpanzee] is better than you," and "Touch your toes." We had no overall sports teacher, but each game was supervised by the introducer. Mr. M S Mustapha, the physics teacher, coached football. Mr. Jones trained and acted as the umpire in cricket. Form 1 class was called "greeners." Every Saturday morning, two or three of the senior boys took us for a three-mile jog and back. It was a military drill that exempted the day students and girls. I do not think everybody enjoyed it, but I could not recall a single student resenting or protesting. We accepted it as part of our training and conforming to the saying that "a sound mind in a sound body makes you a clever student."

We were exposed to a variety of subjects, but religious training played a major part in our lives. One Sunday morning every month, the whole boarding school walked to the church, located about one mile away from school. We usually had our white uniforms on. Rev. Parker gave us a sermon from the Holy Bible. The church was usually packed with people from the two schools, the hospital, the town, and its environs. At the end of the services, we filed back to school as orderly as the army ants. The other Sundays were spent in school. We woke up at 5 o'clock, made up our beds, brushed our teeth, and dressed to go for breakfast at 7 A.M. We went to church at 8 A.M. We dispersed to our respective Sunday schools for Bible lessons. We gathered again in the chapel/assembly hall for a full sermon after announcing the offerings collected from the classes. The main service ended at 10 A.M. to be followed by lunch at 12 P.M. We returned to our respective dormitories at 2 P.M. for meditation or silence. Between 5 and 6 P.M., silence was broken, followed by supper. At 8 P.M. we went to service. We returned to our respective dormitories at 9 P.M. and the lights were off at 10 P.M. The lights marked the end of a typical Sunday and the beginning of Monday classes.

The term ended and within twenty-four hours, the whole compound was deserted except Mr. Jones, SWG, and me. As I walked across the compound to join SWG, I heard a shout from the principal's office: "656 Gandi, why are you roaming the school?" I froze for a moment but gathered strength and answered, "I am going to help Mr. Gandi at your house," and then there was total silence again.

Mr. SWG was no longer a student at Kayima School when he took us to school. However, he was in Form 4 when I arrived in CSS. This meant that he had lost a lot of years. He was never ill and there must have been other explanations for this. He was one of two students on a scholarship given by the UBC Mission. I worked with him in his garden to grow vegetables, sweet corn, and ground provisions (cassava, yam, and sweet potatoes), which we sold to buy books. He was the school clerk; he collected mail from the post office and distributed it. He was the time keeper (rang the bell for indicating the end of periods). He looked after Mr. Jones' clothes. While I was considered as a bookworm, he hardly read or studied. Being a senior and respected student, he was allowed to have a lamp by his bedside in the dormitory. Two or three times a week, he would ask me to spend the night in his bed and would disappear when the lights went out.

The last term had started and the school was back in full swing. During the holidays I made some friends in town. Actually, they had their friends but we were forced by each other to complete a soccer team. The holiday gave me an opportunity to have a deeper look at what lies within and without the school compound.

The school compound occupied almost three acres of land. The land sloped gently down from a hill in the north towards the river in the south. The buildings were located in circles. Staff quarters were more peripherally, then the dormitories and the inner circle taken up by the classrooms. In the centre from east to west was the kitchen, dinning room, the chapel, and the administrative building, which housed the principal's office, the school office, and library. Between these buildings were plum trees, which bore fruits, but few cared for because they were very sour. However, the trees provided excellent nesting facilities for those common and annoying weaverbirds. At the top of the hill was a huge water tank, well hidden in the bushes. About a ten-minute walk from the tank in almost a straight line, a water pump was housed on the bank of a clean stream before it joined the main River Jong. Facing the town and the main road was the football field and racetrack, with a cricket pitch in the centre of it, and then within a stone's throw was the tennis court. I came to spend hours on this hard concrete court.

Immediately next to the principal's residence was a garden with ripe bananas, pineapples, and guava trees laden with fruits of different ages. The garden was hidden behind these plum trees and bushes. One saw a lot of green monkeys on both sides of the riverbanks but were always at the tree top. "In this part of Sierra Leone, people do not eat monkeys," I was once told by SWG. As you walked into the school from the main road, there was a small brick building that housed the electric generator put on and off by the grounds man. Yes, you guessed it, it was sometimes operated by SWG. Between the "power house room" and the principal's home was a strip of land running parallel with part of the road that went around the school. The first part of this land was planted pineapples and the far end covered by more plum trees faded into the principal's garden. Yes, the middle portion of this land was occupied by SWG. On it was a big sign post that said: "There is dignity in labour." To me he was a capitalist in making. The calm-looking River Jong and the semi-virgin forests surrounding the school were next to be explored.

The Christmas term was fast approaching its end. There were many rehearsals for the school play, which this year was *As You Like It*, by William Shakespeare. The end-of-year exams were also upon us. For a student to be promoted to the next class, he/she must accumulate an average of at least 50 percent for the three terms. A small number of us needed only 15 percent or less at the end of this exam to move on to the next class. This was a brilliant policy by the authorities. It reduced the stress of exam greatly—very few students had to do more than their capabilities to move on. Fewer classes, house sports, and play rehearsals took our attention from the examinations. All of these came and went with excitement and relief. A tiny number may not come back for various reasons—health and finance mainly.

Walter was an excellent soccer player. His two feet were equally effective in kicking the ball. He lived in a house with the rest of his family. The father was a retired primary schoolteacher and his mother a homemaker. He had an older sister, Margaret, and two younger brothers. In his company, I started venturing into the forest. We set traps on the riverbank for fish. I did not think they qualified as being traps. They were made of two strong green sticks, which held a net about two feet long and one foot wide. They were essentially similar to the nets used by women in Kayima and Fanema to fish in little streams and stagnant pools. The net was made of "thread" woven from palm leaves (yet another use of this plant).

We had six of these "traps" hammered into the soil with a rock. They reminded me of a series of mini lawn tennis nets. According to Walter, "when the river overflowed its bank, fish came to the land to feed. One or two was bound to be trapped in the nets as the water rose and when it receded." We forgot to check the traps because we became involved with other activities. Two days later, we came back for inspection. There was a moderately large fish in one of the nets, dead from exhaustion. Another trap had a big fish but it was all bones. Walter suggested it must have been eaten by other fish, which I call "the law of nature." He managed to convince me that we actually did catch more fish but they were taken away by some men.

River Jong was almost the size of Baffin River in Yormandu. In either situation, I only just made it with a stone thrown to the other side of the bank. This was my test for the suitability of swimming safely across a river. The results were as follows: drop in the river meant keep away, hearing a noise produced by a falling rock meant that I could swim across it but with some difficulty, and if there was no noise, then it meant that safe crossing was possible. In the case of River Jong, I decided against trying to cross it. I had no reason to cross it in any case. Like River Baffin, it too had a ferry service and private canoes were available.

In the last three weeks of the holiday, SWG allowed me to go back to Kayima. The following day I boarded a truck to Bo and then the train to Segbwema. I saw the trains many times but had never been in one. The ride was memorable. I had my head outside through the window, enjoying the cool breeze on my face and the steam mixed with smoke into my nostrils. I stayed with Joseph and family. He stayed in school to repeat the year because he did not pass the CEE. During my absence he looked after Alice for me. During my two days in Segbwema, I ran into a few of my classmates who had either returned from their new schools or stayed to repeat the year. We all bragged about our achievements but not failures. All the same, the reunion was just exciting. All good things must come to an end, and so I left for Sefadu on board a Land Rover pick-up van

Chapter 13

Form 2 in Mattru Jong, 1966

I went to stay with Uncle SJW. Mr. John O'Connor sent for me.
The MERIT system was introduced.

I spent the early part of the holidays in school with SWG. One of the main reasons for my staying was to help him in our gardening to harvest and plant new seeds. The rains and many weeds were here, but they were easy to uproot. I spent few days in Kayima before proceeding to Yormandu to be with Uncle SJW and Mama Mary.

Kayima, as usual, was abound by visitors—students, dropouts, the being part of it, etc. There was a lot of food after the ceremonies in which the boys and girls joined their respective societies that made them men and women respectively. Somebody opening the school reports that came in the mail created no problem. The whole town knew that I came first in my class and so too the results of the other students: pass or fail. This created a kind of an atmosphere of friendly competition. Now, I too had something to crow about: French. I tried to pass on my learning of this great and new language, but it was met with ridicule. Fasuluku Sankor was the greatest offender who compared my French pronunciation of "four" sounding like pulling a heavy load at the end of a long rope. No wonder I was disappointed when Latin was no longer being taught in my school when we started our first year.

Mama was happy to have me back. I continued with my house chores but the evenings were not wasted, as I had a lot of reading material. The holidays were over a month ago, and I had no prospects of going back to school. Uncle SJW, in the company of Mama, was not worse than a timid cat. He was never capable of making a decision to send me back to school, although I had over-heard him say that I was bright and liked school.

Two months had elapsed and Uncle SWG turned up. He was sent by Mr. John O'Connor, my history teacher, to bring me back to school. Uncle SJW and Mama Mary agreed to let me go. I am pretty sure they would have sent me back to school if they had the money.

I was back in school after two months and I was on my feet again in two weeks.

My class now had thirty students, the top ten from each of the three classes. There was a demerit system in the school but for the first time, the authorities introduced the merit system. One morning, by the order of the principal (Mr. Jones), the senior prefect collected nine of us in front of the assembly. He was as ignorant as we were about the assembly. The nine of us were the top three from each of the previous classes. The principal announced the names and it was going to be an ongoing practice. Each of us was fitted with a badge with "MERIT" written on it. Afterwards a student from Form 1 asked me what "MERIT" meant. "'MERIT' is the opposite of 'DEMERIT,'" I responded. Then I went on, "You should know DEMERIT because you have accumulated a few already. DEMERIT is given to students who failed to do their homework, were late to school, were caught speaking vernacular in school rather than English, and were noisy in class."

Any student accumulating ten or more demerits was sent to detention but with a difference. He (because girls never get demerits) spent the day with the grounds men cutting grass or trying to kill the weaverbirds using a catapult. The stones were to be directed away from the classrooms, but one particular student found pleasure in aiming his stones at the top of the roofs of classrooms he should have attended. I have never met any of the boys skillful enough to kill any of these birds anyway. I did.

I will like to indulge the reader in my obsession for these birds—yes, these birds, the weavers. These medium-sized birds seemed to be everywhere in Sierra Leone. I had a love/hate relationship for them. I hated them because they killed the most versatile palm/coconut trees. I hated them because they made life difficult for me in the rice farm. I hated them because they were difficult to catch for food. Yet I spent hours observing them in their colonies.

They have the ability to weave a complex nest. They nest in colonies, making them noisy, gregarious, and polygamous with elaborate courtship rituals. Their chicks and eggs attract snakes. They can strip down palm (including coconut) trees of their leaves, leaving them for dead. In Fanema, the best part of a little boy's day in a rice farm is scaring these birds away. They love human habitation, but I found it difficult to see what they offer to mankind. The colourful male (yellow with black strips or brown with red strips) spent days building a nest and only to pull it down when he failed to attract the smaller, less colourful, and fastidious female. He would then rebuild the nest using both feet and its hard beak but less laboriously than before, presumably leaving the final touches to the future partner. The adults were untouchable. On the whole they successfully defended their nests from the tree snakes and chicken hawks. However, they had problems with the villagers.

Before the rice harvest, the town chief ordered censorship of the colonies. On the day of attack, some men with baskets made of palm tree leaves attached to long sticks were placed at the entrance of the nests. By shaking each nest, the female who had been incubating either the eggs or young ones flew into the basket and were trapped. The next step was to empty the nests of its content (eggs and babies of different ages). Nearly matured babies would escape but only to be caught by enthusiastic boys like myself. Eggs, babies, and adult birds were shared among the villagers as food. Within weeks the colonies had reformed as if they had recruited new members from other colonies. On the other hand, the farmers had succeeded in saving a few more rice and corn grains from these birds, the weavers.

I was still curious to know why I had not seen student activity on River Jong. It was calm and quiet as it made its way to Bonthe Island. I was told that it was full of fish and cockles. The answer was on a wall in the chapel. At eye level was an inscription that said: "Greater love hath no man than this than to lay his life for his friends" (Psalm 12). As there was no official announcement banning students from bathing/swimming/diving in the river, various explanations were given to explain the meaning of the inscription. The most commonly repeated version was that "a group of students went across the river in a series of canoes for picnic. On their way back to school, one of the canoes capsized. Some of the students escaped. However, one of the escapees went back into the water to save a few of his friends. Apparently he did but he himself drowned, probably from exhaustion."

A month or so in school, our respective classes had gone. The first test results were interesting. No one student came first in all the subjects. I maintained my grip on French and biology but did fairly well in the other subjects. We were quite competitive in our academic work, but the majority of us became involved in sports. I took to table tennis, which I played a lot in Segbwema. My next interests were in lawn tennis, soccer, and cricket.

The tennis court was made of concrete. It was bounded at each end by tall wire nettings. It was situated in front of the school between the strip of land containing SWG's garden and the main road. It was a death trap for birds, particularly wood pigeons. In their attempt to escape human predators, they flew straight into the nettings, resulting in suicide. Sahr John, Jonathan Sharkah, Sorie Sesay, and I spent hours on that court every week. We preferred lawn tennis to football because it took less time and we were able to go back to our studies. However, none of them maintained it at a competitive level.

Chapter 14
Form 3 in Mattru Jong, 1967

*Miss Tucker, the French teacher, left for home. I developed
pneumonia and Uncle SWG took me to Freetown for treatment.
I visited my grandparents in Fanema. I sat the Junior Cantab
Examination.*

I returned to school in high spirits. At the end of the final term last year, I
went straight back to Kayima. I developed restless feet and was soon off to
Fanema. I had unfinished exploration to do there—the cave, Uncle Tamba's
farm, learning to play the top, and above all to travel around the section with
Grandpa. Unfamiliar but delicious foods were always on offer.

I arrived in Fanema when the moon was at its peak of brightness. Late afternoon I walked to Wordu. I spent a night at the usual willing family home
before proceeding to Fanema the following morning. As luck would have it,
I ran into two men heading for Fanema. We had rice and groundnuts for
supper intermixed with storytelling. They literally doped me to sleep because
I could not keep up with them. Sahr Moiwo was the funnier storyteller of the
two men.

"Do you know why four-legged animals enjoy drinking water but two-
legged birds do not?" he asked. "One day God summoned all the birds and animals to come before him. The dry season was at its peak. The sun's ray and
the clashing of horns of fighting bulls were setting fires to an already sparse
grass. He promised to provide plenty of water for all of them but they should
not be greedy. Each of the animals on four legs had a mouthful and stepped
aside. When it came to the turn of those on two legs, they would not stop. The
punishment of this disobedience was that birds drank water but only a sip at

a time. For the next sip, they looked up to God and pleaded for mercy. They were granted their wish but promptly interrupted after another sip," he continued.

They woke me up on the first sound of the clock bird. The walk to Fanema was pleasant. At the start, the ground was cool due to the morning dew and so too was the air. The rest of the journey was under the branches of the trees. It was wonderful to be in their company. They had no care in the world; all their jokes and stories were all about animals and birds they lived with. I learned from them how to catch weaverbirds red-handed.

Grandpa Joe, Grandma Fembawa, and Uncle Tamba were all home when I arrived in the village. For the first time visiting Fanema, I felt terribly ashamed of myself. I brought nothing for anybody, although I was profusely apologetic about it. "Remembering to come and see us was more important. You are still a school boy," each of them assured me.

The next morning I was off with Uncle Tamba to his new farm. He was in the middle of clearing for the next plantation. On arrival at the farm, we scared a hawk off its catch, a big tucson. "I had something to take for Grandma," I said to Uncle Tamba. He smiled and gave me the impression that I was fooling myself. He did all the work but overall he thought we did a productive day's work. Before dusk, we packed our belongings and set for home. However, "Grandma's bird" was gone. Uncle Tamba smiled again and said, "Yes, the hawk's food." He pointed his finger in the direction of a tall tree and sitting in one of its main branches was a bird's nest. He was just too happy to have the hawk around because the bird's family kept the weaver population down. I thought this was neat, getting nature to do a natural thing.

Two weeks into my holiday, a major event was to happen. Chief Sahr Yarjah had died a few weeks earlier and it was his wake. He was a very good friend of Grandpa. The head of the Sumoe society asked me to join nine of his men. Our role was to visit every big village in our section to collect money, food, and cotton cloths. When we arrived in each village, we chased down chickens and collect clothes left to dry. "All the catches were brought to the community hall. In exchange for their belongings, the villagers paid any amount of money they had or food or cockerel," according to custom. It was during these gatherings the villagers exchanged news. We quickly moved to the next village before news about our arrival preceded us. After one week of this, we got back home with our collection. It was a bumper harvest and the leader extended a special thank-you to me. However, he thought I was a bit unorthodox because I chased the chickens into the verandas. This was not allowed. People came from afar and near. He was a popular chief and loved by his subjects. After a successful ceremony, we all left for our respective villages.

The holidays were almost over, and I had not achieved even half my goal. A few men from the village invited me to go bat catching. I jumped at it. The hunt took us into a cave. It was exciting, not because of the catch but Fanema was named after this cave. When I did bid goodbye to my grandparents, they gave me the impression that this was my last visit to them. A week prior to my departure, Grandma tried once more to put some flesh on me. She ordered a goat to be killed to fatten me but yet again, she failed. My visits with them over the years have taught me to appreciate the things offered by nature to man. Many phenomena occurred that were (and are) beyond my understanding. What made the head of a goat disappear when offered to the spirits could not be explained by my limited scientific knowledge. Events like these subconsciously pulled me to Kayima and Fanema, repeatedly.

I came back to Mattru to start school on time. The third year in school was a dreaded period for administrators. The students were cocky and behaved badly. It was interesting, though, that my group hardly received DEMERITS. This was most probably because we were preparing for the Junior Cantab examination. For me the school year shortened very rapidly by two major events.

Firstly, Miss Tucker left for home, USA, after an unpleasant episode. She had punished one of the senior boys for bad behaviour. This boy managed to mobilize some of the other boys to attack her. They physically manhandled her, but she managed to escape to the hospital, where there were other expatriates. She eventually came back to school, but things were never the same again. She became disillusioned and returned home. It was a personal loss to me. She left in the middle of the school year. We were preparing for the Junior Cantab examinations. I was her "teacher's pet" because I was likeable, obedient, and hardworking. However, I continued to communicate with her in both French and English.

Luckily, within weeks another French teacher arrived. Mr. Frank Palladino, her replacement, was an American Peace Corps from New Jersey, New York. We became instant friends. He was curious and wanted to know everything about Sierra Leone, including the food and people. He got down to learning to speak Mende and Creole.

The second major event was my getting ill. I was woken up one morning with high fever, productive coughing, and right-sided chest pain. I was breathless but I walked over one mile away to go to the local hospital. While there, Dr. Solomon Pratt saw me and made "a working diagnosis of malaria complicated by tuberculosis." He ordered a male nurse to stand me under a cold shower after which they admitted me on the ward. I had injections in my bottom and was given tablets to drink. Mr. SWG went into action.

Within a week, he took me to Freetown. I stayed at the Mission House, managed by Mr. and Mrs. Cox and family (Douglas, Darling, and Darlene). It was a friendly reception, and for the first time in my life I was given a room similar to that seen in the movies. The Coxes were a Godsend for me. To complete the work force was Mr. Harry Fillie, who was "the man of all trades and master of all." He only had a few years in primary school and left because of no school fees. All the same, he managed to teach himself to read and write. Mr. Momodu Koroma hailed from the north of the country and was the night watchman. Both men were the icing on the cake. Everybody in this mission equated their duties to their lives.

The house was located on a terraced land alongside the Mount Aureole. The view was spectacular, as we saw the whole of the western shoreline and part of the city. All of this gave me hope that I was going to get well.

The following day, Mrs. Cox drove us to Connaught Hospital to see the chest specialist. The doctor was from Ceylon (now Sri Lanka), and he looked professional. After examining me, he sounded my chest and concluded that I had severe pneumonia but could not determine the cause. He ordered a chest x-ray, a microscopic examination of the sputum and blood, and Heaf and Mantoux tests. He prescribed injections given to me on my little flesh bottoms and tetracycline to be taken by mouth every six hours. At "home," he advised Mrs. Cox to treat me "however as having pulmonary tuberculosis." Within a week of treatment, my condition improved and Uncle SWG returned to Mattru.

The Coxes took me everywhere—church services, youth meetings, outings to Lumley Beach. Mrs. Cox discretely advised me to sit alone and to cover my mouth with my left hand whenever I coughed. The blood tests showed infection, the sputum was negative for bacteria, and the chest x-ray demonstrated right-sided pneumonia. On May 26, 1966, over six weeks after our arrival in Freetown, they declared me as having no tuberculosis. "All the tests are negative for TB." Everybody was happy for me, and Mrs. Cox was the happiest and the most relieved. I returned to school after almost three months of absence.

I, but not Mr. SWG, had completely forgotten about the Junior Cantab examinations. All the same, I read every day and continued to write my diary. In my absence, Uncle SWG had entered me for seven subjects. Unfortunately, he could not remember the seventh subject, geography or arithmetic. He entered me for geography, which I came to be aware of when they discovered that I was not in my seat in the exam. Overall, I thought I did well except geography for which I was not mentally prepared. A month later the school year had ended.

For the first month, I stayed with Uncle SWG at Mama Ada's home. Mama Ada was one of the cooks in school. Living there was Auntie Sophie Caulker with her daughter, Juliet. She had met my uncle while in Jaiama Secondary School, Nimikoro. However, they went their separate ways after graduation. I took off for Kayima.

For the first time after Yengema, I met with my sister, N'Gundia Monde. She had grown up to be a delightful woman. She was beautiful, tall, and very dark. She always had a serious face. She had two bat ears similar to her father's. She was living with Grandma Feeyo. We saw each other quite often then but never discussed our mother. I guess neither of us could say much about her.

After three weeks in Kayima, it was time to head back to school. The new school year was due to start in one week.

Chapter 15
Form 4 in Mattru Jong

I passed the Junior Cantab examination. I started the first two weeks of the new school year with a suspension. I became a school prefect. I acted in Shakespeare's Othello.

As I alighted from the truck, a student approached me. He was excited and all smiles. He said, "Congratulations, you people did proud to our school." This was the Cantab result. My group apparently did extremely well. Habib Mohammed and Mohammed Conteh each passed with seven subjects. Sahr John and I passed six subjects each. In my case geography escaped my certificate. It was the best result for the school in its history.

On New Year's Day, I left Kayima early in the morning for Yormandu. I opted to go on foot instead of by public transport. It took about a day but I usually had more fun. I was up at about four and on the road within an hour.

The first hour of the journey was on open dirt road and the rest followed a trail. The first part had to be done early, when it was cool and there were no vehicles to raise dust. On the road, there was everything to see, especially with time on one's side. Not long after 12 noon, my first excitement arrived. Until then the journey followed the usual pattern, rallying messages and news from one village to another.

I was warned about the repair work being done on the suspension bridge ahead. However, three miles off course would have allowed me to cross the river lower down by boat. It was difficult to explain why I ignored the advice, but I arrived at the disintegrated bridge.

Somehow, I had to get to the other side of this wide river to continue my journey. I picked up a smooth stone (about the size of a pigeon egg) from the ground and held it between my thumb, index, and middle fingers of my right hand. I threw the stone towards the opposite bank of the river. I heard clashing of the stone in the branches. This gave me a rough estimate of two hundred yards to swim.

The current was, however, very fast because I could see branches and fallen trees flying past me. I walked up the bank for a mile and stopped. I took off all my clothes and sandals. I made them into a bundle, which I tied on my head. I took to the fast-running river.

With the help of the current, I dogpaddled to the other bank, the point of crossing for normal people. The first group of villagers standing on the bank ran away.

They thought I was a ghost. They had never seen anybody so brave and probably stupid like me to take the might of River Seima. It was probably unwise, even though I may have swum the same length of rivers in Fanema and Yormandu.

I arrived in Yormandu at about 5 P.M. but Uncle SJW had left for Sefadu to be with the rest of his family. I spent the night with Uncle Paul, who had become a changed man. He smoked a lot and drank heavily. He played Draft with all sorts of characters for most of the day. He was very good at the game and almost became addicted to it. There was no money exchanged for hands, but they just enjoyed beating each other at the game. The next day, I left for Penduma, the old Koidu Town.

In Penduma Uncle SJW was again living with his first wife, Kumba Regina. Auntie Kumba had a variety store called The Shop. She sold soft and alcoholic drinks, cigarettes, and other items found in such stores. It was an excellent meeting place for most of the young men. These men spilled over from New Koidu Town (Sefadu) and neighboring villages to mine diamonds.

Those who had more money to spend sat in the parlour. Others, either by design or lack of enough cash to get rid of, stood outside with their drinks and cigarettes in their hands. Life here, to me, was no different from that in Sefadu—total chaos.

On January 4, I left for Mattru via Bo and Bumpe. On leaving, Uncle SJW gave me forty Leones (Le 40) and Auntie Kumba two Leones (Le2). Bo was the largest city outside Freetown. It had a government hospital, four large successful secondary schools, two cinema houses, etc. Despite all these facilities, it was an extremely boring city. For me it became only a transit port to and from Kono. This meant that on each occasion I stayed with a different family or friend.

I arrived in Bumpe the following day. I had the option to stay at Reverend Sharkah's home or with Zealia and family. Everybody was home at Zealia's and so I opted to stay with them. Zealia spent little time with me, as her boyfriend was in town as well. As usual, the family was kind to me. In the afternoon, one of the boys went to watch football with me. Bumpe Secondary School was playing against a team from one of the secondary schools in Bo. We thoroughly enjoyed ourselves. The following day I was off to Mattru, my final destination hopefully for the year. Two of my village mates were now in my school. Kumba Mei (of the Owl and Pussy Cat fame) entered Form 1. Dominic Fasuluku, my classmate in Kayima, who joined us to do his O'Level exam. We spent a lot of time together.

For the first two weeks of the new term, I was under suspension from school with Dominic and a few other boys. On the last evening of last term, pandemonium broke out in my dormitory. Mr. SWG called in the principal, Mr. J Allen Kpenge. On arrival, he ordered Mr. SWG to make a roll call. All those not in their beds and the names of the ringleaders were taken. Dom and I were not in our beds but in the company of Doris. At the end of his closing speech on the last day of the last term, Mr. Allen Kpenge announced our suspension. This sentence for first-time offenders by a one-man court was probably too harsh and unfair. There was no appeal—the principal was the final arbitrator. The power of the principal was to be demonstrated soon again.

Back in Mattru, Sahr Mafinda came to my rescue. I stayed with him in town during the suspension. Dom joined us in the second week. This period was painful and hard, but we made the most of it. It was hard because we depended on another student for food and all three of us slept on one bed. It was painful because we saw other students go to and come back from school. We spent the school hours in the public library and visited Doris and Auntie Sophie in the evenings. To make life more difficult for us, I had to take Dom to the hospital on three occasions because of high fever. We were finally readmitted to school on January 17 and then to classes. Three days back in school, the principal summoned me to his office.

Mr. Allen Kpenge selected me to represent Bonthe District in Moyamba against Moyamba District at lawn tennis. I was to pair with Terry Sam, who was my classmate. But the question of turning down the request never arose for many reasons. The principal's request or command was sacred and had to be obeyed. Besides, there were other many reasons to accept the request.

It was an honour to be chosen to play for a district. I had never been in a boat or to Sherbro Island, the home of our first prime minister, Sir Milton Margai. In Moyamba I would most likely run into Zealia.

Six, three doubles, members made up each team. Our team had a playing captain, Mr. Jalloh, a generous businessman. The sailing down to Bonthe was exciting. For half of the day we saw either side of the Jong River as it meandered towards the sea. I saw colourful birds I never saw before fly off and red crabs disappear into their burrows. The monkeys and baboons were not scared of us. As they jumped from tree to tree and shook branches, they looked straight into our eyes. With their hairs standing on their backs, they seemed to be saying to each other, "We are the kings out here and let them catch us if they can." We will take the challenge another day.

At about 4 P.M., we were out at sea—no trees, no land, and no apparent life. Looking around for the first time, I read the boat's name, *Malls' Boat.* There was only one lifeboat but no life vests. I saw an old oil drum marked "DIESEL." I was scared but I dared not show it. The rest of my days in

Centennial would have been hell if Terry were to become aware of my fears. Without exaggeration, he was an irresistible teaser. To him every human endeavour offered a joke. Within another two hours, we could see land and this was Bonthe, the capital of Sherbro Island.

The main industry in Bonthe was fishing. Most of the people lived along the coastlines. They boasted of an excellent UBC Mission School, which provided most of the girls in CSS and BSS after the Common Entrance Examination. In fact, the student who topped our group came from Bonthe. There were other interesting places, but time was against us. The next day we set sailed to Moyamba in a smaller, less noisy, and faster boat.

Terry and I won our match. We had played against two American ladies—Peace Corps teachers. We were about equal in skill, but they started off badly. They picked up their game in the second set, but it was too late. The overall score was in our favour, two sets to one. Late afternoon Terry and I went into town with one thing in mind—to visit the girls' school.

The layout of the school was similar to, but more spacious than, CSS. We met with Zealia, who showed us around the school. We received a bonus by visiting Madame Ella Kobolo Gulama, the only woman Paramount Chief in Sierra Leone. She was impressive. "These are not real but imitations," she said as she watched us eye the apples, pears, bananas, and pineapples, neatly arranged in a basket placed in the centre of a large table in the living room. This was the first time either of us had ever seen artificial fruits. At about 8 P.M., we attended a party organized in our honour by the host team. The following day we were off to Mattru via Bonthe.

Back in school there were a lot of changes. We now had a new English teacher, Mr. Becker, and new students in my class. Mr. Becker graduated from Njala University College with a B.A. in education. For me classes had started again in earnest. I attended all the classes, took part in sports in the afternoons, and worked on my books after supper. I also enrolled into a new course, First Aid. Mr. Downing, the biology teacher from England, organized and taught the subject. At the end of the course, he issued a certificate to each successful student. He was also responsible for the dispensary, and he was very happy for me to continue treating sores.

Centennial Secondary was strong in everything. We did well in public examinations—Junior Cantab and General Certificate Examination at Ordinary Level. We took part in sports and this year was no exception. We had inter-house tournaments in cricket, soccer, table tennis, track and field games, and English drama. The newer two additions, volleyball and baseball, were equally represented. We dispatched BSS at soccer but got hammered by Ahmadiya Secondary School at baseball.

It was not all study and play, but I got involved with people I cared for most. I replied to John's letter immediately after receipt. I always looked forward to hearing from John. His letters were philosophical, underlining the fact that there was a lot to gain by reading. The other letter was from Miss Scullery in USA. She was on the panel that gave scholarships to students in

CSS. Dominic and I nursed each other from malaria attacks. I visited Doris and Sophie for a few hours after school. My next stop was Sorie Sesay. Sorie became my best study mate. We were both doing the same subjects at O level examination. I did French in addition. We would solve some problems in additional math, physics, and chemistry before leaving for school. Mr. SWG gave me a lot of laxity—he demanded little of my time to work in the garden, which was surprising. The general impression was that when I left the school compound, I went to see Doris.

Mr. SWG was unpredictable. One day he designated the Sick Parade to me. Two days later, he verbally attacked me with regards to having an affair with Doris. Zealia's mother was concerned that I was seeing Doris too often. I was at a loss because Doris and I were good friends but there was no sexual relationship. It was shocking but somehow I was not surprised at Mr. SWG's sudden outbursts. Life for me just went on as usual. It was not so simple for Doris.

Mr. SWG threatened Doris to take her to the police for having an affair with Francis. How was she to prove that she had no affair with Francis? We found the whole situation confusing and ironical. I helped Doris with her schoolwork, which gave me an opportunity to revise my examinations. We were both doing well in our class examinations. Our pants never came off.

I continued working in the Sick Parade because it was enjoyable. The first-aid course was going full throttle ahead. Somehow I had found myself playing more lawn tennis than other sports. My excuse was that tennis was less demanding on time as compared to soccer, running, cricket, and the like. This was probably the main reason. But also true, I was away in Freetown too often for check-ups. A week or so resulted in losing one's position in a team. In any case, I had also become involved in a new game, badminton.

This new game called feathers was introduced by Mr. Waragheese. Mr. W came from India and was an excellent physics teacher. All of us who took to badminton were good players in ping-pong or tennis or both. Like Mr. Palladino before him, on introducing the game Mr. W provided everything that went with it—net, posts, rackets, and shuttlecocks.

Soon after the end-of-second term examinations, there was a staff meeting. They named the school prefects—Mohammed Conteh as senior, Lucinda Quinn as assistant, and seven others, including myself, as dormitory prefects. The appointees were very good students, but I doubted our abilities as leaders with one or two exceptions. The appointments marked the beginning of the Easter holidays.

While other students left for their respective homes, I went to Freetown for yet another doctor visitation. The Coxes returned home at the end of their contract. We (other missionaries, students, church members, and the workers) loved them dearly. Their departure was a personal loss to me. They qualified as "my other parents." The Medfords replaced them but they could not fill the Coxes' shoes. I arrived on Friday and saw the doctor the following Monday. Living in the annex of the Mission House on this visit was Max King. He was attending the Albert Academy at the foot of Mount Aureole. It was said that, "A-level students at the end of their examinations just walked up to Fourah Bay College." The school had a reputation for excellent results in O- and A-level examinations. After two days with Max, I did not think he had a hope in hell to crawl past the first step to FBC. Max was not a nice boy. For his keep he was supposed to work with Pa Harry Fillie after school. He took no advice from him and was rude to most people, except the Medfords.

The end-of-year school play was appropriately produced by the English teacher, Mr. Becker. The play was *Othello* (one of Shakespeare's tragedies) in which I acted as the king. Samuel Lunsai from Form 3 played the part of Othello. He was not particularly very good at his schoolwork and when chosen by the teacher, I never thought he would pull it off. There were a lot of lines to remember. He was brilliant. In fact, he had a standing ovation.

Chapter 16

Form 5 (Final Year) in Mattru Jong, 1969

Uncle SWG left to study in Bo. I stayed with the physics teacher. I did marginally better in the final than the mock exams. I went to live with Pa Harry Fillie in Freetown.

This was the final year at Centennial Secondary School after which we were on our own. At no time during the five years of study were we warned what was in the outside world. In one of his masochistic moods, Mr. Lavaley, the principal, invited the whole class to his office. The purpose was to complete application forms for admission to one of the universities. It took him three hours to go through the motion during which time we stood and he allowed no student to sit.

After Form 3, we had chosen our subjects for General Certificate Examination at Ordinary Level (O'Levels). I had chosen seven subjects (all sciences, ordinary and additional maths, English, and French). This year was extremely important to me (and the rest of my classmates), but for the first time in my life I felt lonely.

Uncle SWG had left at the end of last year for Bo to study for his teacher's certificate. For most of the time we lived together, I wanted my freedom from him. Now that I had my freedom, I did not know what to do with it. I missed his nagging, his advice, and his emotional and financial support. Dominic had completed his O'Levels and he was no longer around. Granted, Doris Mei and Sahr James were still around, but they too had their friends. Most of my mates had paired off to study together. I did work with Sorie Sesay but not consistently. He was a day student and I had to journey home by him to study.

Fortunately, I pulled myself out of this state of self-pity and got on with my revision.

At the end of each year, the principal invited a guest to give the graduation ceremony speech. The guest speaker's speech followed that of the principal's. Last year one knew that Mr. Allen Kpenge was leaving us. He was burning down the bridges as he crossed them. When appointed as principal after the departure of Mr. Jones, great things were expected of him. In his first year, he introduced and taught economics. All the candidates passed, although none had distinction.

He received his bachelors and master's degrees in USA. He was not a churchgoing man. His one-hour speech was a reflection of a frustrated man. At first, he gave account of the achievement of the school in sports, public examinations, and the steady increase in the student population. Then he went berserk. "The missionaries only taught us to read the Bible," he said. I found this confusing considering his previous utterances.

For example, two years previously, Mr. SWG called him to the Dining Room (DR) because we, the boarders, refused to eat our breakfast. We thought the food was poorly prepared. He walked into the DR and everybody stood. "I cannot believe some of you people. In your homes, you eat cassava and palm oil for breakfast. In this school we offer you everything, including bread, milk, and sugar," he commented. We instantly ate our food without any fuss. We were fully aware that he had no difficulty suspending "naughty students." He did leave at the end of his speech and was replaced by Mr. Lavaley, a graduate from Njala University College.

Last year, I became one of the school prefects. My responsibilities were to supervise the Form 3 dormitory students and the cleaning of the toilets. I did badly at both of them. My administrative technique was completely different from that of Uncle SWG. Gentle persuasion as adopted by me failed. One day, Mr. Lavaley summoned me to his office in the middle of my biology class. I followed him to the boys' toilets. Most of the bowls were blocked and the walls half-heartedly cleaned. He ordered me to supervise the cleaning after school. He also ordered me to distribute a toilet roll to each toilet daily. His reasoning made sense: "Using toilet tissue instead of hard paper reduces blockage. Blockage costs the school a lot of money." I took this as a personal attack, but he treated all the other prefects the same way. He proved my point; my class was good at passing exams but bad at administration.

At the beginning of this year, Mr. Lavaley introduced the "mock exam," which was unheard of in CSS. He warned us that in a month or so prior to the "real exam," there would be a "mock exam." Any student who failed that exam would not be allowed to sit the real exam as a school candidate.

Another Easter term had started, and all the prefects were relieved of our duties by a new set of appointees. This was an excellent traditional practice. It allowed us to concentrate on our forthcoming examination. I again emphasized, "Besides, my group was bad in administration. We were excellent at passing examinations."

Mr. Waragheese gladly offered me a spare room attached to his quarters. The room contained a spring bed covered by a cushion made of dry straws, an electric light bulb, and a desk. The room was ideal for studying because it was quiet and peaceful. Sahr James or Doris Mei hardly came around to visit me. This was probably because I was now living in the teachers' quarters, which were out of bounds to students. This isolation was not limited to me; other students had disappeared to study in isolation or in groups.

The mock examinations came and I did not do well in them. Mr. Lavaley quickly posted the names on the school notice board. He reminded us that the candidates who failed the examination "would not attempt the real exam but as external candidates." However, after an emergency staff meeting, he changed his mind. He informed us again through the bulletin board that we were allowed to sit the exams. We were never counselled but left on our own devices.

The final examinations came and went. We the graduates were now faced with an immediate problem. This was the acquisition of two different outfits for graduation—a two-piece suit and a traditional top and bottom fittings. We wore the traditional outfit during the prize-giving night. Traditionally, the suit was worn during church service followed by speeches. Not all of us could afford these outfits and it caused a lot of distress. Some of the students just made it through the last five years. Despite these financial difficulties, all fifty of us attended the ceremony. Among Sahr John, Habib Mohammed, Mohammed Conteh, and Musa Mansaray, they received more than 90 percent of the prizes.

A week later we had a night of disco at the town hall sponsored by all the graduates. I invited Doris Mei and Ms. Mini, the domestic science teacher. It was a lovely evening. A few days later, I went to visit Uncle SWG in Bo. I spent a month with him during which time we worked on his maths. As expected, he was finding it difficult to study. This was his first year in the training college and I held little prospect for him. He was a doer, an administrator, and not a student. After a month with him, I went to Sefadu.

In Sefadu, I found myself travelling between my sister's and her husband's home for food and Uncle SJW's home to sleep. On waking up one morning, something told me that I was wasting my life away. The next day I was off to Freetown. Pa Harry and I had become father and son over the years. In fact, I had stayed with him on a few occasions during my hospital consultations in Freetown.

He lived in New England Ville, and he was just too happy to have me. A few weeks later, the O-level exams came out and I did marginally better than the mock exams but not good enough to enter college. I immediately entered for evening classes to improve my grades. John wanted me to go back to school, but his advice came too late. As expected, the school did very well and probably came first in the country.

Chapter 17

From Freetown to Dublin in 1970

I was now living with Pa Harry Fillie. GCE O-level results came out. I met with my mother after fifteen years. I developed recurrence of my chest infection in Dublin.

The present diary, *LETTS BROWNIE GUIDE DIARY,* was worth Le0.53. I was once a scout. It had the photograph of Lord Baden-Powell of Gilwell, Chief Scout of the World and founder of the Girl Guide Movement. The cover was made of leather and easily carried in the back pocket. I bought it from the only bookshop in Freetown.

The first day of this year was on a Thursday, a public holiday in Sierra Leone, including Freetown. When I came to live with Pa Harry in New England Ville, I befriended Mr. Albert G'Bondo, a primary schoolteacher living three doors from us. He was living in a rented accommodation made of concrete bricks. This contrasted sharply with mine—a common association as seen in neighouring Dworzak. In this city, the very poor and the very rich lived on the hillsides overlooking the best scenic views in Freetown.

My living quarters were nothing more than "a matchbox standing on four wooden pillars." It was a recipe for fire disaster. It had a door, no windows. The roof and walls were made of the same material: corrugated tin. It was one of four such buildings in this compound owned by Mr. Joe Abibu, a seaman. He was a handy man on deck who worked for three months at sea and then one month off.

On this day Mr. Albert Gbondo gave me ten cents when I was about to leave for my compound. Mr. G'Bondo must have been in his late thirties. I used to call him a Christian man; he was kind and quiet spoken. He left a few months later to further his studies in the United States of America.

The day's events for the early part of the year followed almost the same pattern as most other days for me in Freetown. I studied in the morning until 10 A.M. I would then cook for Pa Harry and myself. Prior to my arrival, he sent his wife, Musu, away to her parents. He lived opposite my living quarters in similar building materials. He had two rooms rented from Mr. Joe Abibu. Out of his meagre allowance/salary from the mission, he paid for our respective rents and the food. He also paid rent for his older brother's son, Samuel, whom he thought was a failure. We were God-sent for each other. We became father and son.

After cooking, I studied for the rest of the afternoon and then went down to the Prison Officers' Tennis Club. Before the arrival of the men after work at 5, I would play table tennis with the local boys. Thereafter, I would become a ball boy for the big people. This group included active and retired lawyers, medical doctors, university lecturers, prison inspectors, etc. In short, most of the players had "BA," being away or back to Africa. Play stopped at about 6 P.M. (the beginning of darkness) and then drinking time, Heineken or Three Stars beer, cool Coca Cola, etc. For our reward, we were allowed to play among ourselves (the ball boys) using the men's (no women in the club) rackets and tennis balls.

One evening, I managed to talk with a Mr. J E M'Bayoh. I was ashamed of myself for failing to recognize him because "all children are expected to recognize grown-ups." In 1965, he was the feature speaker at a graduation ceremony in CSS. At that time, he was adorned in his academic gown. He was also known as the first Kono man to have a B.A. (bachelor of arts) degree. He was a medium-built man, an up-country man who had done well as a civil servant in Freetown. He was well respected back home as a secondary schoolteacher.

"My son is in Prince of Wales doing his A-levels in the sciences. Do you know him?" he proudly asked me.

"Not really because I have not actually started there yet because they want me to improve on my O-Levels. That's what I'm doing now with the aim of starting in September."

"What do you want to be after A-Levels?" he curiously asked me, as I sounded so confident.

"I am going to be a surgeon," was my response. This was my usual ready-made answer for the same question.

Then one evening, a new tenant appeared in the compound. I watched him cook one afternoon and he was clumsy at it. He was like a "fish out of water." Being a boy, the women in his family must have done everything for him. One evening we got to talking. He graduated from Bumpe Secondary School, the other secondary school (the first one being mine) established by the UBC Mission. He got the best grades from his school at O'Levels. He came to Freetown to do technical engineering at the Technical College in

Brookfields. What a surprise; we hit it off instantly and Pa Harry was even happier. I became the cook for the three of us.

I later learned from Alfred Sam Foray that I could enroll in his college to do evening revision courses. I did this and it was an instant success. There I met with Gerald Mathews, my friend and former classmate in CSS. I was repeating math, chemistry, and physics. I topped in all classes—a reflection of the good foundation we had in CSS. Gerald's father eventually employed me to be his son's tutor. We just became study mates.

I kept in touch with Doris and Zealia by letter but did not with any of my relatives. My days had now become fully occupied—study, cook, study, and tennis or revision classes. On weekends, I would either visit Gerald or Dominic or go to the cinema. Then I lost the cooking rights to Auntie Musu. She was recalled from up-country. This was a welcome relief.

On Thursday, Alfred and I attended Parliament on Tower Hill to watch the parliamentarians' debate. It was disappointing. Our school debate was even livelier. The majority of the parliamentarians were reading newspapers or chatting among each other, and the legal adviser always passed written message(s) over to the prime minister, Siaka Stevens. He would then proceed to read the answer posed by the opposition. We never went back.

Most of my activities became greatly affected because of recurrent chest infections for which I received Penicillin injections from Mr. George. Mr. George worked at the Connaught Hospital as a pharmacist. I also made frequent self-diagnoses of malaria fever, followed by the administration of tablets bought over the counter as suggested by the dispenser. Whatever little pocket money I had went to my health. This must have been an additional reason, consciously or subconsciously, that pushed me into becoming a medical doctor.

Alfred, like me, enjoyed studying. After tennis, we studied together until 1 or 2 A.M. with the help of the kola nut ("academic night cap") and the radio music in the background. Mariama Musa joined us one evening. She lived with her family in a brick house a further door before Mr. G'Bondo's. She too was revising for her O-Levels. She also enjoyed our company, particularly the way we interpreted Bible stories. She repeated the sayings of Alfred, like "Jesus was the first cannibal because he gave his body to his disciples." Miriam had a much younger sister, who was violent verbally. One day you were friends and then a day later she developed a dog-and-cat relationship with you. She was both kind and quarrelsome. Those evenings were productive. We shared the cost of the kerosene for the hurricane lamps.

It was not all study, cook, fetch water from the communal standpipe, and play lawn and table tennis. I read few books, including *In Another's Likeness, Perfect Murder Case, The Lonely African, Hastings's Cases in Court, Lucky Loser, The Biafra Story, Typist, Red Head, The Scarlet Letter, Assignment Malta, Murder Has Been Done, Communism American's View, Murder on Night Ferry, Beloved Come Back, Against the Wind, The Hammersmith Maggot, Dark Days in Ghana, Zambia Shall Be Free, Bayonet Point and Facts About Israel.*

Alfred and I entered for the "Soviet Quiz." The Russian Embassy in Freetown organized an educational week for USSR. The authorities invited all candidates to write an essay on any topic about the Republic. They had their library opened to all competitors and were offered reading materials for two weeks. The winner received a return ticket to visit the Soviet Union. Alfred and I won a book each.

The Sierra Leone Open Tennis Tournament was here again. Mr. Mathew, a lecturer at FBC, asked me to team up with him in the tournament. He came from India. We surprised everybody because we got to the semifinal stage. At the end of the game, a well-dressed male spectator approached and gave me a ten-shilling note, which I have at the time of writing this book.

One day Pa Harry and his wife left for Moyamba. They went to collect their son, Henry, from the wife's parents. Henry happened to be their only son or child, for that matter. They had had three boys before but all died before the age of five. They came back a week later with Henry. He was unwell and the future for him looked bad. Together with his mother, I took him to see a children's doctor privately. He examined and sounded the child. He prescribed some medicine and we left. He made some progress after a week.

"Well, there is always a first time." One Monday afternoon I went to visit Dominic on my way home from the American Library. He had "a little something going." I had a pint of 3-Star Beer. Less than an hour later, I started vomiting and everything around me went in circles. I just wanted to lie down on the floor to overcome this unpleasant feeling. I got home in a taxi and promised myself never to do it. This I have done up to now. Two days later, I went back to the library to continue reading *To Be a Tennis Champion*. It was actually on the life of Rod Laver of Australia. It was an exciting book because it was an autobiography and about tennis.

On Thursday, I received my exam results from the Examination Council. I passed all four subjects with good grades. At least the results entitled me to do my A-Levels at the Prince of Wales School. Mr. John O'Connor received a transfer from New York to Dublin. He and his wife invited me to join them. Of course I accepted instantly.

In the meantime, I received USD50 from Mr. John O'Connor to apply for my passport. In less than two weeks, Dominic was able to obtain one for me through "a relative" who was the head of the Passport Office. The subsequent weeks were full of physical activities. I needed to have my vaccinations (cholera, smallpox, yellow fever, etc). I attended an interview at the British High Commission for a visa, which was not required, as Sa Leone was a member of the Commonwealth.

According to John, to enter college I needed character references. Mr. Albert Metzger, the lawyer, from tennis readily gave me one. He was generous in his recommendation as if we had known each other for years. He had more confidence in me than I had of myself. My hunt for more references got me to Mattru Jong and this was disappointing. Miss Nancy Hall, my former English teacher, stated that as a school prefect I was very cooperative but there was no mention of my academic achievement. Mr. Alan Lavaley, the principal, quarreled with me for not coming back to the school to improve my grades. I found this surprising because a year earlier he almost stopped me from doing the exams. He wrote that I was a top student but was held back because of poor health. This reflected on my disappointing exam results. He said that I was a fine tennis player and that I played for the school and Bonthe District. He did not commit himself in any way. Reverend Parker, who had taught me religious knowledge, never said yay or nay. I waited outside his classroom for over two hours, but he never came out. My next stop on the way out of Mattru was at the hospital. I went to see Dr. Solomon Pratt, my medical doctor and friend. He sent his attending nurse to ask me to wait. He came out three hours later and flatly announced his refusal to give me a reference. His argument was "You will die in the cold." I had three character references out of a possible five, not bad.

On Wednesday, October 21, I left Freetown for Sefadu by road. It was the rainy season and the roads were bad. The journey took us just under eight hours. The Bedford truck had six wheels, and there was no mistaking when they got into potholes. On two occasions, the driver let us all out of the truck to drive across the road, buried in mud water and stretching for over two hundred yards. We then walked across the river to join our transport. I was amazed to see very few capsized trucks along the route. However, arrive we did.

This trip was meant to bid goodbye to my family, but it had a mixed outcome. Aunty Regina, after many years of separation from Uncle SJW, was back at home. Unfortunately, she came back to revenge. She came back to collect what was due to her and also their son, Wilson. She considered me as one of the privileged during her absence. Therefore, I came back empty-handed. Mr. M'Bayoh, my brother-in-law, gave me fifteen Leones (Le15). Tamba Sama Monde, my pal in Kayima, donated a few Leones and introduced me to Mr. Bonzo. He was rolling in money because he just hit a jackpot in his mines. He discovered a "big stone." He was generous to the both of us. My next visit took me to Kayima, where it all started. I was well received.

I stayed with Grandma Feeyo, who had various families, including two of her grown-up children living with her in her own house. She was as hard-working and industrious as ever. Her love for me remained unshakeable. She ordered one of her chickens to be killed for me. My stepfather was happy to see me but could not help financially. I finally went to bid goodbye to Grandpa Joemende. He was a shadow of himself. He was well but as a chief, there were very few people around him.

The following day, I went to see Mr. T W Johnny, my teacher who taught me to write with a nib-pen on a sheet of paper. He was still teaching but on the side, he reared pigs and grew vegetables. The following day I left for Sefadu. I confidently told these people that I was going abroad "to study surgery." Sometimes being naive may be helpful.

My curiosity got the better of me. I agreed with my sister to go and see our mother. She lived with an older man, both doing subsistence farming. We spent two nights with them during which time she wept on and off. We never discussed the reason why she abandoned us, my sister in Yengema and me in Kayima. Her concern was how to pay for my plane fare to a foreign country. Although we did not see each other for over fifteen years, I saw no change in her. My sister resembled her very much. She was a very dark woman and she had a limp in her right leg due to a chronic leg ulcer. Neither of us had little to say to each other. Three days later we bid goodbye; N'Gundia stayed.

After a night in Sefadu, I took a bus to Bo. I stayed with Uncle Samuel, Daniel, and Wilson. Uncle Samuel was in a teacher's college while Daniel and Wilson attended one of the secondary schools. I am not sure what my family thought of me going abroad to study. They gave me the impression that "we should wait and see." However, non-family members were more receptive, generous, and encouraging.

I got back to Freetown and started packing for Dublin, Ireland. Alfred and Dominic were always there to support me. Dominic had his older brother living in England and so he knew about the cold climate in the United Kingdom. He accompanied me into town to buy warm clothes and suggested I tried them in a refrigerator. If comfortable then I was ready to go to England. Like Pa Harry they were true Christians—happy with me when I was happy, and they shared my pains.

On Friday, December 11, I left Freetown for London. Pa Harry, Alfred, Dominic, and Joseph Lamboi were all there to see me off at the Paramount Hotel. The bus took the passengers across the ferry to Lungi Airport. John was waiting for me at Heathrow Airport. After some refreshments, we went on another plane, this time to Dublin. Patricia and the two boys, John and Michael, were waiting for us. We had corned beef, new Irish potatoes, and orange juice for lunch. "Oh, it's wonderful in London" was an entry marking my first day away from Sierra Leone. I left its shores on a jet plane, as sang over Sierra Leone's broadcasting service.

John had done a lot of groundwork. He had made an appointment to meet with the registrar of the Royal College of Surgeons. Dr. Harry Cunningham was honest with me; John was disappointed but I was not. He thought I was qualified to enter the school but I might not enjoy the study. He said that the majority of the students would have had B.Sc. degrees, others with A-Levels, and the Irish students had Higher Leaving Certificates. Based on his advice, I was willing to spend another two years in secondary school.

Less than a week in Dublin, my chest infection came back. My chest became tight, developed coughing with sputum production and probably compounded by malaria. John took me to a chest specialist who made a working diagnosis of bronchiectasis. He requested few tests to include that for tuberculosis. In the mean time he ordered chest physiotherapy and oral antibiotics. The recovery was instant just as the onset of the infection.

My first Christmas in Ireland was an enjoyable one. For Christmas, I received a wristwatch and two pens. For the rest of the year I played with the boys, read every available book in the house, and wrote back to friends like

Dominic, Alfred Foray, Joseph Lamboi, and Pa Harry, but none to any of my relatives. I also tried to explore my surroundings. We were living at Tudor House, Monkstown, in a suburb of Dublin. It was a huge house with a well-maintained garden to play and not for growing food.

Chapter 18

First Year at St. Andrew's College, 1971

I was accepted at St. Andrew's College, Dublin. I met with other Sierra Leone students in Ireland. I had a lung operation. The O'Connors returned to USA.

John donated this year's diary to me. It came by the way of a surprise. John was very good with surprises, making it a point of duty to bring a treat for each of us each evening he came home. Pat had left for Boston a week earlier. Mrs. Coughlin was the home help who looked after Michael when I went to collect John Jr. from school. On a good day, walking to John's school took me just under forty-five minutes and was enjoyable. However, at this time of the year (early January), the weather was cold, wet, and windy, causing me to cough more. I always came back with John by bus.

I prayed that the year would get better. I visited the Physiotherapy Department at the St. Laurence's Hospital for chest physiotherapy. Miss Kelley, the physiotherapist, turned out to be a good teacher. We were both pleased with my ability to do the exercises on my own. The exercises made me feel better. When I got home in the afternoons, I would play with the boys until John got home at about 7 P.M. I continued to read whatever was available, including *The Betrayal of Africa*.

The other wonderful thing about John was his ability to take us for long drives on weekends to see restored and ruined castles, caves, lakes, and farmlands. On other weekends he took us to Navan, the Kells (with a round tower, high crosses), Ardee (with castles), Drogheda, and Swords. The boys and I enjoyed these drives tremendously. Our most commonly visited location was at Glenda Lough. It gave the boys, particularly Michael, a chance to run riot in the open fields. I saw snow for the first time. We all made snowballs and pelted them at each other as in the movies. The outing was wonderful and the scenery was breathtaking. On getting back home, John helped me to compose a letter of application to St. Andrew's College.

I ran out of reading material in the house, and so I joined the public library at Dun Laoghaire. I borrowed three books *(The Cigarette Smoking Habit, Zoology,* and *Biology)* following registration. I received three letters from home one day, one from Pa Harry. His only son and child, Andrew, died on December 20. I felt very bad and sorry for him and his wife. I could do nothing; I had no money, was not yet in school, and was dependent on John and Pat. I wrote a long letter of condolences.

On Sunday John and I went for an interview with the principal of Presentation College. The school was less than thirty minutes' walk from home. We were both very disappointed when we were told that being non-Catholic, I could not be admitted to the college. We left hurriedly.

Subsequent weeks followed, and each day followed almost the same pattern. After breakfast my trip would take me to the hospital for chest physiotherapy, recommended by the chest specialist. On getting home, I took over the babysitting from Mrs. Coughlin. We entertained ourselves by doing hide-and-seek, playing soccer, and sorting jigsaw puzzles. We had no television or radio, and so I exhausted them to sleep after supper.

I wonder how I would have survived in Dublin without the guidance of the O'Connors. To go to hospital I had to take two buses, one from home and one from city centre. The first bus was almost empty from my street. The passengers walked in and took their seat in complete silence without saying good morning. The seat next to me was the last to be taken. They left the bus in the same blank face they came in with on arrival at their destination. Before boarding the next bus, I would say good morning to every black person I made eye contact with on the pavement, but they too looked at me as if I was insane. John reassured me that it was normal in all big cities and "you will get used to it."

John finally made a breakthrough. Apparently, he tried various schools to take me in for the Leaving Certificate Examination classes but was unsuccessful. We got a nod from St. Andrew's College. I was late on the first day at school because of traffic delays. I was internally excited. I attended geography, maths, and English classes. None of the topics were new to me; I had done them before. During change between classes, I was approached by one of my classmates, Timothy Mansfield. Tim was from the warmer parts of Australia, and he seemed adjusted. I also found him to be knowledgeable, bright, and friendly.

Would you believe that only after one week in school, I wanted to go back home because I found the classrooms to be very cold? Apart from Tim and less than a handful of students, the rest of the boys were not very serious about their work. The teachers seemed to be doing all the work for them. But above all, the majority of the boys called their teachers by their nicknames. This was unknown in all the schools I attended back home. Not to be outdone by Tim, one day Mr. Duke stopped me in the corridor.

Mr. James Duke was the headmaster (principal). He reminded me of Mr. Alan Jones at Centennial Secondary School. He was heavily set and wore an academic gown over his three-piece suit. He had an air of authority, firmness, and fairness. The geography, maths, English, and chemistry teachers also wore their gowns. He officially welcomed me to the school. He gave me no fore-warning about what to expect or how to behave. I took an instant liking to him.

The days were now becoming shorter and shorter; twenty-four hours were not enough. I attended school every day, went to the hospital for chest phys-iotherapy twice weekly, and played with the boys after tea until 8 or 9, their bedtime. I would then work in my room until 12 midnight or later.

Tim became a real friend. I wanted to do physics but couldn't because the times coincided with the biology classes. He suggested I went for "grinds," or extra classes, instead. He told me that other students did grinds even in sub-jects taken in school for their college entrance exams. It was difficult to explain why we never discussed the subject again. He too must have been taking extra classes.

One mid-morning Mr. Duke walked into the maths class. My teacher told him that I was in the wrong class, as I was far ahead of the other students. I was transferred to the honours (or additional maths) class. I joined my new maths class the following Friday. My new teacher was an older man and more serious than the previous one. There were only five of us all planning to enter university. This meant the students were highly motivated to do well. In order to keep up with the other students, I borrowed an hour or two hours from the other side of midnight.

Patricia returned from the States. She looked well and the boys were ex-cited to see her again. I worked harder on my schoolwork with little or no in-terruption from outside activities. I had few friends, probably because of my accent and I did not use deodorant. John helped me with the later problem in his usual diplomatic way, by inviting me to go shopping. On the list were two varieties of anti-perspiring deodorant and Dettol. David Knaggs became my friend because most of our classes coincided with each other on most days. With regards to my body odour, he was not as diplomatic as John. I was ex-tremely grateful to him when one day he said to me, "Look here, Francis. You have a very good personality and everything about you is good. But your problem is that you have a bad body odour and so everyone tends to stay away from you. So why can't you do something about it?"

I did something about it, and the effect was dramatic. I had more students sitting and talking with me. The classes became more interesting. Our English teacher did not have long to go for his retirement. He strolled across the fire-place as he taught his subject. He was quite good at his subject. On a cold day, the boys complained that he blocked the heat from them. My new maths teacher was yet another dedicated teacher and quite experienced.

Unfortunately, he solved most of the problems by himself and hardly turned away from the board. The French teacher was a middle-aged man who behaved like a Frenchman. He looked younger than his age. He never gave weekend homework because he thought that weekends were meant for recovery from the week.

Most of the days followed the same pattern. I went to school in the morning and then back home in the afternoon to play with the boys until they went to bed. I stayed up to study until 12 midnight and then was diary writing. During one of my checkup visits to St. Laurence's Hospital, I ran into Martha Margai and another lady. I overheard them talking in Creole and I introduced myself. Two days later, I got a telephone call from Charles Margai. Mr. Margai invited me to meet with him and some of his friends. John was extremely happy for me that I was able to meet with some students from my country.

I gladly accepted Mr. Margai's invitation to attend his party on Saturday night. There were a few Nigerian students and a few of his relatives. Charles was the son of Sierra Leone's second prime minister, Albert Margai. Samuel and Martha were the children of Mr. Samuel Margai, the younger brother of Albert. Charles and Samuel were law students but never got on well with each other. Martha was studying medicine at TCD. The other guests at this bottle party were students in the different institutions in Dublin. It was a wonderful night out viewed from two aspects.

Firstly, I was able to eat some West African foods different from those prepared by Pat. Pat was equally an excellent cook. The second front was, and probably, more important to me. I listened to what everyone had to say about his achievements in their various studies and of female conquer. These talks gave me that extra desire to enter medical school. At the end of the party, I accepted an invitation from Charles and Martha to stay overnight. I got home early the following morning.

I spent many more Saturdays at Charles' flat. He was an excellent cook and a social butterfly—he liked people around him. This was easy to understand because he came from an extended family of successful politicians. Sir Mitton Margai, Sierra Leone's first prime minister, was his uncle. His other uncle, Samuel Margai, was a government minister. Charles was also a fine table and lawn tennis player. I never won against him at any card game.

Each time I got home, the studies became intense after first making sure the boys had gone to bed. Pat did not seem to appreciate these going-ons with me and I was confused. She said little to me; there was no discussion, but she commanded me to do my duties. To me living with them was a piece of cake—collecting the milk bottles, taking the garbage bags on my way to school, cleaning the dishes and tidying the kitchen, and babysitting—for me.

John's parents came to see us in Dublin from New York. John was a mirror image of his father. John Sr. gave me a hunting knife in exchange for a piece of coin. He said it was an old tradition among farmers in America. I still have the knife at the time of writing. The visit was brief and when they left I shed tears. Not to be outdone by his father, John took the boys and me to the car races. It was my first experience ever, and I enjoyed myself thoroughly. I did some studies until the usual time, 1:30 A.M.

I spent a lot of time with the boys. I enjoyed their company. They were two contrasting children. John, the older, was gentle and liked to read. Michael, on the other hand, was athletic, rough, and fearless. But like all children, they were blind, selfish, and merciless. They did not know when they were tormenting me. I must say that I did my best for them; I kept my temper in situations that would have tried the skill of St. Francis of Assisi.

In the midst of all this, the chest ailment that haunted me in my last years at CSS had recurred. The chest physiotherapy given to me by Miss Kelly and the antibiotics prescribed by the specialist were no longer effective. The doctor ordered a bronchogram (x-ray examination of the bronchial tree), which demonstrated that the middle lobe of my right lung was affected by a constrictive condition. In consultation with the surgical team, it was decided that I would benefit from a lobectomy (removal of the right-middle lobe of the lung). On getting home that night, I discussed the operation with John and Pat. Pat was totally against it. John was supportive of it, and I was excited about it. Her argument was that I was not sick enough to warrant surgery and that the operation would be very painful and risky.

I was admitted to the Richmond Hospital late afternoon on Monday. "I got into my bed and continued reading *Charwoman's Daughter.* Becoming a bit anxious about my lung operation, I wrote to Uncle Samuel and Pa Harry. I explained in detail with diagrams what the doctors were going to do. I jumped into bed after a bath with a book. I did some reading and finally dropped off to sleep. As I went to bed I thought about my new birth," as recorded in my diary. The following morning I was given a shave and a nurse gave me the pre-medication by injection into my buttock. With regards to the operation, "I should have been nervous but was somehow excited because for me it was a new birthday," being my last entry into my diary.

The operation was a success according to the nurse in charge when I came around in the intensive care unit. The following day I was moved to the main ward. John visited me every day, except when out of the country, and as always a morale booster. I had twice daily chest physiotherapies, which were useful. The pain-killing medications were extremely inadequate, but I dared not complain for two reasons.

The majority of the patients were worse off than I, as they had chronic lung diseases complicated by cancer. Others suffered from smoke-related diseases, bladder cancer, leg pains at rest or on walking, and chronic bronchitis. Secondly, I did not want word to get to Pat that I was in tremendous pain.

My other visitors included Charles and his girlfriend. One week prior to my discharge from the hospital, Pat and the boys came to see me. I was discharged home on the twenty-fourth post-operative day, although I was allowed to go shopping in town every day one week before the final release.

With Pat's encouragement, John enrolled me into the boarding school. It was going to be difficult in many ways, but "I will soon adapt myself." I started classes again on September 7, but this time we had a new student, a South African of East Indian parentage. He was about my age and he too wanted to study medicine. Naturally, we started studying together. One month later, John got a transfer to New York, working with Chase Manhattan Bank. It was a promotion.

Midterm holidays came and there was nowhere to go, but Mr. Duke had already made arrangements. I stayed with the Childes, an elderly couple, in Sandymount. George was in his mid-seventies and his wife probably two years younger. George had a museum in the attic in which he kept old books, souvenirs, and antiques, etc., which were neatly labelled. He was now finding it difficult to climb up the ladder, but apparently he used to spend hours there before and after his retirement.

As the new term progressed, I made more friends but mainly in my class. Cengiz Sarakayali was from Turkey, Stuart Whitney from Canada, Abiye Obenje from Nigeria, and of course, David Knaggs, an Irishman. With a new lease of life in me, I continued to do well in my subjects and played more games like running, playing tennis, playing soccer, etc. Unfortunately my outside friends, including Charles, had all left Dublin. The boarding school lent itself to studying and this I did. On Saturdays I went to the movies and Sunday afternoons after attending church service in the morning, I went on mountain hikes around Dublin with Cengiz.

The end of the year was fast approaching. Mr. Duke was determined not to leave me out of the activities. He let me read a passage from the Holy Bible during assembly. He let me do this a few times until one day he called me to his office. Two Sundays from yesterday, St. Ann's Anglican Church was broadcasting to the nation over RTE Radio (Radio and TV, Eire). They wanted me to read a passage from the Bible on that day. I did and it was a success. I got invited to other churches through Mr. Duke.

I spent Christmas with the Childes and as usual, George was wonderful. He gave me instructions by saying, "You must always respect your book; never leave it face down on an open page but use a book marker." We had a visit from their son and daughter-in-law. It was a deserving break. I was ready to start the new term.

Chapter 19

Second Year at St. Andrew's College, 1972

I spent the summer holidays making hay and silage. I attended a youth Christian camp in Arklow. John withdrew his financial support. Apollo 17 went into space.

In anticipation of the school reopening in a few days' time, I went into town for a haircut and then to Eason Bookshop to buy a Shakespearean tragedy book. Thereafter, I went to see a film, *Puppet on the Chain*. Overall, it was a productive day.

Going late to bed late last night, I woke up late this morning to have breakfast and clean the dishes. I continued with some studies. I stayed home today to read a book, *Frankly Speaking,* because it was wet, cold, and windy.

I decided to stay indoors to do some studies. Everyone appreciated my living with the Childes. Mrs. Childes did the cooking, I washed the dishes, and George worked in the garden. Bill, their son, and his wife enjoyed visiting us often. After doing some work, I joined George to work in the garden. I played with my tennis trainer on the street. After tea, I continued with my work.

The Easter term had started and I was back in school. I now put my whole concentration on the TCD entrance examination. They eventually came on May 1. Every topic I revised appeared on the papers, but most of it escaped me during the exam. The French aural examination was poor although, at least in my mind, I did well in the written.

On May 21 (Sunday), Mrs. Phyllis Fairbrother invited me for lunch. This was the beginning of a lasting relationship. Phyllis was a widow who had no children. She looked after foreign students by providing them accommodation, breakfast, and supper for a reasonable fee. She was a cousin of our school cook, who unknowing to me arranged the meeting. Mrs. F and I hit it off on our first meeting.

I decided then to move in with her. I discussed the proposal the following day with Mr. Duke and he was in total agreement. On June 21, 1972, Mrs. F picked me up from school. It was easy to move because I had little belongings—tennis racquet, school and casual clothes, two pairs of shoes, and books (and diaries) forming the main bulk.

Mrs. F came originally from the country and had many relatives there. One such relationship was the Notleys. Mr. and Mrs. Charles were farmers living in Eyrecourt, twenty miles from Galway. They wanted somebody to do some odd jobs in their farm. I jumped at the opportunity and on July 7, I moved down to Co. Galway.

The farm was huge, specializing in corn (oat, rye, and barley) and cattle. They also had a vegetable garden, which produced literally everything—fruit (soft and hard) trees, vegetables, etc. Behind the main house were farmhouses, which housed the tractors, chicken shed, and various storerooms. Further behind these was a reasonably sized pigsty. This place was paradise to me. The Notleys had one daughter, who was studying nursing in England.

I felt comfortable in the garden, and Mrs. N was happy with this. Every morning I started work at 8.30 A.M.—weeding, clipping the hedges, mowing the lawn, and painting the gates. Within two weeks I ran out of work. So I joined the workmen to make silage. The smell of green grass in my lungs was addictive. Venturing into the storeroom one afternoon, I discovered an old bicycle but perfectly functional. This discovery marked my exploration of Eyrecourt and its environs.

The Notleys were Protestants and went to church every Sunday. I spent a lot of time with Mrs. N, who enjoyed driving around with me to meet other church members like the Nethaways, Hodges, and Kennys. These long drives were enjoyable. One such drive took us down to Shannon. The scenery was brilliant. It was a reflection of the true Ireland—all greenery.

One morning Charles had a surprise for me. "Will you like to go with me to a sheep auction?" was his request to me. I drove in the back of a tractor to Birr. It was my first experience, and I found it extremely amusing and amazing. Luckily for us, the day was bright and sunny. My day was completed when Mr. C offered me a baked potato with Kerry butter in its centre.

After work, I went for my usual ride. I found myself in Banagher. I ran into a group of boys all younger than me—we played tennis and went fishing in a boat on River Shannon. We caught nothing but we didn't care.

When working with the men, I tried to hold my own. Unfortunately, the end of some of the days left me with back pains and hundreds of little cuts in my fingers. I did well against the farm men during hay making and cleaning out the stables. We joked most of the time.

I had spent a month already with the Notleys, and my relationship with them had been nothing less than a son and parents. After dinner, Mrs. Notley invited me to join a Christian camp in Arklow at her expense. I had attended such a camp at CSS, and so I jumped at it.

Mrs. Notley drove the Nethaway children and me to Arklow. We spent the night with the Mitchells. William, the head of the family, was the brother of Mrs. Nethaway. There were two girls (Christine and Rachel) and two boys (Richard and Robert). Christine and I started an instant romance.

On Saturday, we (Christine, Helen, and I) went to camp. I shared a classroom (used as a bedroom) with nineteen other boys. The girls had all gone mad over me even though I was older. I guess being the only "black child" in the camp, I was the centre of attraction. I did not particularly enjoy all the attention, but it was fun.

We (Christine and I) escaped camp and went for a walk. I enjoyed her company. She was, of course, younger than I was but probably more experienced with handling older boys.

I acted in a play written by the organizing vicar's wife, Margaret Smith, set in Kenya. It was the product of the drama class headed by Naomi, a literature student from TCD. I became an instant star at the end of the evening. "All 37 girls kissed me on the cheek." This marked the end of a successful summer camp.

Mrs. N came to collect me, but I opted to stay for another week with the Mitchells. The next few days were all fun. We played table tennis in the village community centre and lawn tennis in an abandoned family estate.

On Monday, July 31, I had my first practice drive with Bill. It was a joke and yet dangerous. I drove in gear one all the time. He stood out on the lawn and gave me instructions.

What an exciting day. Christine, Rachel, Richard, John, and I went for an early walk on the neighouring hill. It gave one an eye-catching view of the farming lands below. Richard and I drifted off on returning home.

Mrs. Notley came for me to go back to Eyrecourt. I found myself being depressed a day after returning. I spent the whole day doing all I could about nothing. It all seemed as if I had no space for me on the Green Isle. What a frustrating and depressing day.

September started on a Friday, and I snapped out of my depression.

There was no more work for me at the Notleys', and so I moved to another farm owned by the Finneys—a couple and two children.

The farm was enjoyable despite the hard work that I was not afraid of. We weeded between the turnips.

The week came but it disappeared quickly because I was beginning to love them. The wife was a schoolteacher and played the church organ. They worked hard and ate well, including wild ducks, young spring lambs, etc. They were self-sufficient (probably true of all the farmers I visited thus far) in foods.

Back again with the Notleys, I joined the men to work in the farm to make more hay, silage, and painting. These tasks are no longer difficult for me.

Mrs. Notley's brother was a church minister who lived in Whitehead, outside Belfast. A few weeks ago, he visited us with his wife and a son. They invited me to visit them in Belfast. You guessed it; I jumped at it.

I hitchhiked a ride to Roscommon, from where I took a bus to Belfast. At the bus station, my guests (Rev. Bournes and wife) met me for a delightful scenic drive.

I found Northern Ireland more developed than the Republic and the people just as warm. The church members were extremely friendly. I played tennis at the local club. I accepted the invitation to talk to groups of thirteen- to fifteen-year-old children in a Go-Club. The question-and-answer sessions were more productive than the "lecture."

On the following Thursday, we visited the Stormont, the House of Parliament. We could not enter the building because there was no government. Northern Ireland was under direct rule from Westminster. However, the landscape, the flower gardens, and the driveway were breathtaking. Seen at night with the lights on, it was majestic.

I woke up this morning with respiratory tract infection as suggested by productive cough but no pain or shortness of breath. A general practitioner who did not charge me, as I was a student, saw me. I played tennis later in the day.

I went for my usual bicycle ride around the city. I sustained a big laceration on my right foot at our gate. This did not, however, prevent me from playing tennis later in the day. I felt better today, two days later, from the chest point of view. The infection was short-lived.

Today, September 22, I caught a bus from Belfast to Roscommon. I then hitchhiked to Eyrecourt. The whole trip was an exciting and a long-lasting experience.

I finally got to Dublin and then faced reality. A typewritten letter from John (first ever) was waiting for me at home. In essence he wanted me to go back home. There was no need to ask why because the reason was obvious—too much drain financially. I completely understood his position, considering he had two young mouths to feed and a wife to support. However, the question of going back to Sierra Leone as far as I was concerned was not for discussion. John's response to my letter was as follows:

Dear Francis:

I am not prepared to send you the money for the plane ticket because when this has been spent, you will need more. Francis, you are not aware of the costs of what you propose is well over 100 pounds. Practical necessity dictates a different course of action for you. Your delaying in not realizing and accepting this only compounds and confuses your situation, making everything that much more difficult.

Let me know what your plans are.

John

My response was as follows:

Dear John:

Thanks a lot for the twenty-five-dollar cheque. I will ever remain regretting it should there be any misunderstanding between us. A letter could be misunderstanding. I am not trying to be aggressive or ungrateful as indicated in your letter. What in reality I was trying to say is that it is my responsibility to follow my own interests. John, I have already entered for the exam because I feel that I can make it. I will not be able to feed myself should I go home without a single certificate. I know you will find it difficult to understand my feelings. You might feel that I am just trying to make things complicated and do not understand your position. Should I get my exams, I stand a fifty percent chance of getting a scholarship. At the moment, I have more than a sixty percent chance of getting the exam in May. I think it is an opportunity I must take. This is my case. It is risky but it will worth it.

> *I still need your help.*
> *I have nothing more to say but to say hello to everybody.*

Sincerely yours,
Francis

Then as it had happened many times in my life, Mr. Duke telephoned me to meet with him. John had written to him a month earlier prior to writing to me. He had gone into action instantly. Mr. Duke called an emergency staff meeting during which time he managed to convince the staff members to support me for a year. Apparently, he had no difficulty convincing the teachers because they were confident that I would pass the Leaving Certificate Examinations.

I was now back in school and still living with Mrs. F. On Friday, December 1, I got a call from John. He was in Dublin for a few days and invited me for lunch in his hotel, the Jury. He ordered room service and they brought up a lot of food, but neither of us enjoyed it. "I am pessimistic," he said when I told him that I was going to be a surgeon. He gave me twenty pounds on my way out and we bid goodbye.

Charles Margai and I had become close friends. I enjoyed his meals. Although I never won a card game or table tennis against him, I beat him to pulp at lawn tennis.

I was on top of my studies and had many people as friends to keep me happy. The Hollinsheads in Dunglaire, Mrs. F, Charles, many tennis partners, and my country folks were all available to help.

Mrs. F did not have television, and so we had both become avid radio listeners. Our favourite show was *The Archers* on BBC Radio 4. On Thursday,

December 7, they blasted *Apollo 17* into space. We went over to our next-door neighbour to watch it on television.

This was interesting. In 1958, my school in Kayima moved to its present location. I was intimately involved in that move.

At the end of the school term today, there was a huge fair in preparation for the school moving to its new location.

I went to spend Christmas with the Mitchells in Arklow

The nights were extremely cold but the company was wonderful. Some nights we will play scrabble until 2:30 A.M. I also did a lot of reading—*The Evolution of Life, Passing Examinations, The Fall of the Sparrow, They, Running Blind,* and *Rat Race.*

This year marked my third Christmas in Ireland. On each occasion, I found people to be generous. The Childes gave me a scarf, and the Irish Rotary Club, through Mr. Duke, sent me ten pounds and many Christmas cards.

Chapter 20

1973 at St. Andrew's College

I broke my relationship with Christine, and Rachel broke hers with me. My mother, first parent, died. George Foreman beat Joe Frazer, and Casius Clay beat Joe Burgner in boxing. Ile Nastase lost to John Smith in the Wimbledon finals. I finally arrived in medical school.

The first day of this year found me with the Mitchells in County Wicklow. Like previous days, I stayed up late and woke up late. I completed reading *Jungle Fever* and started reading *The Art of English*. As a form of a breakaway from reading, I decided to do letter writings. I wrote postcards to the Notleys, Nethaways, Chucks, and Childes.

Included in these letters was that to my cousin N'Gundia. She had written me a week earlier, announcing the death of my mother. I told her about my feelings towards my dead mom—all she gave me was life, making her my first parent. Looking back on this statement at the time, I thought it was un-Sierra Leonean. As it is said in my tribe, "There is no bush into which you can throw a bad baby."

In essence, I did not know who my mother was. All I knew was she was a woman, a Kono by tribe, gentle, and kind. When I was two years in school, she disappeared. I last saw her in November 1970. She cried when she saw me. I still had the natural love for her in spite of her abandoning my sister and me. Nevertheless, before she left us, she gave me a halfpenny coin, which meant nothing to me. What was my sister's first reaction on the passing of our mother? I do not know.

Over the Christmas break, I stayed with the Mitchells in Wicklow. Although I broke my friendship with Chris, I still enjoyed being with the family. The credit for binding the unit together must be given to Mrs. Mitchell. Despite their meagre income, they managed to send both girls to a private boarding school.

I completed reading *Mutiny on the Bounty* the night before, which meant late rise. However, soon after breakfast, Richard and I found ourselves wandering off to Wooden Bridge, a little village some six miles away from home. There was a trout farm there. It was exciting to see the same type of fish in clear-water ponds at different stages of their development. They sold us two— arrow-picked by Richard. We got home late that night, but surprisingly nobody showed any concern.

Today (January 4) was my turn to entertain everybody with my home food. Fortunately, I had brought with me from Dublin: grounded cassava leaves, dried hot pepper, and palm oil. It was delicious, according to my hosts, particularly Richard. Richard refused to eat his normal supper the following day, hoping to have the leftovers reheated. I felt satisfied, too.

I got back to Dublin a few days later. The following day I was up early to clean my bike and then went for a ride to college. On returning home, I wrote letters to John O'Connor, Martha Margai, Rachel Mitchell, Alfred SamForay, and the Burkes in Eyrecourt. I spent the following days visiting friends: Mr. Keegan (geography teacher and assistant school headmaster), former classmates Cengiz from Turkey and Stuart Whitney from Canada in TCD, and Charles Margai from Sierra Leone. All these events were to remind me that "you are back and get started."

Having completed the preliminaries, the term's work had started in earnest. Charles and I played tennis after which we prepared lunch. I got back home before it became dark (6 P.M.) and worked on organic chemistry for the rest of the evening.

I received a letter from Richard Mitchell reminding me of our fun time in his village. I doubled my efforts on the revision, as I was meeting Rachel the next day. It was nice to be with Rachel. We talked about everything, including our schoolwork, but our relationship was completely platonic. The only time she got into an argument with me was over the spelling of "exam" for "examination" during the game of Scrabble. I knew "exam" was acceptable in Scrabble, but when challenged I lost my confidence, compounded by the fear of losing my turn. I backed down and she won by getting rid of her pieces to overwhelm my score.

Today (Saturday) was fully packed. After breakfast, I visited Charles and joined in to prepare lunch. Moses joined us later. I collected Rachel from the city centre to join us for lunch. Everybody enjoyed the meal after which we played Scrabble. I escorted Rachel into town, where she boarded a bus to school. I liked this girl. She was quiet, pleasant, and gentle—a complete contrast in character to her younger sister, Christine. Chris was outgoing and knew more about boys. The oldest brother, Robert, was a private person, probably because he lacked confidence, having dropped out of primary school. Like Bill, their father, he was a motor mechanic. Mrs. Mitchell was the brain behind the running of the household. She charged the customers and collected payments from them. Bill's real name was William, but he preferred to be called Bill. Bill managed to retain his English accent after so many years in Ireland. He did all the mechanical repairs of cars, farm machines, etc., for most of County Wicklow. He gave me my first lesson in driving without getting into the VW van himself; it was either fear of me or he did not trust his repair.

Prior to our moving to the new location, I rescued a junior boy from a bully. News got to the parents, and they always wanted me to visit them at their home. After a church service one Sunday morning, I took a ride to visit them at Sutton. It was a long ride. The wind from the sea always blew against me. The ride took me along the coastline, separated from the sea by a strip of land. This strip of land between the sea and road had few buildings but mainly greenery turned into parks. On arriving at my destination, Emeka and I went for a walk along the sea. Unfortunately, he was fat and unfit, and therefore walking was no fun for him. Mrs. Chuck was a very kind and generous woman. She was the boss. She took to me instantly, most probably because I took interest in her son. In one full swoop, I met with the rest of Emeka's family. Emeka's older sister had arrived from a boarding school and his younger brother was home. Mr. Chuck was an executive living in Nigeria who sent his children to be educated in Ireland. To complete the family, there was a beautiful woman, probably a few years older than me, who was the house helper. I spent the night with them on the kind request of Mrs. Chuck because the weather was horrible—gusty wind, cold, and wet. After supper, we spent the rest of the evening watching television. Mrs. Chuck dropped me with my bike just outside town on my request.

The following Sunday I went to see the Childes. While there, they gave me the present diary, *Collins' Gentleman's Diary, 1973*, being aware that I kept one. It contained the map of the London Underground rail. It had other useful information but mainly about the United Kingdom and Northern Ireland but nothing or little on the Republic of Ireland. We watched a fight for the WBC belt between George Foreman and Joe Frazier. George Foreman won.

I got to school well on time for my first class of the day. I covered many topics between classes. I got home before Mrs. F could finish preparing supper. We had a visit by Mrs. F's niece, who was up from Galway visiting her daughter in the hospital. I later discovered that Mrs. F repaired a hole that appeared in my school pants a few days ago. This woman, my second mother, and I hit it off the first day she invited me for a Sunday lunch. We supported each other in every way. Before going back to my room to continue studying, I telephoned Rachel. Mrs. F interviewed an Irish man today as the next lodger. I was excited about the idea of a third person coming to live with us.

Another weekend had arrived. After lunch and having completed my ironing, I took a ride down to Dalkey (eight miles away) to meet with RH. We went to the Methodist Church Hall to watch a game of badminton between our local team and that of the police. We lost by three sets to one. We woke up this morning at Paddy's home and after breakfast, we went to play badminton. We came home for lunch and then back to play more games. In late afternoon I drove back home at #1 Whitebeam Avenue in Clonskeagh.

Getting out of bed the following morning was difficult. Every muscle ached and every joint movement was pain. I must have played a lot of badminton over the weekend. I met with Michael O'Gorman, the new lodger, at breakfast this morning. He was in his early thirties and this was his first experience staying away from home. He was born and grew up in a village near Galway and was employed in Dublin. He was pleasant and looked athletic. He played tennis and I promptly invited him for a game on Saturday. Sometime later, I got a phone call from Moses to say that he had got himself a girlfriend. "I am happy for you and I would like to meet her," was my response.

Going to school today was tough; it was a freezing, windy, and wet morning. I stayed back in school with a few of my classmates for extra lessons in chemistry with Mr. McCardle, who had taken a special interest in me. He wanted me to get the necessary grades to enter medical school, as he considered me as his best student. The one complaint I had about our teachers was that they stopped teaching when the exams were just around the corner. On my way home, I bought a bottle of a cough mixture. Winter was surely here; streets were covered with wet black snow. However, I was reassured that "things are worse in England." I had to strip naked in the toilet, as I was soaking wet with icy water on getting to school. After math, I spent the rest of the day working on biology. I got a card from Rachel today, and I called her at about 8.30 p.m. The following day was essentially the same but with slight variation. Mr. Duke invited me to his office to sensitize me with a prospect of a grant. I played badminton after school and then did two hours' work before leaving for home.

After tea, I walked down to the local pub to watch the fight between Casius Clay and Joe Burgner. I did not enjoy the fight at all. As I walked into the pub, an Irish man approached and insisted on buying me a drink. I reluctantly accepted the offer (a glass of orange) and this was a mistake. He would not move on. He was biased and totally against Burgner, who was "white and English." Clay won easily.

I had planned to stay home this morning to study but found myself in school. I had a long one-to-one session with Mr. Treanor, my advanced maths teacher. I spent an equally constructive time with the biology teacher (Dr. Frewin). The geography teacher (Mr. Keegan) arranged or organized a film on the Great Barrier Reef for the class. Mr. Keegan was a practical man but far from being a good teacher. He once took us to an expedition to Connemara, the barren land. Overall, the day was satisfactory for revision. I ran into Mr. Duke prior to end of school, who had asked me to see him next week to discuss the subjects I would be offering at the next TCD matriculation examinations.

After a quick bath, I went down for breakfast. One had to be quick in the bathroom, as there were now five of us. The days allotted to me were Wednesdays and Saturdays. I read somewhere that raw egg was good for you. I poured two down my throat this morning, and it was not a very exciting breakfast. As it was now becoming a routine on weekends, I ended up at Charles' flat.

I helped him to prepare lunch. John, Moses, Ken, and Violet joined us later. I collected Rachel from town to complete the company. Charles was indeed a social butterfly because he enjoyed the company of admirers. His uncle, Sir Milton, was the first prime minister of Sierra Leone, followed by his father, Albert. I would not be surprised if he turned out to be a politician back home. He knew all the tricks in the book of how not to lose any game, particularly cards, Scrabble, and table tennis. He had just completed his study from law school. His father was a lawyer.

The mornings were getting extremely cold but were not a deterrent to school attendance. I was fifth highest in the last biology examination; I did just about all right but I needed to do better. I got home at 6 and after tea worked until 10:30 P.M. Again, through Mr. Duke's influence, I read a few selected verses from the Bible over the radio as part of the Church of Ireland's annual broadcast to the nation. I studied in an unheated room, as they turned off the central heaters because of the midterm holiday. Again, cold or no cold condition was not a bar to passing this exam in May.

After breakfast, I spent the rest of the morning studying, mainly geography. At 3:30 P.M., I went to Trinity College, Dublin, to collect application forms for the exam. I bought a book, *The Burren,* to read and a "missing you" card for Rachel. I dropped in by Charles, who gave me his old suit. The weather had improved marginally, but for how long? I did no serious studying today, but I read my book. I was also heavily laden with food. Unable to keep my eyes open, I dropped off to sleep almost immediately.

I fell off the bike this morning on my way to school. This happened because I was hasty and more focused on the schoolwork ahead. I sustained no injury; luckily, the open roads of Belfield Campus UCD were empty. I did some productive work in biology at school today.

Today, March 2, Friday, was exciting and probably because of it being Rachel's birthday. All the same, revision on my exam subjects went on as usual. I got a call later in the evening from Rachel to thank me for the birthday card. I went to bed this morning at two. I was caught up reading a novel, *Europe,* a common occurrence. After breakfast at nine, I did my laundry and studied until early afternoon. I dropped in to see Charles and then went into town to take Rachel out to a theatre to celebrate her birthday.

Today's events revolved around the exam: studying and the completion of application forms for a bursary from the Sierra Leone High Commission in London. I attended various classes and worked on my math before coming home. I reluctantly wrote to John to ask for pocket money.

This is how I spent my money (in pounds and pence) over the last three months:

Stamps	0.36
Glue	0.08
Drink and fish	0.42
Writing pad and apples	0.17
Lunch	0.33
Sundries	0.77
Telephone call to Rachel	0.02
Telephone call to Charles	0.02
New pair of trousers	2.15
Belt	0.71
Bus ride	0.04
Loaf of bread and telephone call	0.09
Mrs. Chuck gave me	0.50
Bus ride	0.08
Church offering	0.06
Postage stamps	0.11
Bike spare parts	0.11
Sundries	0.37
Postage stamps	0.54
Books	1.40
Telephone	0.02
Bus ride	0.04
Telephone	0.02
Bookshop visit	1.39
Date with Rachel	0.54
Marmite	0.34
Cinema and passport photos	0.75
Sundries	0.40
Bus ride	0.30
Church service	0.60
Lecture	0.10
Telephone	0.04
Soap	0.32
Postage stamps	0.12
Bus (with Moses)	0.10
Bus (to Dalkey)	0.20
Cooking	1.00
Theatre (*Pirates of Penzance*)	0.25
Food	0.50
Tennis shoes	2.50
Sundries	0.65
Bus ride	0.24

Postage stamp	0.04
Bus ride	0.16
Telephone call	0.06
Bus ride	0.16
Telephone call	0.04
Telephone call	0.02
TOTAL	**19.23**

I must admit that this indeed was a reasonable expenditure, a well-managed budget. I never borrowed money from anyone.

The ride to school this morning was a pleasant one, as it was warm and sunny. I was enjoying schoolwork as usual but much more so because I was ahead of most of the boys. I was, however, aware that the majority of the boys had no desire to go beyond secondary school education, as their parents were wealthy. After school I dropped by Charles' to pass on a book left by his friend, John Thomas. After an hour with him, I left for home and went down to work on geography.

Mrs. F gave me a letter at breakfast from Trinity College Dublin (TCD), which offered me a place in medicine, of course depending on my matriculation results. This was a bit of an encouragement to work even harder.

Events of the rest of March and early April followed a similar pattern—ride to school after breakfast, studying in the reading room between lessons, and back home to eat and do more studies. The weekends composed of doing my washing, meeting Rachel in town, and then going back home via Charles' flat to do more studies. However, one weekend, Rev. Smith of the Arklow camp interrupted my routine.

After school on Friday, he collected me and we were off to Eyrecourt. It was a request made by Mrs. Audrey Notley. I always enjoyed going down to this village. I normally stay with the Notleys but split my time with the Burkes and Nethaways as well. Rev. Smith showed a film produced from East Africa after which he gave a talk. He asked me to comment. I spoke about the practice of Christianity in Sierra Leone, which went down well as suggested by many questions and answers afterwards. After breakfast with the Notleys, I rode the farm bicycle to visit the Nethaways, where I played cards with the boys. On my way back home, I dropped in to see the Burkes. I got home at about 10:30 P.M. and went straight to bed. I went to church the following morning and then after lunch, Mrs. Notley gave me a lift to the train station in Ballinasloe bound for Dublin. The weekend succeeded in taking my mind off studies. Despite the intense revision and in the middle of mock examinations, I had time to meet with friends for various reasons.

I went to the movies with Rachel on Saturdays after first playing tennis with Dermot. I would meet with Moses at Charles' flat for a good meal with card games and Scrabble. During the bus ride to Sutton to visit the Chucks on the occasional Sunday gave me the opportunity to read. Karl Sorenson, a classmate of mine, occasionally played table tennis with me. He too wanted to do medicine at Trinity College Dublin, TCD. Like myself they gave him space on the proviso of passing the exam. His father was the American ambassador to Ireland. He was sure of himself but quite bright. He was always trying to beat me in the tests with some success. He, however, failed at tennis.

We now had a new lodger, John Thomas. His stay was short, as he was in Dublin attempting a postgraduate examination in law. At the same time, Mrs. F went to Scotland for her annual break. She left me in charge. My responsibilities included looking after the plants in the greenhouse, reheating the well-labeled foods each day, and taking the dustbin out every Wednesday.

During the week, Mr. Treanor, the additional maths teacher, invited me home to do some revision. After a productive two hours' work, I rode farther on to Dalkey to visit the Hollinsheads. I helped Jackie with her maths homework and then went back home.

The real examinations were now in full swing. They were going fine so far. One day Mr. Duke invited me to his office. "The University College of Dublin, UCD, has offered you a space in the medical school depending on your results. Should you fail to secure a Sa Leone Government scholarship, the Bank of Ireland is willing to give you a loan to be repaid without interest on graduation." Mr. Duke was a man who believed in the principle that "all human problems can be solved by humans." A week later, the letter of rejection from the SLHC arrived and it read:

Dear Mr. Saa Gandi:

RE: APPLICATION FOR BURSARY FOR ACADEMIC YEAR 1973/1974

I refer to your application for a Sierra Leone Government bursary to continue with your studies during 1973/1974 academic year and regret to inform you that your application has not been successful. I sincerely hope you can now make alternative arrangements.

Best wishes for the future.

Yours sincerely,
S.H.A. Sawyer
For Head of Chancery

I think Mr. Duke saw this letter being posted to me from London.

The exams came and ended abruptly. This was not fair when one considered the effort and time put into the preparations. This was now a closed book. The next hurdle was to get a summer job. Mr. Collin, one of my classmate's fathers, offered to help. I was in no luck even after his recommendations. It was now July and the weather was glorious—hot and sunny with longer days.

I played more tennis, looked after Mrs. F.'s garden, read books (*How to Influence People, A Grain of White Keane's Big Maggie, Bandoola*), and watched television, mainly sports, including the Wimbledon final between Ile Nastase and John Smith at the Overseas Students' Club. Nastase (from Rumania) had all the ammunition to win but lost the game.

On Wednesday, Mr. Duke came to my rescue yet again. The lawns around the school buildings were covered with stones, the gates required painting, and the school needed a caretaker. He thought it was a hard job but I told him, "I will make it easy." I offered to do it willingly without pay. Mr. Collin was to be my supervisor. He got me a self-contained caravan (a single bed-room, a kitchen with a gas cooker, and a sitting area). I moved in over the following weekend. It was a perfect arrangement for me. I did my own cooking, learned to drive a tractor, read a lot in the evenings, and played tennis every Sunday morning with Dermot Delaney on the UCD grounds.

After weeks of stone picking, I leveled the ground and sowed the seeds. Within weeks, the seeds had sprouted without any watering. The young grass called for the rains and the heavens opened for two days. New stones grew— free and half-buried. Two more weeks of hard work saw the lawns cleared of stones again. Another week passed and the new lawns were ready to mow. I enjoyed the mowing—beautiful, smooth lawns and the pleasant smell of cut grass. Being aware that I would be going to college soon, the authorities em-ployed a permanent grounds man.

I enjoyed working with Paddy, a name he preferred. He was in his fifties and might not have completed secondary school education. He once told me, "You can do an honest day's work without killing yourself." It was wasted advice because I went on with my duty as ever before.

Come what may, somebody was going to pay my college fees. Mr. Duke was going to make sure of this. He had secretly approached the secretary/trea-surer, Miss Maureen Cloake, of the Overseas Students' Club about getting sponsorship for me. She promised to find a way once admitted to one of the medical schools in Dublin. I continued to read for entertainment such books as *L'Abri, The Fall of the Sparrow, Running Blind, They, Killer Mine, Rat Race,* and the Holy Bible. I was still living with Mrs. F. She visited me often with homemade biscuits and cookies and by the same frequency, I took a ride by her. Neither of us believed in the telephone, especially if the distance could be made by either walking or riding a bicycle.

I had become so involved with my assignment that a few things happened with little notice to me. There were no telephone calls from, or meetings with, Rachel. Visits to Charles became fewer and far between.

"What goes around always comes around." On one Saturday morning, while collecting yet more stones, a group of boys from the neighbourhood threw stones at me. I evaded all the stones and just smiled. They were angry with me probably because I watched the compound with hawk eyes and never allowed them to jump over the walls. They reminded me of a similar episode when I was about their age in Kayima. Three of my pals and I had thrown stones at a stranger who came to live in our village. He was easing his bowels in the bushes. He was an Arabic who called prayers at the local mosque. He lived alone and kept to himself. At the time, we thought it was funny and we meant no harm. I can now understand. It was annoying and unnecessary.

The following Saturday the boys came back. Unfortunately for them, things turned out worse. I was a natural stone thrower. Thereafter, they never attacked me physically but verbally.

Mr. and Mrs. Keegan asked me to babysit their two children, Clare and Andrew. Clare became the first girl admitted to the school. They lived in a house at the entrance of the school. Like Mrs. F, they had no television and so I did more reading (*Roaring Boys*).

August 15 was a Wednesday. A white envelope was waiting for me at Mrs. F's. With shaky hands, I opened it. They were the exam results. I passed all the subjects, four with honours. This qualified me to take up all my offers, but I opted for the Royal College of Surgeons (RCSI), assuring that I could only come out of there with a surgical degree. For a treat, I went to see a James Bond film, *Live and Let Live*, in town the following Saturday. The results opened the flood gates for letter writing—to the Mitchells through Rachel, John, Martha, the Notleys, the Burkes, Stuart Whitney, Daniel, and Miss Cloake.

It was ironical that here I was offering financial assistance to Charles to return home and asked Daniel to go back to school with the assurance that I would help him. I continued with my work in the schoolyard, played tennis in between, and babysat for the Keegans. I started reading another book, *The School Rebellion*. I never accepted pay from the Keegans because it was my appreciation of their assistance to me, prepared excellent meals on their return, and gave me the opportunity to tell them my life history growing in Kayima. I visited Mrs. F on weekends whenever the opportunity arose. She had become more to me like a mother.

On September 10, Monday, I received my letter of acceptance from the RCSI. Finally, I was now a medical student! Two weeks later, the University of Galway accepted me but into the School of Natural Sciences. Depending on my grades at the end of the first year, they would admit me into medical school. I rejected it outright because of the obvious risk; I did not do so well at exams.

Most of my duties were moved indoors. At 7 A.M., I cleaned out the toilets, emptied the dustbins, and opened the main gate (the eastern entrance). Mr. Keegan opened the western entrance. Yet again people would not mind their own business.

Fellow students reminded me on many occasions that I was doing a degrading job. Yes, it was hard and messy work, but it was the job that was going to determine my future prosperity.

Out of the blue, I got a letter from Rachel ending our relationship. I would have loved to find out why but failed to contact her after many trials, including telephone calls, verbal messages, and visits home. It was probably my fault through neglect. Without my diary, I probably would not have been able to separate one day from another.

The first few weeks in medical school were treated the same way as I did in the last months of revision for the Leaving Certificate and matriculation examinations. I acquired all the recommended books (old and new) and attended all classes. Each afternoon on getting back to school, I helped the caretaker to clean out the toilets, particularly in changing the hand towels. I became an expert in changing those towels. I continued to babysit for the Keegans.

While still living in the caravan at St. Andrew's College, I played tennis in the evenings at the Monkstown tennis club. The friendship between Dermot Delaney (DD) and I grew stronger. Without fail, Dermot and I played three sets of tennis every Sunday morning at the UCD grounds. He was a pleasant man and only spoke when spoken to. He lived with his elderly mother. He looked like a student and in his own words, he was "young in spirit." I learned from him that he, like many others, paid a weekly wage from their salary to the Catholic Church, for what I don't understand. He was a new-car dealer. John finally wrote back, congratulating me on getting into medical school. He also enclosed a cheque for one hundred dollars.

Christmas was fast approaching. I passed biology with distinction and got ordinary pass in physics and chemistry at the end-of-term examinations. Mr. Duke kindly allowed me to go down to Galway for my Christmas break. My first term in college was a success; I worked hard for my living, kept up with the schoolwork, had good times with my former school mates now in faculties of their choices, and played tennis regularly with DD, and at last I had succeeded in beating him on alternate weekends.

On Friday, December 21, I arrived in Ballinasloe by train. Mrs. Jean Burke duly collected me for Eyrecourt (my second home). When I (probably the first African here) first arrived in this village, the distinction between Catholics and Protestants (fewer but apparently wealthier) was obvious. The two never mixed; they tolerated each other. For instance, the cemetery was divided right in the middle—the Catholics on one side and the Protestants on the other side side. However, during that first visit, I gathered the local children to play football (soccer) on an open field. It attracted both boys and girls. At other times, those children interested in tennis played with me and the Burkes children (three boys and two girls). The tennis court belonged to the Burkes, who were Catholics. At other times, we went swimming and fishing in the River Shannon. Then suddenly, families started inviting each other to each other's homes. The warm reception and the great respect for me had always drawn me to Eyrecourt and its surrounding villages. This visit was no different. I spent my time equally with most families until my departure on December 27. On the last day of the year, Mr. Duke and I completed a loan agreement form for my course.

I had little but was always willing to share whatever I had with whosoever needed it. I had a sense of vocation to becoming a doctor and that had made me charitable. I could make no mistakes: sex, studying, playing, etc. I was also aware that life did play tricks on one because one did not necessarily get what one wanted.

I am not sure what prompted me to write the following letter:

The Royal College of Surgeons in Ireland,
ST Stephen's Green,
Dublin 14,
Republic of Ireland.

Christmas, 1973

Dear Fellow Students,

It will be an obligation to me to answer questions from you or attempt to advise all those wishing to study in the United Kingdom or the British Isles as a whole. I will be of more assistance in the fields of Medicine and Sciences. To start with, you could not be in any better school than Centennial Secondary School.

We must say many thanks to our past and present teachers.

Sincerely yours,
Francis W SaaGandi
School Prefect, 1968 - 69
Centennial Secondary School, Mattru Jong
Sierra Leone, West Africa

Part Three
Undergraduate Education

Chapter 21

1974 at St. Andrew's College

I entered medical school and then became a blood donor. Three IRA bomb blasts in Dublin killed 23 people. Mr. Harold Wilson became Prime Minister of Britain and Mr. Richard Nixon resigned his post as President of USA.

Mr. Keegan gave me this present diary as a Christmas present. At the right-lower corner of each page was a prescription drug advertisement. It contained other pieces of useful information for my studies. I dragged myself out of bed this morning later than usual; it was cold and wet. At about 1 P.M. I took a bus to Dalkey, paying 0.20 pence on the invitation of Christopher's parents, the Westrups. It was a wonderful New Year's Day dinner, and I was sure the rest of the year would only get better. Christopher was one of the quiet but bright boys in my class at St. Andrew's College. He gained admission to TCD for a degree course in mechanical engineering.

Lectures had started but surprisingly, few students attended. For me each day followed the same routines to the point of monotony. After lectures, I went to play badminton and then visited Stuart. Stuart Whitney lived with his mother and two sisters. He was in my class and now reading social sciences at TCD. We spent a lot of time together. Pa Harry wrote me a letter to say that things were "getting badder and badder in Sierra Leone." Daniel wrote, too, to narrate the hard times for him in Switzerland. I was happy to listen and empathize with them, but I could not afford to get involved emotionally. I had resolved after a year in Ireland that "emotional involvement results in im-potence and failure." I believed that I had to get myself into a position that could allow me to help others. Therefore, I had to focus on getting into medical school in the first instance.

I took all my lecture notes today in a notebook, which I rewrote after reading the designated textbooks. This was time-consuming and I quickly abandoned the technique. "After tonight's revision, I have concluded that it was a waste of precious time to rewrite notes," I observed. On waking up this morning, falling trees covered the whole school compound. Overnight, there was gale force, which was the worst I had ever experienced thus far in Ireland. I helped Mr. Keegan to trim off the branches, and he got the experts to come in the following day to do the rest.

After a morning's hard work, I went to play tennis at the Overseas Students' Club (OSC). I ran into a classmate of mine, Errol James. Errol was from Trinidad but did his B.Sc. degree in Canada. He did not have a nice time there and was bitter. He looked sluggish when he walked but he was quite strong. I took an instant like for him. He was pleasant and not full of himself.

It was now the middle of January, and the boarders had started returning to school in dribs and drabs. They delayed the reopening of the school because of the Middle East Crisis. The boys looked less tidy compared to their return in September. In college, I ran into another Trinidadian, Phillip Tang. He was of Chinese origin and was quite intelligent but lazy. We became good friends and we studied together on some occasions. He lived with his older brother, Lawrence, in a semi-detached house.

I received a letter from Dan today, and there was something familiar about it—the strong desire to leave Sierra Leone. A year or two ago, I was asked to go back home because it was getting too expensive for my parents. Over a year ago, I advised Dan to stay home and I would support him there financially but he left for Switzerland. Now he was out of money. I was able to understand his position.

Today was the day I normally took a bus ride into town on completion of my duties in school, but I decided to ride instead. One reason for this was that I had no money. It was another rewarding day in college. In biology we dissected earthworms. My dissection was accurate and the drawings were very good, but the process was rather slow. I again suggested to myself, *Be accurate but be fast.*

One morning Mr. Duke asked me to meet with him in his office. I had no idea what the meeting was about, but somehow I felt it was going to be for a good reason; he always gave me good news. He shook hands with me on entering his office and said, "You have won a Sierra Leone government scholarship but to start from the 1974/1975 academic year. Dr. O'Flanagan, your registrar, and I have decided that you should move back into proper accommodations. Living in the caravan was bad for your health and not conducive to studying." I was over the moon.

I moved back to Mrs. F's on March 4, the day Harold Wilson was asked to form the next British Government, after his Labour Party won the general election. We were able to carry all my belongings in one carload. Until my moving back to Mrs. F's, the daily routines for me had been to open the school gates, have breakfast, take a shower, and go off to college on my bicycle. I spent the times between lectures to study in the library. At the end of the last lecture, I studied in the library for two hours and then went back to St. Andrews.

One day, I received a disturbing letter from Daniel in Switzerland; he was in serious financial troubles. I wrote at the time: "It disturbed me greatly. Daniel is not only my brother but also a friend. He took a decision contrary to my advice. I had advised him not to come overseas until there was going to be a steady income from home. I am not blaming him. But what's disturbing is, I cannot sit down and watch him perish, yet I can do nothing about it." I did do something about it.

Since my arrival in Ireland in late 1970, life had been more than good to me. I had always wondered what would have become of me had I lived in England or USA. Through Cengiz, I made a few friends at the Turkish embassy. Patricia, a Nigerian girl, brought me a pint of milk. I got lifts into town on very bad mornings by a milkman, the local grocery man, and one of my college professors, for example.

An unknown man kept my glass filled with soft drink for over two hours while watching Mohammed Ali fight Joe Frazier on a big screen in the local pub. Mr. Keegan gave me a blood pressure measuring machine donated by a Dr. Johnston, who remained unidentified. I entered tennis tournaments paid for by my club. The Rotary Club continued to invite me to their dinner meetings. I had easy accessibility to the watering hole, the Overseas Students' Club. Above all, I was able to attend all lectures and tutorials.

In the biology lab, we completed dissecting the frog and our next agenda was rat dissection. These dissections seemed to come to me naturally because I had skinned rodents in the hundreds while in Kayima and in Mattru, I was the butcher man for wild animals (monkeys, grass cutter, etc.). The reasons for doing so in both circumstances were completely different. In college, I did dissection with the ultimate aim of understanding the human anatomy. In Kayima and Mattru, I did so for food. I was finding schoolwork exciting. "Education is a right but in my case, it is a privilege. Am I overstating this fact or being over-sentimental? If the latter is the case, it makes me human." I was daydreaming again.

So far this year I had played a lot of tennis. I played against DD on weekends and during the week, I played against Errol or for my club. DD and I had thought that Monkstown Tennis Club had "gone crackers." We, however, agreed that the expression "The land over the hill is greener" was far from true. During our club tournaments, the majority of the clubs were far from being greener lands.

There were now three of us living with Mrs. F as lodgers. Chris was a psychiatrist from Canada. He had lived with Mrs. F while a student at RCSI. He originally came from Ceylon (now Sri Lanka). Mrs. F left me in charge of her garden while she was away visiting relatives in the country. I also took over the cooking. Today, St. Patrick's Day, I prepared a curry meal for the three of us. While at the table, Chris gave me pieces of advice, which included, "There are times when Mrs. Fairbrother will make some patronizing remarks." I had made the same observation and told him so. However, we both agreed that she did not say them with malice or premeditation but out of ignorance. He went on to say, "Anytime you are offended by her words, read the Book of Psalms."

St. Patrick's Day came and went in previous years completely oblivious to me. One of the main reasons was my total commitment to entering into medical school. This year, however, I decided to find out more about St. Patrick. He was born and lived in Scotland until the age of fourteen. At that age, pagan raiders captured and took him to Ireland as a slave to herd and tend sheep. During his captivity, he turned to God by praying. "He preached and converted all of Ireland for over forty years." Legend had it that he banned all snakes from Ireland; I am yet to see a snake outside the Dublin Zoo in Ireland. Mrs. F came back from her break and looked quite rested. She was more than happy with me for looking after the other lodgers, front and back lawns, and above all the vegetables in the greenhouse.

I understood all the lectures, I participated in all the tutorials, and I explained difficult topics to colleagues with clarity. Despite my total commitment to work, the test results so far did not reflect these inputs. I got an excellent grade in biology, a fair grade in chemistry, but a poor grade in physics. Between 12 midnight and 2 A.M., the time I wrote down the day's event, I found myself in a soliloquy.

"What is my purpose in life? Am I what people make me to be? In the first place, I am a selfish person. This is so in my lavishness of affection for people I call friends. In return, if not consciously, I expect the same thing and that makes me selfish. In my dreams, I have visualized myself as being a very successful doctor and writer. I have seen myself faced with responsibilities, which are within my capabilities. Learning from experience, looking after children of relatives and friends without falling victim of misunderstanding, is just beyond my imagination. I do not think anybody knows that I have two faces. By that, I mean, at times I am openminded while at other times, I am rigid in my stance. It is not that simple. One adverse effect is therefore: a slow thinker most of the time." That explained why I often remembered the answers to questions posed by examiners on standing to leave the examination table.

I had made many good tennis friends/partners so far this year. I played occasionally with Errol, often against Erdem, Stuart, and my club members, but most consistently with DD. DD and I played every Saturday or Sunday or both mornings, only interrupted by bad weather. DD and I had been playing tennis for over four years now, and that was where our relationship ended. We met on the courts if the roads were not bad for me to ride. Otherwise he picked and dropped me home in his car. Neither of us had made any attempt to invite each other home. Since the collapse of my alliance with Kumba Mei, my involvement with people (male or female) became restrained. Everybody was my friend and no more. I enjoyed solitude life much more than mixing. It had, in a way, made me a better man. I was stable—not easily annoyed, content, and not necessarily selfish, not anxious, and able to control my emotional feelings. All the same, I needed the exercise to keep me well.

I replied to Daniel's letter, telling him how I felt disturbed by his dilemma and a contrasting letter to Martha, thanking her for her consoling letter and a postal order for five pounds. I was a friend to everybody in the small Sierra Leone community in Ireland since arrival in 1970. When everyone left, the relationship went also except for that between Martha and me. She was a student nurse in England, but she treated me as though I was her younger brother. She had been studying medicine at TCD but left because of lack of financial support.

One other event that happened to me was my resolve to being a volunteer blood donor. They accepted me as a donor on passing the tests. What prompted me to keep going back was the treatment given to me. At the end of each session, each donor received a royal treatment—a few jars of beers (and Guinness), biscuits, and a cup of tea or coffee. I bought a copy of *Animals Parasitic to Man* to cover the subject in parasitology. The majority of my colleagues thought it was a waste of money. "Unfortunately, it is too late to change now; I always bought and read books," was my response.

I had never had difficulties with authorities, an observation made by Miss Hall, my English teacher in Mattru, in her letter of reference. I attended a meeting organized by the Irish Anti-apartheid Society at the Shelbourne Hotel. The leaders wanted us to stage a protest demonstration, but I refused to attend. The president of our Student Union interrupted the first lecture one morning to explain why we must not attend morning roll calls. He argued that one did not have to attend all the lectures to pass the appropriate examinations. Majority of the students agreed and the motion was passed. I disagreed. But buying all the books and attending all lectures and tutorials did not make me pass all my exams at first attempt.

At the end of two sets of tennis, we sat down on a bench provided by the Herbert Park authorities and talked. Errol accused me of being antisocial. He then went on to say, "You are friendly, warm, and cheerful, but not actually social. You don't go to discos, you have no girlfriends, and you hardly attend bottle parties. All you talk about is schoolwork and tennis." On reflection, he was perfectly right, but the remarks made little difference to me.

I read many books outside schoolwork and on many occasions, I found myself daydreaming. "I've in my thoughts to go back home at the end of the second year so that I can work in different hospitals and to see my grandparents' home in Fanema. At the same time, I'll meet the different doctors for advice on folk medicine. While visiting home, I'll gather all the necessary materials to write my autobiography. I expect a lot of stumbling blocks along the way, but I'm determined to jump them all."

During the lunchtime hour, between lectures, today, Friday, May 17, I attended chest physiotherapy at the Richmond Hospital. I rode through City Centre back to college. The traffic was chaotic to say the least because of a rather prolonged bus strike. As I chained my bike to the railings, I heard a huge explosion in the direction from whence I had just arrived. I later learned that a bomb had exploded and it had killed twenty-three people and wounded a score of others. The Irish Republican Army (IRA) admitted to causing the three bomb blasts on O'Connell Street. That day in Ireland became known as "Bloody Friday," and I assured myself, "The almighty reminded me that I had a role to play in society and so I was spared from injury or death." Fifteen minutes earlier, I was in a stationary shop next to one of the pubs.

Occasionally, during the lunch, Phillip and I would walk on the lawns of St. Stephen's Greens opposite the college. "It was a lovely day and the scenery was fantastic. Many people like us just strolled while now and again young couples lay down on the lawn, kissing, or a brightly coloured duck climbed upon the back of a less coloured one in the pond and the monochromatic flowers in partitions add to the beauty of the place."

Mrs. F had become my true other mother. She had many students before me but never became attached to any of them as she had with me. There were many reasons for this, but the obvious ones to me were that we loved gardening, we regularly attended our respective church services, and our lives were simple. She left one weekend for a week in Galway. She left a lot of signs on different jugs in the fridge that read: "soup for two," "soup for two days," "frying," "curry," "cold meat for Sunday or Monday," etc. She arrived two hours before either of us got home. To prove that there is dignity in labour, she made a bouquet of flowers, including her favourite, the water lily, which gave a memorable, pleasant smell resembling a "perfume factory." She produced the flowers herself. She was observant for details. If there were any notices or messages to be delivered, she exploited our weaknesses to the fullest. She left Mike's information under the biscuit can in the kitchen. She laid mine under the newspaper in the hallway.

The final-year exam results came out, and I became a casualty. I clearly passed biology, failed chemistry by two percent, and failed physics by three percent. Some of my mates were surprised and disappointed, but I accepted the results and was ready to start revision in three weeks' time. In the interim, I made appointments to meet with the respective professors. "As life goes on, I have come to convince myself that I was born to succeed. I have to labour for everything that comes natural to other people. "Noone weathers the storm by storming at the weather." One good piece of news was that the Dublin bus strike was over but the fares went up by 20 percent.

This year was a mixture of good (less) and bad (more) news. It was announced that the first "test-tube" babies (three of them) were born in a British hospital. This was followed by a coup d'etat in Cyprus. The coup leaders said that the president was dead but his supporters said he was still alive. Richard Nixon resigned as President of the USA over the Watergate scandal and Gerald Ford was sworn in as the thirty-eighth president. "Our long national nightmare is over," he declared during his acceptance speech. The flooding in Bangladesh had taken many lives.

On a day like this, bright and sunny, I was usually out playing tennis or going for a ride. Yet I couldn't; my ambition overrode my physical pleasure. As I sat on my desk, pondering over my chemistry subject, reaction mechanisms, a wasp squeezed itself through my upper window. At the end of a five-minute (probably shorter) flying around, it decided to take its leave. It couldn't because of the glass window, and that got him frightened and excited. By coincidence or design, at the same time, another one tried to get in. This, I thought, was equally true with human beings. One group in one hand had and didn't want it and on the other hand, another group didn't have it and would do everything to get it. I was not sure what prompted me to write like this—thinking too loudly or a reflection of my position. But whatever the situation I was in, I had got it out of my system.

Revision for physics and chemistry became easy and fun. Anna Bofin and I became friends. Anna was one of the daughters of Professor Bofin, professor of pathology. She was repeating physics and so we studied together. The alliance gave me the opportunity to detect my weaknesses. I knew the core knowledge of the subject, but my presentation in examinations was poor. Erdem, my tennis partner from Turkey, had to repeat his first year of chemistry. He was studying natural sciences. He was bright but would not study. I gave him tutorials, which again assured me that I had a good grasp of the subject. All three of us passed with flying colours, and within a few weeks, the new school year had started. It gave me the satisfaction of being able to help friends achieve their goals. To crown it all, Martha passed her nursing exam and sent me a ten-pound note. Alfred wrote to tell me that he had been granted a permanent visa to the USA.

For the non-repeaters, it was difficult for them to unwind but for us, the repeaters, we just dove into anatomy, physiology, and biochemistry, with no difficulties.

Chapter 22

Year Two at Royal College of Surgeons, 1975

The Sierra Leone student population had increased. I visited David and Cen in London. I moved into a flat away from home. I met with Maria Theodore and sister.

For most Sundays of 1974, I went to the Methodist church on Leeson Street after tennis. We shared the building belonging to the Church of Ireland, whose services were earlier in the morning. It was natural to attend church services in Kayima, Yengema, and Segbwema. It was mandatory, as a boarder, in Mattru. At St. Andrew's, it was optional. My main attraction to the church was and still is to read the Bible and listen to stories within it. Despite my long exposure to the church by competing in Bible quizzes, heading Sunday school classes, going to camps, etc., "I do not know how to pray."

While at supper on January 1, 1975, I mentioned to Mrs. F that I wished to try living on my own in a flat at the end of this academic year. My reason was that coming back home every day for supper at 7 P.M. was becoming too difficult for me. "I like to stay in the library after classes before coming home," I went on. Although very disappointed, she gladly accepted.

During our first anatomy demonstration with Professor Rooney, one of the students fainted. He shouted, "Catch him!" as the student went down. Apparently, this happened during every first demonstration. He told us to buy a pair of scissors, dissecting forceps and a scalpel and blade. "I have finally arrived," I quietly said to myself. The next day, dressed up in my white coat and fully equipped with my instruments, I was ready to go to work. With the help of Cunningham's *Anatomy Manual,* I dissected out the upper limb. My table-mates were just too happy for me to demonstrate the various structures.

Errol and I became closer, particularly in anatomy. His girlfriend, Erica, from Canada was visiting him in his flat. She used to find it very entertaining when she watched us doing surface anatomy on each other. She was a pleasant and bright person. We enjoyed her company during the two weeks she stayed with Errol. One day on our way to Errol's flat from tennis on my motorcycle, he asked me to stop outside a shop. For the first time I was introduced to Kentucky Fried Chicken. I told them that it tasted like roasted termites. They were extremely amused. They later introduced me to a meal in a Chinese restaurant.

Despite work and exercise, I kept in touch with my other Sierra Leone students, in particular the two beautiful nuns and the two schoolteachers. Sister Clare Stanley bluntly told me, "Why do you people find it so difficult to approach us?" I said, "This was true because you are different but exactly how, apart from being nuns, I don't know."

Today in physiology, we learned about the workings of the sphygmomanometer (the blood pressure machine). At the end of the lecture, I approached the lecturer for further explanation. The consultation did help, and this approach became my trademark in all the subjects. He recommended a couple of books for further reading. The next day I bought two of the books! We enjoyed measuring each other's blood pressure and pulse rate. My hunger to read and to exercise every day stayed almost the same. "A doctor who works hard to keep well should appreciate his patients' dilemma. He should be in a better position to alleviate his patients' sufferings. This should be the responsibility of all medical doctors—brilliant or not-so-brilliant," as I reasoned with my diary.

The lecture today on the central nervous system in physiology was difficult to follow. I went off to the biochemistry tutorial feeling disappointed. Biochemistry was not too disappointing. The lecture was on digestion and absorption. Lectures closed to biology always go down well with me. This good feeling was only brief. The next lecturer, like himself, always got under my skin. Nevertheless, I had to like all the lecturers because their subjects were important in determining progress.

Returning home one afternoon after church, I could not resist reading again *Chemistry of Life.* When I first read it a year or so ago, it made no sense to me. This time around, it was light reading. It was during periods like these when I went into mind wandering. "I am hoping to visit home in June 1976...."

During my morning run, I found that it was rather bright in the middle of winter. I was able to see more objects at a longer distance. It must have been a sign of good things to come for the rest of the week. I passed the biochemistry test and had no difficulty having my card signed by the senior lecturer in anatomy. In physiology, the professor showed us how to use the stethoscope. To demonstrate its use, he lifted the back of Vijay's blouse. It was so spontaneous and quick that she had no time to resist but was extremely embarrassed, to say the least. We went on to learn the cornerstones of examining a patient: inspection, palpation, percussion, and auscultation. I turned to Errol and told him, "We are fast approaching the hospital gates." The more involved I got with my work, the less I wanted to have any social relaxation—partying, having a steady girlfriend, etc., was all out of the question. The exceptions to this rule were running, hiking, and playing both table and lawn tennis. My aim was to succeed in life. But what is success?

"Success is something that some people acquire. Some are born with it and for some people, it is forced on them. A cynical person will at once ask, what's the difference? As far as I am concerned, there is a hell of a difference. The only problem is that I don't know where to lay the distinction. One of these days when I succeed in my career, I shall define that big difference." However, for the moment, I had a problem.

My exam results were unpredictable. I was either in the top three or in the last few. Exams were not made for me. I was excellent at demonstrating anatomy to other students, postgraduate students, and clinical surgeons from Richmond Hospital. I therefore had to change my style of studying to be successful in exams. On the whole, I knew the answers.

Erica left for Canada, and life for Errol returned to normal. We studied together quite often but his resident girlfriend, Juliet, was never keen on our alliance. I received two surprises in the form of a letter, each from David Carmichael and John O'Connor. John was in Dublin and invited me for supper. The reunion was exciting to me. However, I learned from him that he had divorced his wife, Patricia. John was a saint to me, and I was sure the separation was the work of Pat. From Sierra Leone to Dublin, I had never heard him raise a voice against her. He looked uneasy when asked for explanation, and so I abandoned it. David invited me to London.

I thought I must be a true bore to Juliet. I was always after Errol to study or revise lectures. Saturdays were the worst days. We worked together for most of the evening, and then he hurried off to see his girlfriend. They went to the movies, and I continued with some work. I usually got back to my flat at about 12 midnight and at 12:30 A.M., I wrote and talked to my diary.

"Is there any reason to think aloud? I do not know why but I know it is possible. I thought about people who have written masterpiece autobiographies. What were their qualities? Do they have to be great? Did they just state facts about themselves with little attention to the style and medium in which written? Will my story be boring and best forgotten in the bottom shelf? It is needless to worry about this now; write the book and the readers will decide."

I have now become the longest-living Sierra Leonean in Dublin and all new arrivals tracked me down. I enjoyed this role. I visited the two latest arrivals, Mary Martin and Teresa Alfred. I invited them to have dinner with Mrs. F and me the following Sunday. I attended a lecture given by a professor from Leeds University. He was a wonderful speaker and the title of his talk was

"Christianity in Medicine." I learned from him that "patients are not cases but people."

The dissecting room had now become my relaxation room. At the end of the physiology lecture at 12 noon, I walked down to the anatomy room to do some dissection. Our oral exam results were up. I got the third-highest grade. Well, that's encouraging. Keep it up, Francis. Actually, the credit must go to Errol for tolerating my pestering. He too passed with a five percent better than the last exam. The following day my colleagues on our table gave me a standing ovation. The professor and senior lecturer were happy with my dissection and henceforth my body was used for demonstration. On getting home that evening, I wrote to Erica, Errol's girlfriend, thanking her for supporting us.

Today was another Sunday and as usual, I played tennis, attended church service, and then went back home for lunch. Chris joined me at the table some fifteen minutes later. He was greatly apologetic. Chris was a psychiatrist, but I often wondered whether he was the doctor or patient. Both of us were seated at table and eating quietly. Then suddenly he would start thinking aloud. He would then pull his medicine container from his pocket. After fidgeting with the content of the bottle, he would come up with one tablet but after he had spilled most of it on the kitchen floor. Mrs. F could only add more mystery to Chris's state of mind when I enquired.

I arrived in London alone on the invitation of Mr. David Carmichael. I read David's note to the letter but ran into all sorts of trouble. I only had Irish money on me, but the ticket man understood my dilemma; he accepted my coins. I got into the underground but where to get out was like a maze to me. Going around and around continued for three hours. A porter finally rescued me by directing me to the right tubes for my destination. I was collected from the North Ealing Station by David, who was overflowing with apologies because he sent me the wrong information.

In London, I was like a fish out of water. Yet there were many familiarities about this city. These must have come during classes in Sierra Leone, from reading, and a small amount from the cinemas. David was a bachelor and was once the secretary to President Kwame Nkrumah of Ghana. He behaved like a philanthropist, reminding me of William Wilberforce of the slave trade fame. He enjoyed the task of rescuing foreign students from jams. He was an excellent cook and fun to be with. As time went by, I learned that he belonged to a club I called "Company of Bachelors." Professional bachelors visited the apartment quite frequently, and we returned the visits as well. I admired them because they seemed to do more for more people and were more devoted to their jobs. I wished I could enjoy both worlds—you see, I needed a female partner. I would be an excellent father and a good husband.

David worked at the Africa Centre, situated at the old Convent Market Place. While at work, he would let me roam the city centre. One morning on our way to work, he said to me, "It is better for an African student to marry a white woman than to marry a black woman from a different background.

The white wife will easily adapt in an African atmosphere because she is already mentally aware of the difficulties. But as for a black girl, say from the West Indies or USA, the situation is completely the reverse, though the alliance may look the most ideal at first sight." During one of my outings, I discovered Lewis Medical Bookshop and without fail, I bought two books, *Respiratory Medicine* and *Passing Medical Examinations*. The Easter holidays were over, and I had to return to Dublin through the Holyhead boat.

It gave me a wonderful pride to have brought something for Mrs. F from London. She was extremely grateful. The wonderful experience in London through David and friends gave me a renewed energy to work harder. I had resolved, "I will like to go on to do postgraduate studies." I just continued with life from where I started.

As the year progressed, I started making active attempts to look for a flat. I enjoyed being with Mrs. F, but I had to go one day and doing so at the end of this school year was as good as any other time. Over ten years ago, Mrs. F lost her husband, Mr. Joseph Kenny. She took back her maiden name, Fairbrother. They had no children. She became a financial beneficiary of a medical school in India. To do so she made and sold jams, sold her garden products, and collected rent from lodgers. She was upset one evening when I got in from college. A speculator wanted to buy her house. "They will only get me out of here with head first."

During the course of the year, I had tapped a summary of each course on a tape recorder. For revision now, I listened to my own voice as I rode my bike and while in bed. Whenever the opportunity arose, I visited the two nuns and the two schoolteachers. The end-of-year examination results came out and they were disappointing, not for me but for those who knew me. I had an interview with the professor in biochemistry before my departure for the summer holidays. I accepted the outcome and was willing to re-sit it in September, just when the leaves started falling. David again invited me to London to take my mind off the exams.

During the few weeks that were to follow, I found myself daydreaming about home. "My grandfather, Tachesumoe (Joemende), was a man of great strength. He had many qualities as a Section Chief. Chief among these was his insistence on communion with the dead, with ancestors (including his dead older brother, whose name was given to me) and defeated princes of his Kawama people. He spent his whole fortune in an attempt to achieve this aim. He succeeded. He was loved, worshipped, and adored by all. Nevertheless, he died as a poor and brokenhearted man. But where lay the justice we advocated for by us all?. He who rules by the sword shall die by the sword. But he who rules with kindness and gentleness shall die with hatred and brutality." He was never paid for his work. I went to him for school fees. I received one pound in coins that had gone green. The money went through the hands of the town chief, the town crier, etc., gathered in front of our house. When it finally reached me, the money felt warm as I held it comfortably in both hands. He dispatched me with a bag of rice, which I sold on the trip to supplement the one pound. I started school in a new blue shirt and khaki shorts—the pair for use in every occasion.

We were joined by Cen Jones, who worked with WHO in Kenya in the second month of my holidays. David, Cen, and their many "bachelor friends" have become relaxed with me and would discuss their homosexuality with no difficulty. One morning while having breakfast with David, I asked him about why he was a homosexual.

"One of the main reasons why you are not married is because of your philanthropist nature," I suggested.

"It is my bisexuality that led to the situation. I got engaged to a very pleasant girl but we called it off. She could not accept me for what I was. It was difficult for people like me to live in a society that strongly opposes the practice. If masturbation is accepted, what is wrong with homosexual relationships? Both are natural."

For the rest of the summer, I had wonderful experiences with London life. David took me to live shows, including Mikado. It was the best show I had seen so far in London. David was not impressed with the replacement actor. I thought to myself, *I thought he was great but having not seen the other, I couldn't argue with him. Even if I did I wouldn't argue with him.* We visited many of David's bachelor friends, some single and some married. According to David, "the golden rule for a heterosexual who has had homosexual experiences should never discuss it with his girlfriend." In the same breath, he said that there were no golden rules.

It was not all study and being in the company of David and friends. I made contact with my "sister," Martha Margai, who was now married to Dr. Momodu Yilla. Momodu graduated from Moscow and was doing postgraduate studies in London. I found him to be humorous, quiet, and bright. I enjoyed reading through the photo album of their wedding. I was now used to the London Underground, and the day's activities were constantly changing. I saw many homeless black people, and this disturbed me. I saw, in the train, three black girls fought with four white girls. The two sets were nuisances to society and should have been locked up. Back in Sierra Leone, I recalled, the African people who came to Great Britain had a plan to becoming a lawyer, medical doctor, or a qualified somebody. They were good in their own home country but by transplantation in the United Kingdom, they could not cope with life in this new environment.

At the end of each adventure, I made a resolution not to fail in my dream. "In the first place, I want to succeed in my career. I will be more tolerant and in this way be able to help those who can be helped. However, before I settle down into full practice, I will at least like to write my autobiography. The purpose of the book will not be to make more money, make a name for myself, or to show the world that I have been there. So far, I have lived a very interesting life. It has been a life that had been full of circumstances or, in a better word, coincidences. The book will aim at bringing out its full theme: *The Child of Two Parents.*

"My first parents include my genetic father and mother, who came together to bring and present me to the world. My second parents are those who brought me up through the world into which I was presented by the first parents. I am grateful to both of them. The hero will be me, naturally. I will be presented to the world for the second time as in the first time, nothing more and nothing less. We learn by our and other people's mistakes. It could, therefore, be a guidebook for the African child."

I received a letter from Mrs. F one morning. In recent times, she had ended her letters to me as "Your affectionate aunt." She was anxious to know where I was going to stay starting next school term.

"What are the qualities of a good African autobiographer?" I asked David one morning while having breakfast.

His response was as if he had anticipated the question a long time ago. "I assume you don't necessarily mean the handling of the language in which the writing is done. A good autobiographer is one who develops incidents leading up to what he is. He does not condemn or justify events. He states things or facts as they are—in their natural state—without bringing trivialities. In the first place, there are very few good autobiographers compared to biographers. Nevertheless, with no hesitation, I'll choose Camara Laye's *African Child*."

I agreed with him. I had read the book in both its original French version and English translation. It is a simple, natural objective book.

I was very happy with myself to be back in Dublin. I was able to bring back a little something for everybody but above all, I acquired a full natural human skeleton from a London osteology department. I negotiated a flat at #130 Tritonville Road, Dublin 4, for twelve pounds a week.

I received my first ever letter from Uncle SJW. In it, he apologized for wronging me in the past. This was my response: "Dear Uncle SJW, you are talking in the past. Daniel is in financial trouble in Switzerland and so is Tamba in Sierra Leone. They need your help. I have reassured both of them that I would help if possible. My scholarship was just enough to cover my expenses. I am fine at the moment and there is no need for you to send me any money." I have forgotten whatever wrong he would have done to me. I reminded him about my admiration and adoration for him and that we are humans and prone to making mistakes in our lives and those of others.

One day I received a telephone call from Miss Maureen Cloake, the secretary at the Overseas Students' Club, informing me about the arrival of a new student from Sierra Leone. He was David Kanu. Mrs. F agreed to have him as one of her lodgers. He was a premed student and did his primary degree in Lebanon. I felt good that I was able to help.

The repeat September exam results came out and I did extremely well in biochemistry. As I walked along the corridor one morning, I ran into the professor of anatomy. To my amazement and possibly with shock, he said, "Saa-Gandi, have you seen the results? You did extremely well overall, but you seem to find a way in your essays to deviate from the question at hand. This, therefore, costs you precious marks." The professor had a bamboo back and walked with a stoop forward. He hardly spoke to anybody in public. I was extremely grateful for this outburst.

I started the new school year in my new flat. I continued to see Mrs. F every week. I enjoyed her homemade cake and she appreciated my help with her plants. As the weeks went by, she wanted me to come back but I refused flatly. Of course, I wanted to go back for many reasons. Often it was colder inside my flat than outside because of non-performance of the central heating. "The central heating is again not working" (this is what I wrote). "Boiler has sprung a leak. I will try to have it fixed over the weekend. It may not, however, be until early next—it looks like a big job" (this is what Mr. A J Bennet, the landlord, replied). I responded, "The hot water never came on until Tuesday. It was a big inconvenience." I received many friends and visitors to have idle talks, discuss their personal problems, and borrow money. Once every week, I cleaned in front of the building because the other tenants (twelve in all) left their garbage in front of the building the night before collection day. This allowed the foxes and cats to have a field night. These, I considered, were bad for my studies, but I dared not admit to Mrs. F.

The SL student population had suddenly grown, and I decided to have a get-together party. The guests (ten in all) made a good showing. We had authentic SL food and plenty of it. The girls cooked most of the food, I did some cooking, and I provided the drinks and the flat (of my Turkish friends at the basement). It was thoroughly enjoyed by everybody as they ate with their bare hands, cracked jokes, and danced to quiet pleasant music. I naively concluded that this would be it; they wanted more! The most prominent culprit was Alex Stevens. He was one of the sons of our president, Siaka Stevens. He was studying law at TCD. He was a likeable person but extremely lazy and full of talks.

My new study partner was now Isaac Stern. He was a Jew and a strong practitioner of his faith. He lived with his wife and two daughters. We worked extremely hard, but he was not a true student because of his outside commitment. Errol appreciated why I had kept my distance from him this term; his girlfriend, Juliet, had never enjoyed my company. She found me too boring.

There was another reason why we saw little of each other after college. Maria came into my life. We first met at his flat in company with her sister, Andrea, early this year.

While visiting Dublin from Cork, I invited them to stay in my flat. After the first two lectures of the day, I went to collect my guests at the OSC. It was a pretty cold December day. On Sunday I helped Maria with her anatomy. They left at about 5 P.M. for Cork. All three of us felt badly, but all good things must come to an end. Within days of their return, Maria sent me a thank-you letter. I replied instantly to thank her for the letter. I hinted in my reply that I would like her to be my girlfriend.

Isaac and I continued to study together in my flat after lectures. The outcomes of these joint study sessions were unpredictable; we could cover a lot of work or spend half of the time talking about Israel. This morning the foxes and others were at it again. I again cleaned the pavement before setting off to college. Errol, my other study partner, was sitting at my steps when I got home from tennis. We studied separately for an hour and then after a fifteen-minute break we worked together for two hours. Errol decided to make us one of his specialities. Errol was always a good cook.

Christmas was fast approaching and so too cards and letters. I received two letters today: one from Maria Theodore and the other from Grandpa O'Connor. Maria told me that she got through her exams and that she and Andrea would be spending part of their Christmas holiday in Dublin. She never asked to stay in my flat. But like all my women, she let me take the plunge. Grandpa sent me a cheque for USD30. He was keeping well and at his age, he remained employed. I always enjoyed reading his letters and re-plying to them.

"I hope that next year things will improve between me and my four-legged night friends." Today was Friday morning and things had not changed. "Lectures and exams are over for the term, and so I must have a complete rest today. That is a joke. I had a quick shower and went out for a ride. The foxes (I presume) again got at the bins. The tenants facing the street could be seen hiding behind their curtains as they saw me picking their things from the pave-ment. I am used to it because this was the way I was brought up—a houseboy and environmentalist."

To be aware of my surroundings was initiated by my first headmaster in Kayima. I have mentioned this episode elsewhere in this book. He hid a ten-shilling note under a rock that fell on the driveway. After one week, he brought the whole school to make a circle around the stone. He asked one of the junior boys to shift the stone. On picking up the stone, the money appeared. The lesson to be learned from this demonstration was, according to him, "One day you will be rewarded for keeping your environment clean." The reward of maintaining one's upkeep was a result of contributing to one's labour. This was not to be confused with "childhood exploitation by forced labour."

Chapter 23

Year Three at Royal College of Surgeons in Dublin, 1976

I was not a professional tennis player, far from it. Nevertheless, I played tennis almost every day this year. I passed all my clinical examinations and driving test. I began understanding women.

David invited me to a New Year's Eve party held at a nightclub. All the partygoers were men. When the clock stroke 12 midnight, the men went crazy, and glasses with champagne went up with cheers, followed by kissing and hugging. The atmosphere was electric and filled with clouds of smoke. Smoke and my lungs did not make a good alliance. David noticed my uneasiness and he nicely suggested that we left.

Now back in Dublin, the first person I visited was Mrs. F. Still troubled about my experience with David and friends, I decided to keep things to myself. For yet another time, we talked about my returning to live with her, but I declined.

The first Saturday of the year started busily. I spent the morning playing with Erdem. In my flat, my neighbour dropped in with his girlfriend for a drink. They left soon after the arrival of Bernadette and Andrea. After lunch, we went to see *Jaws*. None of us thought the film deserved the publicity it got. It failed to bring out what it was set out to do. It lacked the real touch of science fiction and the comedy was inadequate.

On Sunday I went to play tennis with Brendan and then went to church. I finally got home at 12 noon but only to find myself reading a book entitled *A Doctor's Look at Life and History*. The book was not a set textbook and one of the reasons for getting me into exam troubles—general reading. I stopped reading when I received a call from Maria inviting me to join her at Errol's flat. Mid-morning, I went for my riding test. I had read all the official booklets on safe riding of motorcycles. Besides, my learner's permit allowed me to ride on my own for the previous one year. My confidence equated with success. The oral part of the exam went well and the practical was a piece of cake. The examiner was full of praise. He instantly gave me my certificate. I hope that this was the start of many more good things to come for the rest of the year. On the last day of the month, I received a letter from Daniel.

His father, Uncle SJW, disapproved of him studying theology. N'Gundia, his older sister, wanted him to send her a present. I was angry with both of them. This was my reply: "Dear Uncle SJW, I write with regards to your last correspondence with Daniel. We must be grateful that he is studying towards improving his quality of life. All he wants is to get on his feet and will probably do law in the future. I know he is your son, but you are being unreasonable to discourage him from doing theology in the University of Fribourg. He is broke, scared, and lonely. Leave him alone."

Classes had not started fully in college, and so I wanted company. None of my study partners were back from their holidays yet. I contacted Teresa, who reminded me of our agreement—to go our separate ways. Jacinta had other plans. "Women are so whimsical. We men always have to give in to them. I guess I deserve it," I opted, or was forced to write letters.

I thanked David for having me over the Christmas holidays and sent a thank-you card to Cen in Kenya. Pa Harry became chief of New England Ville, Dworzak, and their environs. It was a highly respected appointment. I wrote to congratulate him: "I am proud of you." On completing three more letters, I ran into trouble.

I became suddenly hot. I tried to sleep but could not. Every movement generated pains in my joints, including those I was not aware of before. The eyes would not tolerate light. I lost my appetite. Ceaseless non-productive coughing complicated all of this. I eventually dropped to sleep but only to face some weird dreams. In the dreams I was the centre of attention, yet I could not explain what this was all about. Early in the morning, I was well enough to play tennis with Erdem at TCD.

All the same, I opted to stay home for a day to rest, eat, and drink plenty of liquids. I read Maria's letter again before replying. In the letter, she advised me to save myself from the bad weather so that she could poison me. She was playing back to me one of my jokes. We were growing to be true friends, suggested by the evaluation of the similarities and differences between us.

At mid-afternoon on Saturdays, I always managed to recruit a study group. We were to meet at Errol's flat. I invited Eric and Larry to join in. I got there first as always, followed by Eric, Errol, and Larry, in that order. We covered many grounds. Eric was a businesslike worker if the host could sustain his food demand. I had forewarned Errol about this because I had studied with him on many occasions in my flat—"He eats me out at the end of each meeting." This time we could not go to my flat because I had Alex Stevens living with me. I eventually ventured to go home and only to find Alex entertaining our two nuns, an Irish girl, and David. I concluded at the time, "Alex had no chance of completing his law degree course."

Maria dropped in from Cork for the weekend. We spent these weekends revising, eating, and then going to the movies. This time an old classmate of mine at St. Andrew's dropped in to see me. I was shocked. He had changed for the worse. He talked a lot and chain-smoked. His hands shook, probably from excessive alcohol intake and drug abuse. I shed tears for him. He was one of the boys who made life bearable for me during my first year at school in a foreign country. I had since run into two other students, but juniors to us, in similar circumstances. But what was it that made these brilliant students to go astray?

For my Christmas present last year, Cen made a year's subscription for the *Medical Practitioner.* I usually read it from cover to cover, although I understood less than fifty percent of it. Nevertheless, what was new? I spent many "precious times" reading outside my course. I had been reminded many times before. I loved books and they were going to kill me.

I made my usual weekend call to Mrs. F to do any odd job in her garden. I took off to study with Errol and Eric joined us an hour later. We covered what we set out to do in anatomy. On my way home, I dropped in to see one of my Sierra Leone girls, but she was on her way out on a date. She invited me to her workplace the following Saturday, which I accepted. She worked at a nightclub, Lord John, for extra pocket money. I would have been better off staying home. No need mourning now because the harm has been done. Smoke, noise from loud music, and voices and the smell of alcohol filled the air. When I left a few hours later, my eyes and chest burned and felt dizzy. This was to be my first and last visit to a nightclub of that nature.

The lectures were now in full swing. I visited the anatomy lab daily without fail before or after other lectures. It gave me the opportunity to demonstrate my dissected body to both under- and post-graduate students.

This year marked three years of my being president of the Irish arm of the Sierra Leone Students Union of Great Britain and Ireland. The position was only symbolic, as there were no active members. On returning home after one of my hectic days, I received a call from Alex Stevens. Together with David Kanu, for various personal reasons, they wanted to revive the student union. Alex wanted me to respond to a letter from Sa. Leone regarding the union. "It worried me stiff when he said he was doing it for us. What does he think he is? He is a student like any of us. I don't trust him," as noted in my diary. David K, on the other hand, had already composed a letter for me to send to the president and prime minister of SL, saying that we appreciated their work. I was uneasy about this and so I gave up the presidency. The girls were extremely unhappy about my decision, but it was final.

Maria sent me a letter, which was more than welcome; it took my mind off the union. "I am grateful for the scarf you sent me. I do not think you should have bothered. I am not worth it," I wrote in the diary afterwards. "Honestly speaking, I am very fond of Maria. However, I hope I do not fall victim of my unnecessary extravagance (financially and emotionally) towards the opposite sex. She is one girl who is not likely to take advantage of a situation detrimental to the other partner. We shall see: Time will tell."

Isaac and I had worked for the whole morning and part of the afternoon. On leaving he said, "I am extremely happy that I met you." Two hours after his departure, things started falling apart. The central heating broke down, the only telephone in the hall way went dead, and a noisy party downstairs was in full swing. I resorted to my old gas heater and got on with my studies.

I had no transport to dash home for lunch from college, and so I dropped into the canteen. I never enjoyed canteen foods because of their tastes but above all, they were often too expensive. The old lady was not there today and her younger replacements were friendly and generous. Larry, a regular visitor, agreed with me. The old lady was only interested in her money and nothing else.

I got back to the flat after an interclub tennis tournament. Brendan and I won our doubles. As I sat down sipping my coffee, I fell into a daydream. "I tried to imagine returning home as a medical doctor. I know I will be a good doctor because I am always ready to help. Nevertheless, it seems that I will be caught between three worlds, which are not distinct. I will be devoted to my family, work, and writing. Maybe to succeed is to attempt to do it in the above order of things. Maybe I am being too optimistic, but is there anything wrong about that? Probably I am just underlining the characteristics of the younger generation of which I am a full member." A call from Errol interrupted the dream. He managed to secure a microscope. I joined him within an hour and we went through the slides. Errol had become a genuine friend of mine. "The alliance between us has become a real give-and-take. We have come to rely on each other for confidence and psychological let-outs."

I got into the flat later in the afternoon from tennis. I had completely forgotten that Jacinta was in the flat. She was sleeping on my arrival, and I noticed that she had cooked and cleaned the flat. I had not attempted to encourage or discourage her from being my friend. It was wonderful to have her in small doses. She was good with her hands, dress making. "She is a wonderful person, gentle, and not quarrelsome." I wonder what she thought of me, a bore to women.

I spent the rest of the evening listening to two plays on the radio set in South Africa. I became absorbed in both plays: *Too Educated to Be Black but Too Black to Be White* and *Don't Go There*.

On this Saturday, I decided to escape from Dublin. I read all the way to Cork and so I was exhausted on arrival. The girls could not believe their own eyes. But there I was, unannounced, in their disorganized dig. Maria made me feel welcome, but Andrea as usual was only concerned about herself. Maria and I went out to buy a bag for me and then went to Margaret and her two children. Like Margaret's children, I had always enjoyed the company of children. "My good relationship with other people's children may not necessarily translate to mine."

This brings me to women friends. "I find Mary rather fastidious to which she admits. She has fixed ideas about me and therefore difficult to handle. Maria is fun to be with, having a cute sense of humour. Hawa is a naïve little girl willing to learn. Teresa is a bore to hang around with, rather world-wise. At the present time if asked to make a choice, I will go with Jacinta with no reservations."

One evening I received a call from Mr. Duke to announce the death of David Carmichael. It was a mutual friend of ours, Mr. George Vellacott, who had contacted Mr. Duke. George invited me to stay with him during David's funeral. I had always liked George and this short stay solidified our friendship. Before leaving for Dublin, he promised to arrange a summer job for me at his school.

By the end of the term, George got me a job at the Royal Post-graduate Medical School in Hammersmith Hospital. This was a change from the farms of Galway. I met with my new boss, Dr. David Gompertz. He was in his forties, about five feet six inches tall. He was medically qualified but branched into full medical research, biochemistry. He was a Jew. His main interest was in inborn errors of acid metabolism. I commented in my diary, "I think working with him is going to be fantastic." After just a week at work, Dr. DG recognized that I was short-sighted. My role was to be a lab technician.

With one of his colleagues, they divided a cell and asked me to look down the telescope. I had to change the focus of the lens to see clearly, and it was at this point when David suggested I see an eye specialist. The next day I saw Dr. Michael Squire on the recommendation of George. My shortsightedness must explain why I always sat in front of the class giving the impression that I was an overenthusiastic student. I was in a new world when I got fitted with a pair of glasses. Bernadette was in London staying with relatives. I invited her one evening to stay with us. At the time I noted in my diary, "George enjoys good music, good food, but I wish he could stop smoking."

Bernadette and I had decided to explore historical sites in London this summer. I wrote Pa Harry a letter, congratulating him for his appointment as chief of New England and Dwozark. I wished him luck, particularly with two wives in these hard times in Freetown. We visited the International Students' House to which Bernadette was a member. We ended the day on brushing up on our colonial history by visiting Buckingham Palace, Trafalgar Square, 10 Downing Street, Big Ben, and its environs.

It was over a month now in London and no summer job for Bernadette, and so she decided to do a course in typewriting. I was flattered when she asked for my opinion; I was all for it. As for me, I was having a fun time at the lab. David was surprised to see me laugh when he called me Akibo. The tone in which he said it was not offensive. In fact, it was a complement because the name of his best technician was Akibo. I was enjoying myself now, analyzing samples of urine from the wards.

One evening after work, I decided to pay a visit to Ivor Cummings. I had visited him once but in the company of late David. I located his flat easily. "We talked about the death of David. He was a wonderful and great man, and it's not likely that I will ever meet his kind again. He enjoyed doing things for people." We talked for over two hours, touching on the prospect of my visiting Sierra Leone next summer. He jumped at the idea and promised to make some contacts on my behalf.

Martha Margai and her husband, Momodu Yilla, invited Bernadette and me for a weekend. We accepted. Bernadette could not go to sleep because she was cold. She asked me to turn around and hold her and with a quiet smile, and I gladly did. We spent the rest of the morning philosophizing. She came to nearly saying I love you.

"You have been patient with me. We have shared beds many times but you never bothered me for sex."

"My main interest in you is because you are a medical student and intelligent. Your being a woman comes second. I have a great affection for you. By this, I mean love, sex, and understanding. Sex is only an independent ingredient. That is to say that the other constituents can stand without it. I have two other sisters and I am considered as the ugliest of them all. I think this is a big mistake on your part especially [when] you believe in it. You are attractive but you are not aware of it. Thank you so much. You've hit the nail on the head. It's only you and Frank that considered me as I am—a person to share thoughts with and then a woman. I can be promiscuous if I want to be. Your conscience, as a catholic girl like you, won't let you."

What a coincidence! Dominic of Kayima was now working at the High Commission in London as an accountant. He invited me to his home to meet with his wife, who had arrived from Freetown. It was a huge house owned by a Sa Leonean. His older brother, Tom, was there too. There was a Mr. Dunso visiting from USSR and John Kamanda studying law. Gloria eventually joined us in the living room. She looked very black and older than Dominic. She said little. Fatima, the other lady, in the gathering was loud, talkative, and amusing. All the guests and tenants were all from SL living in England for years. They had had little to say nice about the country. Instead, they talked about "these people."

For the past few weeks, Bernadette worked as a dishwasher in one of the hotels on Leicester Square. At 2 A.M. I collected her from work and dragged her to a cinema house. It was a bad decision. We were both tired and sleepy and in the wrong place. Half of the people were sleeping and snoring loudly. At 5:45 A.M. I dragged her to George's flat—another bad decision. At about 10 A.M. I took Bernadette to her dig. George was home when I returned. Before sitting down I started apologizing to him for my behaviour.

"You asked me to get out of my bed and when I didn't, you came back with a girl and slipped into the single bed. You tried to play around with me."

I apologized profusely and gave no excuses. The following day, I dropped an apology letter at Bernadette's dig.

Hi, Berns. I had a sleepless night feeling sick about events that occurred over the weekend. But first of all, George said thank you for repairing the kitchen curtain, cleaning the dishes, and beautifully arranging the flowers. He apologized for his behaviour, but I cannot see what he did wrong. Truly speaking, I should take the whole blame. I took you to a downtrodden cinema house and sneaked you into his flat at an unsocial hour. This was very disrespectful to him. It gave me the feeling that I was just using you and him for my own pleasure. But any attempt now to recount all the events just makes it worse.

So please accept my apologies. Don't think badly of George. It wasn't his fault but entirely mine.

Yours,
Francis.

"In any case one excellent thing came out of it all. George and I have re-solved our differences—he is homosexual and I am heterosexual. We can share everything but sex."

Things had improved a lot among the three of us. Bernadette continued to work in the city. In addition to his nominal work, George gave some of his time to the Samaritans and I was learning a lot in the lab. In addition, George started cutting back on his cigarette smoking and showing interest in tennis, which I played almost every day. Pa Harry was my only contact in SL, and I continued to write to him, narrating my progress or regress. He was not keen about my alliance with Bernadette. "His fear is that my people won't like it. As such, your people will hate or bewitch you. I do not believe in or practice juju. So, I am unlikely to be caught in a net I have never entered. My relatives are my relatives. I expect them as they are and I expect the same of them." Pa Harry's advice was similar to that given to me by David sometime ago.

Autumn was here and this morning, I decided to explore the other parts of the Lammas Park. "The ordinary man is a much happier individual than the man at the top. As I walked in the park, I couldn't resist casting an eye over a group of men sitting on makeshift chairs. There were seven of them well dressed in ties. They were drinking from one large brown bottle. As they ate, drank, and smoked, they talked and laughed heartily. I was impressed and en-vious."

All good things must come to an end. I boarded a train at Euston to Holyhead and then across the Irish Sea in a boat. I had paid my rent to cover the whole summer holidays. On the dot, my property owner was at my door to collect her rent. She gave me the impression that our rent had been increased because her children's school fees had gone up. All the same, she knocked off one pound and twenty-five pence because of me being her best tenant. I made contact with Errol as he too came back from New York. His relationship with Ade was becoming quite serious. They both went to a discotheque the night before. Juliet, his former girlfriend, did not like me around often. So I had to be careful with Ade. They gave me a lift home, and en route I told them that I was studying to be a doctor second to none in SL. Errol made no comment, but he knew I meant every word of it.

In the hospital, Mr. Harold Browne was back from his holidays and so he took us for the ward rounds. He asked me to make a diagnosis of a twenty-four-year-old patient's problem.

"Doc, here is a patient with severe pain in the right iliac fossa. If you were on duty that night, you would get to Mr. De Costa [the registrar] or me immediately. But you would tell me not to spoil my sleep. I would then ask why. You would then say because you played piano on his tummy. You were in essence telling me the absence of guarding and rigidity." I missed the diagnosis completely. I failed to appreciate that common things were common. He asked me to look through the window and announced to the group what I saw in the sky. "Seagulls! Yes, but not sparrows."

I am now gladly happy to pass this fact on to my students and junior doctors that common things are common. Mr. Browne was one of our best teachers. I attended all his classes.

As promised, George came over to visit me in Dublin. He drove in a secondhand car, which we had bought for me during the summer holidays. It was a mini-Clubman, WBL309H, my fourth stage of self-transport—feet, bicycle, motorbike, and now a car. The car was to be called "Woble" from now on. A week or so after his return to London, George wrote me two letters. He sent me my AA Membership Card and clarified the insurance policy covering me in Eire. He also emphasized that I passed my British driving test to give Bernadette and me the freedom of London. His second letter was to thank me for looking after him so well during his stay in Dublin with me. Of course, while I was busy in school, he was busy in town. "He visited the Irish version of the Samaritans, Dr. Harry O'Flannagan [the dean and registrar] and Mr. Duke [my former headmaster and friend]. They all think highly of you."

The final letter of the year was from Saffa Tia. Saffa was my classmate in CSS, but we met again early last summer. He strongly suggested that "we should not get our girlfriends pregnant until completion of our courses." Less than a year later, he got his girlfriend, Anna, pregnant. She banned him from seeing the child, and I never succeeded in bringing them back again. I have seen many similar situations like this since my arrival on these islands. "Do as I say, but do not do as I do."

Chapter 24

Year Four at Royal College of Surgeons, 1977

We spent old year's night in London at a Trinidadian nightclub. Phillip Tang bought my motorcycle. Uncle SWG returned to CSS as a qualified teacher. Bernadette passed the Second Med Exams. I proposed marriage to Bernadette.

The termites feasted on parts of this year's diary before I did this time around. George, Bernadette, and I had a wonderful "old year's night" at a Trinidadian and Tobagonian Union Club. "George had the most exciting time of his life. For the three hours we were at the party, he ate, drank, and danced with charming girls." The next day we drove to Holyhead, bound for Dublin. "We bid George at the entrance of the boat. He was in tears when we bid goodbye. I felt sorry for him and probably moved. I can now accept his affectionate love for me with no offence."

I ran into David K and he briefed me on the last meeting on the SLSU in London. The young ones who should have open minds were still suffering from tribalism. I had warned him about it because I learned that "like all other nationals, they are more nationalistic when they are away from home." I received a letter from Grandpa O'Connor. He wrote his usual pleasant and encouraging letter. He was out of work and sounded very disappointed despite his age at eighty. He once told me that there was no substitute for good health. You should not retire once you are in good health.

I took heart to check for my results on the notice board. I passed all my exams but I think I could have done better. On my way home, I dropped in to see my SL girls, who were staying with the McNealys. Jacinta was there and as usual busy in the kitchen, preparing food for everybody. I got into a conversation with Mr. Mc. I have thought of him as being a happy-going man. He had a son at the basement who "is a hermit and daughter-in-law who smokes too much and coughs with blood and is breathless. My ninety-four-year-old mother drives me up the wall." I felt extremely sorry for him. It is better sometimes, if not all the time, to accept things on their face value.

Before the start of the term, I contacted my study partners: Isaac, Errol, Larry, and Eric. Errol had something to tell me. "It has been a long time since I met somebody as diplomatic as you. You agree with everybody and say nothing evil about anyone." I think that about sums me up. Honestly speaking, I am not aware of it.

The weather so far had not relented. There were still a few months of this to be endured. "It was difficult getting to Blancherstown Hospital for tutorials. It was the second day of snow in Dublin. Snow covered every open space, reminding one of movie pictures from far away. The worse was to follow in the form of melting ice in one's shoes. It was in the middle of this when I accepted Errol's invitation to meet with the West Indian contingency in Cork. The drive was full of events not helped by inexperienced driving. On two occasions, I skidded off the road. We lost the road three times because the road and fields were evenly covered with snow." Bernadette was pleasantly happy to see me but not surprised. "When I could not see Errol at the train station, I knew he was driving in your yellow matchbox."

Falabu, a year my junior, was surprised to see me in the canteen at lunch. "You are so involved with your work that you often forget to eat." He was partly correct. "I have done well this year so far—health-wise. I can probably put the credit on the car, which allowed me to drive home for lunch to eat my own cooked food. I managed to eat three times a day. Despite the hours put into my work and exercise, I never felt tired."

I now had a new problem around the flat. The property owner of the block next door occupied the basement flat with his family. They had two dogs, one acquired two years ago and the other from last Christmas. "The younger dog is often left alone in the garden. He hates it. He will bark and cry for hours on end until allowed inside again. He is not to be blamed for his actions because he wants attention and it is an attempt to keep himself warm. Occasionally the older dog pushes itself through the back door. After clearing his throat, he collects all the bones from their side of the fence and buries them on our side. They had free thoroughfare of the two gardens, both unkempt. Today, I decided not to go to the library but stay in the flat to study. At this same time, the little dog appeared in the garden. To keep him quiet, I bribed him with some of Bernadette's sandwiches. It worked.

"During the medical conference this morning, I was tempted many times to buy a cup of tea, but I resisted because I have already spent this month's allocation for food. Errol was quite sharp today. He answered correctly every question put to him by his favourite lecturer, Dr. Noel, who he thought was the only teacher who said hello to his students. The next tutorial class was in surgery and it was my turn to shine. I answered all the questions put to me on fractures. Errol and I were in a little fight for superiority without being aware of it. May be he thinks so, but as far as I am concerned, he was my booster. It was wonderful."

I received a letter from Finda James, who sent me news about my sister as she saw them. "I saw your sister in Sefadu, but she doesn't look quite well. One can tell on her appearance. She looks very thin. Please try and write to her. I guess too much worries are making her thin. Her children are well. At any time you want to write her, send the letter to me. You know it is not nice for you to ignore her or her husband will feel she hasn't a brother because you don't write to her."

My way of avoiding stress was to avoid writing home. The other letter, which contrasted with that of Finda, came from Bernadette. "Thank you very much for your last letter [when it finally came]. It was greatly appreciated and gave a lot of encouragement. Please keep it up and write more often. You disturb me more when you don't write than when you do. Besides the fact, I do not have you in Dublin for your looks, but just for your letters." What a strange way to show a man that you love him.

Erdem invited me to his flat. He had all sorts of characters with him. They were all foreign students from Turkey, Canada, USA, Australia, Norway, and Spain. Everybody had something to say. "When I say Grandfather had 15 wives, it shouldn't be interpreted from the viewpoint of the First World societies. To Sierra Leonean and indeed many other African states, rural population, working on subsistence farming with only minimal mechanical help, many hands are important. Children become producers if not providers at early age. Besides, only one-third of conceptions survive full pregnancy and the hazards of childhood are quite high. It is therefore understandable that a couple might accept repeated pregnancies as a means of providing enough workers for the fields.

"The common practice of polygamy tends to lead to fewer pregnancies per woman and allows the man to observe the taboo of intercourse with a lactating woman. Therefore, in a set-up like this in my country, it is rare to come across a family who has not recovered from the death of a child. Everything is natural; being born and dying go hand in hand. This is the thinking of the animists; a man dies but comes back as a spirit to protect and guide us from our enemies. We make annual offerings to show them our appreciation of their work. For the Muslims in my society, death is due to Allah. This is probably what Charles Darwin alluded to in his theory of Natural Selection—survival of the fittest." The discussion was excellent during the first hour, but it then deteriorated as the marijuana they were smoking took effect.

"It was a delightful morning and the rest of the day will be the same. Therefore, I invited Jacinta for a drive in the country. We drove through Bray, Greystones, and finally into Glendalough. The scenery, as usual, was breathtaking, but we could not come out of the car. It was cold, although dry. On getting back to my flat, I went out to do some shopping. Jacinta had enough time to go through my photo albums. She didn't like the content. Most of the pictures were of Bernadette and me. She drank and smoked more. She was upset and only giggled to herself. Eventually I got her talking and we were friends again." I gave her a lift to her home and on our way, she said to me, "I think you are too secretive, but I have started catching you."

After classes today, I brought Phillip to my flat. With his help, I started my old Honda 50 motorbike, as he was interested in buying it. I showed him a few tricks to ride safely. As a pillion and teacher, we went around the block a few times. He was a quick learner. We had something to eat and he was on his own back home.

The club tennis winter (Sundays) season was over, and it ended with a bang. "Brendan and I won our doubles with no problem but the team lost. The last time we lost was because I allowed him to continue making the same mistakes repeatedly. Today, however, I played every ball within my reach. Our option now was to regroup for the summer rounds. I intend to play in every tournament this year."

I ran into one of my female classmates today, and we got talking. "She is one of our brightest girls. She passed all her exams and did well in tutorials. She is of Asian parentage from Kenya. She knew everything about everybody—students and lecturers. We never spoke one to one before. She is a ceaseless talker." Probably these qualities made her an excellent student. I did not envy her.

Another Saturday has arrived and the general sequence of events was, "a visit to the launderette, the week's shopping next door, and then back home to cook for the week. I visited Mrs. F, who asked me to do things in the garden she could not do herself (like ridding the iris vines off the road-facing wall). An excellent afternoon tea will follow. I will spend the rest of the afternoon at the tennis club. On getting home I will study until 12 midnight and finally diary writing."

This Friday evening was for letter writing. "Dear Bernadette, I know you are thinking the worst, but they invited you for viva in physiology to prove that you are an honours student. I must admit I did not only love but I adore you. Dear Uncle Samuel, congratulations for coming back to CSS as a qualified schoolteacher. I truly believe that you and Mr. Gorvie will bring the school back to its glory days. You are both good administrators, demanding respect and obedience from everybody. Dear Zealia, thanks for letting me know that your uncle and mine are back in CSS as a team. They will do well. Concerning marriage, I do not think it is worth your while to wait. I now have a girlfriend. You have never been straight with me and it is very difficult for me to forgive you. Time will tell."

I set aside this weekend to writing letters. I wrote to Mr. and Mrs. SamForays, Eyan Manney, George Vellacott, Mr. and Mrs. Dominic Fasuluku, John O'Connor, Ivor Cummings, and Finda James. My other contacts included, "Leslie, I am studying hard for my forthcoming exams. I am enjoying the psychiatric lectures. Stuart, I hope the break in Paris will do you many good. Erdem, I hope your trip to Istanbul via Amsterdam was not too demanding. Spring is in the air in Dublin. <u>Cengiz</u>, TCD has closed its doors on you, but you will enjoy yourself going back home to Athens. <u>Semi</u>, I hope you will find yourself. This is the best move, I think, you have ever made. Good luck."

I was expecting Bernadette over the weekend after her exams. But yesterday she wrote, "I wish I could come up tomorrow or even better to be with you tonight…Francis, thank you very much for helping me through my exams. I know I couldn't do it without your help and support. I feel as if it were the two of us doing my second med exam. Bye for now, and I love you." For two nights in a row, I could not go to sleep easily. "The one reason probably was the anticipation of seeing Bernadette and the other was the thought of the Viva in microbiology next Wednesday." George was over the moon when I telephoned him about Bernadette's success in her pre-clinical examinations.

The psychiatry lectures were over and as usual, I found myself reading outside the course, a recipe to failing exams. Nevertheless, there is a real justification to read on a subject like love. "Love is a pleasant sensation, which to experience is a matter of chance. I equate love between two people to a barter trade. The two lovers found the best object available in the market and considering the limitations of their own exchange values they preceded with the trade. In short, we should only love a person as he or she is and not how we want them to be. Respect as a component of love is achieved only by independence." From the foregone conclusion, we can say that love is exclusively an act of will and commitment.

George secured us summer jobs at the Hammersmith Hospital. Bernadette worked in the Bacteriology Laboratory for a stipend. The Departments of Surgery and Medicine accepted me as an unpaid pair of hands. These were exciting times. George was making a steady recovery from his depression. Bernadette and I saw each other every day both at home and work. We enjoyed our respective roles in the hospital, and the heads were satisfied with our progress. I enjoyed the operating theatre sessions, mostly because most of the head nurses were from Ireland. I learned a lot from them.

One day Berns woke up with painful swollen tonsils. The throat specialist suggested tonsillectomy. During the first post-operative day, on my knees beside her bed, I proposed marriage. She accepted. "This is how you do it, the coup de grace, when the opponent is most vulnerable." George fully supported our announcement, but neither of us could predict the reaction of the folks back home, both homes. Besides the engagement, Bernadette had immediate problems on her mind.

"Did they keep my tonsils? I presume they threw them to the vultures. I told them to keep them through the anaesthetist. If this was the case, then you should have had it. However, tonsils are not like gallstones. What did it look like? Your left one was bigger than the right. Did you miss me? Yes, I did. How much? 100 percent. Am I sickle cell positive? No."

On the second post-operative day, she could only swallow liquids but not solids. She felt weak and hungry. I became worried because Bernadette and food were friends. The cause for the weakness was because of the frequent measurement of the vital signs—blood pressure, pulse, and temperature—even when asleep. Although essential, frequent interruption of the patient's sleep may in fact be a contributory factor in their demise.

"Ivor kept to his words. He arranged a meeting between the General Manager, Mr. Ashworth, and me at the Sierra Leone Selection Trust office in London. I impressed him. Through the accountant, the company undertook to pay for two returned flights for SL. Tears filled my eyes, my dreams turning into reality.

"It was a fantasy to believe that my whole life will be dedicated to my fellowman. I love people but cannot understand them. The same people who raise you up today are the same people who bring you down tomorrow. Let us take Mahatma Ghandi of India and grandfather of Fanema. The people who directly fed on these self-denied men tortured them mentally. No wonder people say that politics is a dirty game. In SL, the practice, I am told, is "me first and country second."

George had stopped smoking cigarettes and substituted them with cigars. The habit was detrimental to all three of us. For my part, I will get him more interested in tennis. He once played tennis until the age of twenty. Berns was now able to stabilise herself on her new transport, a moped. With the help of George, I passed my driving test.

We had now returned to Ireland at our respective posts. "Have I actually exhausted the possibilities that marriage with Berns may not work? Maybe I did. I am an optimist, not necessarily a realist, and so I can't bear the thought of failure. I don't totally agree with her because whatever cultural heritage West Indians have is a modified form of their ancestors— Africans, East Indians, Spanish, and French, etc. The only difference lies in the way we think. I can't define it now but my feelings are that it does exist. Berns and I can make it."

Chapter 25

1978 in Dublin

I formally asked the Theodores for their daughter's hand. Cecilia replaced Andrea's spot with Bernadette. Bernadette and I visited Sierra Leone.

The year started with a bang. In the December 31, 1977, issue of the *Telegraph* newspaper was an announcement sent in by George. On Page ten, it read: "Mr. FW SaaGandi and Miss BM Theodore. The engagement is announced between Francis SaaGandi of Kayima, Sierra Leone, ward of Mr. George Vellacott OBE, of 34 Eller's Road, London, and Bernadette, daughter of Mr. and Mrs. Adrian Theodore, of Diego Martin, Trinidad." This meant that both parents had given their consent to let us jump into marriage.

While in Port of Spain, we visited Mr. and Mrs. Anthony, Jennifer's parents. Jennifer was a student and a friend of Cecilia. Mr. Anthony was a historian and a novelist. He autographed and gave me one of his books, *Green Days by the River,* which I completed reading that very evening after dropping the girls at the airport. Shellie, the main character, in the book reminded me of the author himself.

On coming back to Dublin, I had two women, Bernadette and Cecilia, to look after. I was not able to get into my new flat prior to my departure to Trinidad. I noted then that "The flat was freezing cold; even the walls were dripping wet. Poor Cecilia became even more irritable. It seemed almost impossible for her now to cope with life but she will make it." She was fortunate to have a sister who was totally dedicated to her. In fact, Berns wanted her to do the music examination. I drove them to the airport and en route, I promised them that I would always be available to help.

The holidays were over, and so it was time to face the reality. Somebody helped him/herself to my windscreen wipers. It was dangerous driving that morning to St. Brendan's, the psychiatric hospital. I had to stop many times to wash down the windscreen with water in a bottle I specifically brought for this. "When I eventually arrived at the hospital, I was the only student and the only one in a white coat. This was a mistake. The patients surrounded me and complained about the doctors and nurses. They left me alone when I promised to speak with the people involved." I attended all the lectures and the whole course was quite interesting. However, throughout the course, I was not sure of the future of the patients outside this hospital—the situation reminded me of the Dublin Zoo. "Some of the patients were deep in thoughts as they paced the floor. Some talked and laughed at/to themselves. The majority were unnaturally quiet as they stared through closed windows."

In the face of all this, the days went well. Berns wrote to say that she and Cec were settling down into their routines. All her friends were happy about her engagement. Daniel made it into an honours class and his scholarship continued by the Swiss government. However, he mentioned nothing about my previous two letters to him.

In the last few weeks, I had been bad in my correspondence—the hours in the day were getting too short. So I decided that today, Sunday, after church was "designated letter writing day."

<u>Pa Harry</u>: It was wonderful and sweet of you to have rented a flat in anticipation of our arrival in January 1978.

<u>Theodores</u>: Thank you for blessing our engagement. You impressed me tremendously.

<u>Andrea</u>: I was concerned about your aloofness from the family. Such behaviour could be harmful.

<u>Anthonys</u>: I have completed reading the book you gave me. The story reminded me of life in my little village in Sierra Leone.

<u>Coreas</u>: Thank you for the wonderful reception we had at your home and the time you took to see us off at the airport.

<u>Daniel</u>: Reminder about my previous two letters and parcels I sent him.

<u>SamForays</u>: I sympathized with him for the difficulty he was experiencing with the US Immigration officers.

<u>Mr. Ashworth</u>: I formally wrote to ask for financial assistance to visit SL this summer with Berns.

<u>Cecilia</u>: You can always come to Dublin and I will be more than happy to pay for you both ways. Good luck.

<u>Berns</u>: Thanks for your sweet letter and the lifesaving telephone call. At the end of the day, I had to talk to my diary. Life is indeed ironical. We meet certain people and take to them instantly. However, after a while the alliance collapses. Then there is this set of people whom you dislike at once during your first contact with them. However, when you come to understand them better, the association is almost forever. Let us take for instance the two most important people to me now. I do not think Berns thought much of me when

we first met, but here we are. I am her best friend. I was very impressed by George when we first met at David's because he was excellent at fixing things around the house. We were worlds apart when I knew him better. We were equals fighting for our individual identities. We each attained it and are now father and son. I admired and will always love him.

The college authorities really believed in "a good mind in a good body" for the students. In renovating, they incorporated a squash court, table tennis, billiard table, and badminton and volleyball courts. These came with excellent showers. This meant that one was able to exercise the whole year around. I was also able to save a lot of money from electricity, club fees, and transport. I made use of all these new facilities.

I had committed myself to visit SL this year prior to my graduation. There were many reasons why I had to go. I needed to do a summer attachment, to collect information for my autobiography, to renew contacts with relatives and friends, and for Berns to see her future home. The Friday recording showed that Jennifer wished to be with her friend, Cec. She drove down with me to Cork. She talked all the way down. She met an African student in Dublin, whom she would like to know better. I declined being a go-between. "I always maintained that a third party in a love relationship between two people eventually contribute to the breakdown of that relationship." All the same, we had a wonderful time. Cec worked hard at her books. "Berns is such a wonderful girl—extremely tolerant. She helped Cec in her physics and chemistry lectures," as noted on that weekend entry.

It was a wonderful weekend, but I wondered what the week would bring for me. "I am really in for it. I started with a bout of unproductive coughing, tears in my eyes, airways blocked, and noises from the lungs. These were joined by joint and muscle pains. I played three sets of table tennis before coming home. I loaded myself with Vitamin C tablets followed by a good night's rest. I was on my feet again the following morning." My window overlooked the Donnybrook rugby football pitch, which was still covered by snow.

"While defrosting my windscreen and windows, a lady from few doors up my street asked for a lift. I gladly obliged. She was a widow and lived on the street for over thirty-one years. During this period, she had noticed changes in Dublin life and schools. Despite her age she was well preserved." A lovely letter from George was awaiting me at the flat. "Your parents-in-law treated me like a king while with them." He spent two weeks, including carnival, in Trinidad.

I decided against going to school this week but stayed home and revised my notes in psychiatry. Errol agreed to carbon-copy his notes for me. It was a bad decision because I could not read his handwriting. I dropped in to see my countryman in my old flat. "He was home huddling an old electric heater while watching television. Furthermore, to keep himself warm, he drank whisky and smoked cigarettes. His other investment was a record player." I commented afterwards, "It is ironical that all students from Sa. Leone tend to get their priorities wrong." This is an understatement because he was not a typical student.

"The exams in psychiatry are over and the girls came and went. It was hectic and demanding but a success in the end." A few days later, I received a call from Berns to say that Cec had an acid burn. I suggested she took her to the Casualty Department. It was not serious.

All the same, I begged a lift from Catherine Hurley, my classmate, who was going to spend the weekend with her parents. "I expected Cec in bed on my arrival but she wasn't. The flat was upside down. This is one of the differences between Berns and me. I have an obsessional trait and she believes that things should be left to take their own course. I study all the year around with unpredictable exam results. She studies only when the exams are around the corner and she does excellently in them. I clean my flat daily, do my laundry regularly, and wash the dishes as I cook. It is probably these differences that will make us a perfect couple." She appreciated these characteristics in me and advised me against sharing a flat with Joseph. I would have driven him to insanity because of my obsession for time, tidiness, etc.

"Cec wanted us out of the flat because she wanted to do some work. We could not get into college because all the gates were locked. We decided to go shopping at Roche Supermarket for the flat instead. Cec was unhappy to see us earlier than expected. No wonder the O'Connors wanted me to go to the boarding school. In my attempt to enter medical school, I cared less about their feelings then. Therefore, to some extent, I do understand Cec's position. Unfortunately, Berns has now become the pig in the middle."

Two days after my return to Dublin, I received a note from Berns. "Dear Francis. I am sorry that this weekend was indeed a disaster for you AGAIN, even though it was meant to sort our problems out. I know you are not happy here, but even though you may not realize this, I do enjoy and look forward to your company and presence. I see no reason why you should be jealous of Cecelia because after having to spend a whole week trying to be patient with her, I try to relax with you and then you get angry and inpatient with me. I am left feeling miserable when you return to Dublin at the end of the weekend."

She was perfectly right and I wrote back to apologize. "On the other hand, I am glad that I misfired. It brought to the surface what we were suppressing. The situation was getting out of hand and doing nothing about it. Instead, we just fought and got nowhere. The opportunity arose and we unconsciously grabbed it. I am assured and I love Berns even more so now." Neither of us were willing to go our separate ways this summer. Therefore, when SLST agreed to pay my return flight to SL, we decided to share Berns' fares. In anticipation to our visit to SL, I decided to read any reading material on the country. I read the *West Africa Magazine,* sent to me by George while waiting for my first lecture. "Isn't ironical? The Western World is in the process of banning cigarette smoking in public places while the habit is on the increase in the Third World countries that can least afford it. The magazine noted that 72 percent of Lagos, Nigeria, medical students smoked cigarettes. How will Africa—black Africa, for that matter—ever going to make forward progress when they are exploited by her own leaders and the providers from the developed world?"

According to George and I, "there are three faces to Berns. She can look young, sweet, and pleasant. On the other hand, she can be rough looking, older than her age, and behaves thus. Thirdly, she is capable of being a woman, the boss, and a combination of the previous two faces. It is only time that will tell."

Eric and I had lunch in hospital, "and as his trademark, he went back for a second equally as generous as the first." "Evelyn was home when we arrived. She had already cooked, cleaned the flat, which was not done in a hurry, and in many ways, her obsessive behaviour reminded me of myself. She is pleasant and gentle." At the end of the session, we covered a lot of grounds in obstetrics and gynaecology. The following day Eric and Evelyn met me at the hospital. "They walked arm in arm. Eric read from the *Social and Preventive Medicine* textbook as they cruised behind me to the car. It was a spectacular display of two contrasting characters deeply in love."

I lagged behind in my diary writing for over three months. Granted, nothing extraordinary happened. Everything revolved around otolaryngology, gynaecology, paediatrics, and social and preventive medicine. The exams came and went but not with their headaches. "I did well in social and preventive medicine, passed paediatrics, but narrowly missed out on the other two. The feeling in me was just like disturbing the hornet's nest. In contrast, however, I am fired to devour the two at my second attempt as I have done in my previous failed exams."

We arrived safely in Freetown and were driven straight to the SLST residence. The following day we visited Pa Harry at the UBC mission head office. The once huge buildings in Freetown looked smaller. Otherwise most things remained the same—the streets, shops, market places, and beaches.

Our next stop was in Mattru Jong. Uncle SWG, now a staff member, was happy to see us. "Like the leopard, he never lost his spots. He continued with his gardening, now combined with pig farming. We went to see Mama Ada the following day. She was bedridden with a fractured hip. She now had great-grandchildren through Zealia (and her younger sister)." We made our next and brief stop at the Yillas, Momodu, and Martha, in Bo.

"Two nights in Yengema formed the main highlights of our visit. Our guests took us to various nightclubs in Sefadu and Yengema and were generous with their money. They served us like VIPs. In this part of the country, money seemed to be everything. The passing times seemed to have had no effect on Uncle SJW. He spoke excellent English. We met at N'Gundia's home for dinner, which was greatly appreciated."

We must not forget Segbwema and that was our next port of call. They were expecting us one week earlier. If Nixon could have been raised from his grave and visited the hospital (and its environs) named after him, he would have found little change. "The hospital had no additional building, and I was able to recognize majority of the old folks. The old school buildings were there with their weather-beaten rusty corrugated tin roofs. School had closed and so we could not see the students in action."

There was little to do in Segbwema, but we made the best of what was available. We played lots of tennis, badminton, and ping-pong. I got myself involved in a research team from Colorado State University, USA, who were interested in Lassa Fever outbreak in SL.

Both of us thought the trip was worth the while. I met with most of my relatives and friends, visited my old schools, and became aware of what was expected of us should we decide to return.

Back in Dublin, I had one month to revise for my re-sit. The revision was effortless because I had covered both subjects in full during the term. The exams were easy. September had arrived and the final year had started.

Chapter 26
1979 in Dublin

The light had finally come into view at the end of the long tunnel. Somehow, Dublin was not going to let me go. It was a year of civil unrest—bus, postal, telephone, petrol, and doctors' strikes. Mr. Jack Lynch, the Prime Minister of Ireland, resigned his post.

"I am beginning to believe that history does repeat itself in one way or another. I refer to the strained relationship between Berns and me. We are both happy to look after Cec. However, she is so absorbed in her endeavour to enter medical school that she doesn't contribute anything to the smooth running of the unit. The O'Connors must have had the same problem, albeit less intense, with me."

The new term had started but very few of my classmates are around. I suspected there were two reasons for this: the unusual cold and the pending exam in forensic medicine. The Chinese (from Hong Kong, Malaysia, Mauritius) students like me attended all lectures and tutorials. Mrs. Neville, the librarian, was grateful for my looking after the library while she was away. I was now sharing a cubicle with Koogan in the residence. In essence, Richmond Hospital had now become my home and place of learning.

At lunch today, there were four post-graduate (from Sudan) and two undergraduate students on my table. The older students took no note of us. They spoke all the time in Arabic. I found this extremely disturbing. We, the African students in Ireland, were the ambassadors for our respective countries. It was therefore our responsibility to speak in the people's language and teach them about our culture. In this small way, we would have contributed in the understanding of each other's culture and reduced the tension between nations.

The forensic medicine examination came but I was still lingering around. I was not invited for a viva, suggesting that I passed clearly or failed outright. WBL decided to misbehave today, on the go-slow. We eventually made it to the Groschs' place. Eric and I went into our discussion as usual while Evelyn and a friend prepared supper. We actually took time off to sit and talk with the girls. This was a rare occasion because for Eric, idle talk never fit into his vocabulary. The following day we learned that the exam results went our way. We got into a state of euphoria. Of course, we were fully aware that it was only the beginning.

The bulk of this year's work was centred on general and paediatric medicine and general surgery. We had many lectures in haematology; tropical medicine; ophthalmology; and ear, nose, and throat surgery. My problem with these subjects was that I wanted to specialize in each of them at the end of the series of lectures and clinics. I ended doing more work in them with the resultant unpredictable exam performances.

This morning I gave a lift to one of my classmates on my way to Crumblin Children's Hospital. He was one of our top students and formed the Canadian contingency. I had always admired him; he was pleasant and unassuming. He suggested that I left "the choke on all the time to avoid the frequent stoppages. You might weaken the spark plugs but no other damage will be done to the car." You always live and learn. It worked.

I was again daydreaming. This was one such day. "I wish I was living in a centrally heated flat and can afford the time to exercise more. I almost suffered from vagal inhibition this morning when I attempted to wash my dirty clothes soaked overnight. I wish I had my own washing machine." I fulfilled one of my wishes and that was to visit Mrs. F. Her new tenants, Ahmed, Leroy, and Joseph, had their electric heaters on the third bars. She asked them to go for exercise but they refused.

From the weather point of view, I had always found Sundays to be better than Saturdays. I invited myself to a six-a-side football practice on the park. After my first game, the coach invited me to join them "permanently." He understood why this was not possible. I joined them as often as possible on Sunday mornings, their preferred day. Over the past six years, I had always taped my lecture notes on a cassette and Sunday was the day set aside for this.

The lectures keep coming, unrestrained. There were many of them. Unfortunately, students like me could not tell the difference between the woods and the trees. I attended them all. Some of the presentations were excellent while others remained undetermined. However, how was one to decide whether they were useful or useless lectures? Besides, one can always learn something even from a fool. Mrs. Neville gave me a spare key to open and close the hospital library.

The postal and bus strikes came to an end a few days ago, but for how long? Pa Harry wrote to say that he was sick for the past month. "He could well be dead by now but I do not think so." The belated copies of *West Africa* magazines turned up. I watched my only attraction on the television, *Match of the Day*. I found it the most entertaining show on the gray box. I do not support any club, but watching a deservedly better team win was wonderful. My addiction to wildlife and cartoons on the box were to come later.

"Why do I perform so indifferently in the examinations then?" Along the corridor, I ran into one of my surgical tutors who was all praise for me; keep it up. "I think they are genuine and I believe them. The problem lies with me." It was a tiring but productive day and here I was at one in the morning writing my diary." This is shear madness; I should be in bed sleeping."

After lunch, I ran into one of our registrars in paediatrics, with whom I worked at the Coomb's Hospital. He invited me to see some of his patients "with exam flavour." My eyes brightened up and I was reminded of the good old days. Sarah, a medical student from London, joined in. Sarah and I jelled together in looking after those children. We worked together during the day and went our different ways after 5 P.M. We remained excellent friends until the end of her attachment.

I passed the Paeds Exam but without the honours grade for which I worked hard. I was now back in the company of Errol. In many ways, he reminded me of the late Ivor Cummings. They talked big and were philosophers. They had "the most brilliant friends." I met with one of these friends. He had Bailey and Love's surgery textbook wide open on his laps, a cloud of smoke around his head from a lit cigarette, and a glass of rum in one hand. Louis was sitting at one end of the room having fun with a glass of rum.

I was awake at my usual time of 7 A.M., but the air was too quiet. "There was no blackbird chattering. My window, the only window, overlooked a rugby pitch running alongside, which was the River Dodder. The trees have shed their leaves and the vegetation on the banks has lessened. The empty land and the river were now ready to expose their secrets to me. The sterling and its chicks in my bathroom roof have gone quiet. The seagulls and the duck with her chicks have all gone. There was no snow but it was very cold. Within days, rats and mice invaded the flat. It must be the beginning of yet another winter in Dublin."

The postal strike came back on, and so no letters and no public telephones. Rev. Gallagher from my church kindly asked me to use his phone whenever needed to talk to Berns. I thanked him for the offer.

Mr. Carey, the consultant neurosurgeon, entered the ward from a heavy shower outside. The students and his doctors were all present. He asked the students for their histories on the respective patients, but none did except myself. He was pleased with my presentation and for the rest of the two-hours ward round, he asked me all the questions and ignored everyone else. No sooner did he leave the ward, I ran straight to my car.

As I emerged from one of the optional lectures in college, two of my mates standing in the corridor shouted to me, "Congratulations." I passed the anaesthetic examination with first-class honours. I worked extremely hard for it and on the day, the examiners saluted me at the end of the interview. For the past six years, this had been the pattern—top or bottom and few between.

Friday evenings normally found me in the flat. The weekends gave me the opportunity to do my laundry, eat my own cooked food, and do some form of exercise. I was still awake at 1 A.M. writing my diary. I pulled the curtain and sitting straight ahead of me in the sky was the moon. It was a quarter full with its convex side to the left. It created a spectacular view of a dark background and yellow street lights in the foreground.

"It is almost a month since I last saw Mrs. F. After church, I went to see her and I am glad I did. She had a lot to talk about. She was having a difficult time with my three replacements. She found them wasteful, demanding, and noisy. I did not think that either party could be blamed. I put the blame squarely at the accommodation officer's feet. She suggested to Mrs. F to ask for more money. More money meant better service. Mrs. F was not a businesswoman but a philanthropist. Besides, unlike me, these lads came from wealthy families. I spoke my mind to the student officer, and she listened."

April marked the end of our clinical attachments. I had completed reading and studying Hamilton Bailey's *Clinical Surgery* and so too Davidson's *Textbook of Medicine*. "In Mr. Browne's steeple chase (spot diagnosis) examination, I got almost a perfect score. However, on getting home that evening, I could not sleep. I was fighting with the notion that I had peaked too early.

"The two girls came up for the week, which turned out to be a wonderful reunion. Cec was in good spirits and less tense about her exams. Bernadette cooked most of the time, allowing me to continue with my revisions. The meals were excellent, and Cec helped to clean the dishes. On Sunday, we went to the movies, which was relaxing. In all, the whole week was expensive for me but it was worth it."

I cleaned the flat in preparation for Mom's arrival. Now it was the turn of the medical fraternity to rumble. "Most of our consultants were missing today because they attended the Irish Medical Association meeting to decide whether to protest or not for more pay. I have come to conclude that the only people happy with their lot these days are those on the dole and chronic race-goers and gamblers. It is the government's fault by giving in to the first strikers last year.

"All three ladies are living with me in my flat. I gave up my bed to Mom and the second bed to Cec. Berns and I shared the floor during which time she refused to come near or hold me. The hard cold floor did not help my course, bearing in mind that I am almost all bones. The nights were terrible. On most mornings, I was already awake when the alarm clock went off at seven. This morning I was in the worst of moods driving to the hospital. I was tired and only half-alive on joining Mr. Browne's ward rounds. I stood behind the crowd, avoiding questions. I made a mess of it when the inevitable came; he called me forward, knowing full well that I normally challenge him to ask me questions.

"The final days have finally arrived. I have covered all aspects of the course, enjoyed it all, and had more than average knowledge of the course. Nevertheless, I did not produce the products on the day it mattered. My written was poor, clinical good, and viva weak. Therefore, I failed the final exam. All those who knew me were disappointed, but I refused to accept self-pity. I was willing to start it all over again—an extra year in medical school."

I rejoined the Monkstown Tennis Club. Twenty pounds per year was expensive for an unemployed medical student like me. However, everybody who knew me, including Berns and George, had realized that to get me in a good mood was to allow me to exercise at any time of the day. In fact, Berns found it her duty to remind me of my daily exercises. I tracked down Dermot Delaney, my tennis partner until a year ago. He was now married with two children. The club had three new hard courts, which were previously made of grass. We now had a clubhouse with a ping-pong table. At first, the younger boys turned down my request to play with them because they did not think I was good enough. In the end, they called me home, often to join them.

"My future wife was as supportive as ever. She quietly went about helping me in every step of the way. We drove over to see Mr. Duke at St. Andrew's College. He was in his office and in great form. He listened to my story sympathetically and as usual uttered not a single word of condemnation. He asked for Berns' opinion. In addition, as usual he called the registrar instantly, who promised to help. He advised me not to do anything stupid.

My time keeping was not as rigid as before. I wrote letters and continued with my daily recordings. Tamba Joseph Gandi wrote to say that he passed the school certificate with a Division 1. He actually topped the school. I was very happy for, and proud of, him.

Yillas: Continue with the good work. One of these days, we shall be in a position to give you a hand in your practice.

Tamba: You have done a great job, but it is just the beginning. One thing, though, you do not owe anybody anything. Do not blame our parents; they probably do not even understand your problems.

George: Thank you for coming to my rescue yet again.

Berns: I have always maintained that I made the wisest choice as my future life partner. You probably understand me more than I do.

I ran into one of my medical tutors in the hospital, and he came up with a suggestion. "You are qualified to do the London Conjoint Examinations." George and I jumped at the idea, and he promptly got the application forms for me. I had some difficulty getting the college secretary to sign them.

I moved down to Cork, determined to get a proper flat for Berns. Getting a good flat in Dublin was easy. In Dublin, without the knowledge of the property owners, flats were passed on from graduates to students. Cork was too small for that, and the odds were bad for black students.

I got hold of the *Evening Echo* newspaper, and this was to be repeated daily for one month. "It is disgraceful that such advertisements should be allowed in a small place like this. Attractively furnished ground-floor bed-sitter in an exclusive house, luxurious self-contained fully furnished flat to let, and self-contained luxury flats to let were the most commonly string of words joined. These were exaggeration and overpriced. Another evening came and I bought my usual *Evening Echo*. However, before turning to the ADS section, the picture of Mr. Jack Lynch, the prime minister, on the front page caught my eyes. He had resigned his post.

Between flat hunting, I engaged myself in reading works of Agatha Christie and Dick Francis I had not read before mixed with *World Medicine* magazines. I exercised at the sport facilities provided by the University of Cork, across the road from Berns' present bed-sit. I did discover "ideal flats" but they were either gone or taken up by two working women or "not for you" or too far away from college. These were minor setbacks.

I had to let Berns escape from the hands of her property owner. This divorced lady in her sixties knew about everybody's business to the point of being dangerous. "She invited me one evening to watch Roots by Arthur Hailey on her television. She was all tears for the whole episode. Another evening she trapped me in the corridor and invited me into her luxurious living room for a chat. She had something yet again to talk about our neighbours— the Arabian family. The husband is having an affair outside their marriage. This was because the wife was not altogether nice to him. In the frustration, the wife knocked about the child. I told them to move because this will bring bad luck to my house. However, the husband came down on his knees to beg me and he was ready to stop the affair." This was a clear message to me that we should move because we were not married.

Life cannot be that all bad. "I found a butcher's shop that was willing to sell me oxtail for 20 pence. I gladly got one and probably I should have bought two. It now cost one pound in Dublin because the butchers had realized that it was popular among "Nigerian" people. The long-awaited flat arrived.

It was an attic flat with a window in the roof. It was not too far away from the college or city centre. Considering the many "modern flats" in Cork, it was descent and the rent reasonable. We readily negotiated the price, from sixteen to fourteen pounds a week. Berns was happy with the find and pleased with the negotiation. The following morning, I started cleaning out the flat. It took us a week to complete. The other good thing about the flat was the absence of rats and mice, but there was evidence to suggest their presence. Two weeks later, I ran into the landlord, who tried to remember what he promised me for the flat. I assured him not to worry because he was a busy man.

George telephoned to say that he was back in London from his enjoyable break. Soon after, Cec telephoned to say she had no money and was hungry. I telephoned Mrs. F to give her 10 pounds, which I would repay on my return to Dublin. We drove up to Dublin the following day with Berns at the wheel for most of the way. Surprisingly Cec was cheerful and chatty. For Christmas, she gave Berns a jumper and I got a Collin's Diary for 1980. John, my next-door neigbhour, left his keys for me to make use of his one-channel black-and-white TV. I had never looked forward to Christmas but I would do my best to enjoy it at least for the girls. It was expensive and painful to see people spending money they did not have.

Nowadays it is difficult to say who is not striking in Ireland. Occasionally a few letters will get through. One such letter was from Uncle SJW. He had stood for the vacant position of Paramount Chief in Sando but was "forced to withdraw." His wife's mother and aunt passed away. He also announced the death of Uncle Paul. Paul never seemed to have recovered from the one error he made by leaving Segbwema for Sefadu some fifteen years previously.

George was a man of business and he did not like people who could not make decisions. He wanted me across in London to get on with things. I was beginning to get angry with him, but I knew it was all for my future. Berns, Cec, and I sat down in my flat, waiting for the arrival of 1980. Somehow, I felt in my bones that it was going to be a year of excellent things. We knelt down to pray and vowed to work harder.

Chapter 27

1980 in Dublin

I passed the London Conjoint Examinations. Berns and I graduated from our respective schools, jumped into marriage, and became employed in the same hospital as interns. Ireland won the Euro-Vision Song Contest for the second time. Borg won the finals at Wimbledon.

"At 12:01 A.M., Cec, Berns, and I drank to the New Year. I woke up the following morning with terrible stomach pains, most probably due to the Trinidadian rum. It was my turn today for a haircut. Berns cut my hair and successfully had it shaped."

I left Berns alone to do her revision. I found myself in a cinema house. Even in a little city like Cork, people still support each other according to racial line. I refer to the *Rocky II* movie. The audience stood and cheered when it was the turn of Rocky to beat up his African opponent. The director must have achieved his/her aim. I got home and changed to drop in at the Malting (University sport building) for a game of table tennis, a shave, and a shower.

The sailing across the Irish Sea was rough and I had little sleep. The immigration officers were meticulous in their effort to prevent IRA invasion. When I arrived in London, George was relaxing in front of the box. He had our rooms repainted, window curtains changed, and the laundry machine replaced. He looked well and cheerful. This made me extremely happy, giving me the assurance that all was going to be fine.

On January 7, I attended my first job interview at Hackney Hospital, East London. Before the interview, George and I created my first curriculum vitae and Mr. Selwyn Taylor, with whom I had a summer attachment at Hammersmith Hospital, agreed to be my referee. I was offered the post of locum house officer but with little pay because I was not qualified. To me it was a Godsend in that I now had the opportunity to look after patients. It was also the beginning of this thing in medicine—must have "your primary before training, no employment without experience." "Berns was pleased with the news. I promised to sign my first cheque in her name. We both laughed and anticipated the day."

I arrived an hour earlier in the morning to be briefed about my patients before the departure of the substantial jobholder. I would have arrived even earlier but a police officer stopped me by breaking the traffic rule—I mistakenly took the wrong turn. He looked at the map opened on my laps. Ignorance of the law was no defense. It was an outdated map of London. Dr. Tunstall-Pedoe, the consultant physician, was impressed with my presentations. At the end of the ward round, he invited the team for a drink across the street. I was beaming with joy when I got home to George. We spent the rest of the daylight on the tennis courts.

Dr. Pedoe enjoyed doing impromptu ward rounds, but he always found me with a patient. "Today the goings were slow, but I am getting the hang of things. After breakfast, I went to see my patients. I am a good doctor; I willingly listen to their problems and do something about them." Unfortunately, the same nagging reminder keeps coming up, and that is, "Without a hard paper to show for your hard work, you are nothing."

Berns sent me a letter but I could not read it, as George was waiting for a game of tennis. He was so determined to improve his game that he was actually halfway there. We played three sets and he managed to win three games. That was a great improvement. While waiting for my turn for a shower, I read Berns' letter. "It was a lovely and sweet one. She was able to express her feelings much more to me on paper than in person."

I took a day off to attempt the Conjoint examination. I sailed through, reminding me of the good old days at Yengema, Segbwema, and Mattru.

A day before the end of my present contract, I received a call from the recruiting officer wishing to extend the contract but this time in urology. I jumped at it. I am at present a practicing urologist, suggesting that I may have developed my interest in this field at this time.

My new team members included Mr. Whitfield, consultant, and a female registrar originally from China. My first day in the unit was spent reading about, and meeting all, my patients. I thought Mr. Whitfield was quite good and I took in everything he said. The registrar was very sound but she could not make instant decisions. She diddled-dabbled with decisions on many occasions. At the end of one of our clinics, Mr. Whitfield wanted to know how much the hospital was paying me. When I told him, he thought they were exploiting me because I was doing a better job than the substantial doctor had being doing. The administrators reminded him that although I had passed my exams, he had not been issued the certificates. One day I ran into Dr. Pedoe-

Tunstall along the "marathon tunnel" named by me. He was blunt with me and suggested I went back to Dublin and get on with my exams. "You have a great future as a good doctor and so don't waste it doing locums." *This is amazing,* I said to myself. *I thought these people just wanted their work done.*

I looked forward to weekends in London, especially with George. We did our shopping then, watched sports on television, and played tennis in the evenings. It also gave me the opportunity to meet with other students from SL through Dominic. One evening, Dominic took me to a disco organized by the Sa Leone people's club. Free entry ensured excellent attendance. The organizing committee appointed a team of judges to judge a Miss Sierra Leone Beauty Contest. The clear winner was a young lady who was pleasant and bright. The committee would not acknowledge the win, let alone give her the prize. What was the reasoning for the refusal? She was not black but of Lebanese descent. What a disgrace. Born and bred in SL but being discriminated against by her own people, who ought to know better.

The end of spring was in the air while George and I continued to play every evening, weather permitting or when on call. Eric dropped me a line to say that they had a little baby girl called Eleanor. It was wonderful to hear from the Groschs. I felt good.

I came back to Dublin to join the final-year students during tutorials. "Richmond Hospital seemed to have undergone a series of structural improvements. The once bumpy road to the Geriatric Unit had been tarred. I gave none of my new classmates a chance to take pity on me.

"I was sharing my flat with Cec, but she was not a good companion. She hated shopping and did not enjoy cooking. I cleaned the flat while she went out to practice on her piano, a renewed interest. She worked hard on her books." It was just as well because all my study mates passed their exams and moved on. Isaac Stern was in similar boots with me.

He tracked me down for us to resume our studies. He sent his family back to Israel and he was now living with another Jew. "I can imagine how difficult it must be for Isaac, as he once owned a home but now sleeps in another man's sitting room for 35 pounds per month. We took a break and watched the Euro-Vision Song Contest on television. Ireland won for the second time in ten years. It was a satisfactory day in many ways.

"June has arrived, and I have finally made it. It was a hazardous journey but I am safely home. The rest is just history." I contacted Dan but he was still brooding over the death of his father. All the same, he was happy to hear that both of us got through our exams. "I attended the party organized by Dr. O'Flanaghan, dean and registrar, for the final-year students. The food and service were excellent, speeches boring, and the company uninteresting." Mrs. F and Berns, as guests, attended my graduation day on June 6. Both women looked radiant.

"I drove down to Cork the following day on my way to London. I slept through the whole journey, which was never unheard of before. I would normally read for one of my pending or failed exams. The Pembroke crossing was comfortable and the boat quite clean. We are now in Wales. Six miles gone past a filling station, I ran out of petrol. The exercise was good for me and luckily it was a dry and warm afternoon." George and I could not attend Berns' graduation but she had Dad, Mom, and Cec at hand. We all got together in London.

"George got a flat for the family at Du Cane Housing. I had hoped to join them but my lady will have nothing to do with it. It was wonderful being with Berns again. Unfortunately, she kept me at arm's length. Although I understood her stand about no sex before marriage, it was often very difficult to appreciate the logistics. There are times when circumstances outweigh our desires. To wait for the right time and place makes life unnatural." This afternoon I received a note from the Conjoint Board of Examination, indicating that my diplomas would be forwarded on receipt of 58 pounds. The following Saturday, we watched the tennis finals between Bornj Borg and John McEnroe. Borg won in the fifth set. It was sunshine in my heart."

Another big day was fast approaching. We set out our wedding day for July 20, 1980. We bought our wedding rings on Ealing Broadway and had our names engraved on the inside. The rings were cheap, but that was the best we could afford then. We had hoped that in the distant future we would invest in better-quality rings. I still have mine. Our first time in the USA found us spending the night on the cold floor of the Miami airport.

The day, July 20, 1980, finally arrived. Father John Theodore married us at the Crystal Stream Catholic Church in Port of Spain, Trinidad. Dad Theodore became the master of ceremonies afterwards. He asked me to say a word or two.

"Well, well, well. We have finally made it. I never thought that it was ever going to happen. But one of my aunts once told me that it was worth waiting for the best. I agree with her now but not then. Ladies and gentleman, on behalf of my wife, which incidentally is less of a mouthful than my fiancée, I thank you for coming to share this moment with us."

Tobago was our next stop for our honeymoon. We spent two relaxing days in Scarborough, the capital. "We are both now appreciating the fact that we are married. This means having to be together almost all the time and doing things as a unit. It will probably be difficult initially but not impossible. Like most things in life involving two people, success of a union depends on the motivation of the individuals. This is our time to prove it," taken from my diary.

We had spent three days with George, and it was time to start our internship on August 1. We arrived in Hull two days before the start of our new jobs. "What a transformation, at least in terms of accommodation. We lived in our respective bed-sits in Dublin/Cork; we are now living in a three-bedroom house. The Humberside Health Authority, Hull, now employed us as house officers. The charwoman (now called housing keeper) was at the door, prompt to make our beds. The sector administrator welcomed, and gave, us our documents. We spent the rest of the afternoon exploring the city. We liked it and we are going to enjoy it." The training was going to be six months in medicine and six months in surgery.

The four months came and went fast but were successful from my point of view. My wife viewed it differently. Summer ended abruptly into winter unlike Dublin, where autumn slowly lingered into winter. This was the first day in December and the roads were covered with ice. "The house was freezing when we got home, but we had to eat. Therefore, I set about cleaning the house and settling down to cook. I let Berns settled down by the TV and fire. After eating, I went straight to bed, as my unit was on emergency call the following day."

I got into the wards an hour earlier than my registrar. He normally said hello to me but this morning he seemed preoccupied with something. He went for a job interview yesterday but did not get it. "I wasn't particularly surprised, although disappointed. The consultant was an Indian. The other candidate was an Indian. Of course, the Indian consultant chose the Indian candidate. The only way for immigrants to survive in this country is to stick together. The Indians have done this well," he volunteered. The day was not hectic and just as well because he was not in the best shape of mind.

Getting home the following evening, I contacted George. He sounded well and had planned to spend Christmas with Josephine, his sister, in Canada. I collected Cec from the train station and she had nothing but books. Apparently, she had a successful term in Dublin. Berns and I attended a "Sherry Party," organized by the Lord Mayor of Hull City, Mr. Alex Clarke. He was short and heavy, and I took an instant dislike of him. However, at the end of his speech, I tracked him down to chat. He was pleasant and knowledgeable and so was his wife. They invited all the Sierra Leoneans living in the Hull area to sensitize us about their aim of twinning Hull to Freetown. It was not a completely useful meeting. Bernadette and I were cold.

The final entry this year follows. "After a boring two hours at the local Catholic church, Berns went to bed with only her shoes and coat off. I got out of bed earlier than usual. I made myself breakfast and sat by the fire to read this week's *British Medical Journal*. The girls put the pork and pheasant into the oven and we went to the wards to wish everyone a Merry Christmas. On getting home they continued with their cooking."

Part Four

Postgraduate Education

Chapter 28
1981 in England

*Bernadette started in geriatric medicine and rheumatology. I
moved on to orthopaedic surgery.*

Unfortunately, this year's diary had been completely destroyed by the termites.

We successfully completed six months' internship in medicine at the
Kingston General Hospital, Hull. During the six months, we were exposed to
haematology and geriatric and general medicine. We spent hours on the wards
and less time at home. We gave the next stage of our internship in general surgery the same effort but this time based at the Hull Royal Infirmary. It was at
this point that we decided that the two of us could not stay in hospital medicine if our marriage was to survive. We decided to go our separate ways.

Berns opted to go into community medicine while I stayed in hospital
medicine to chase a surgical career. Berns started off in geriatric medicine and
rheumatology. I applied for the Orthopaedic Senior House Officer (SHO)
post at the Royal Infirmary, Hull. There were three consultants and an administrator at my interview. They short-listed four candidates and all turned up.
They offered me the job. "So far I have done well in all my interviews; no
doubt they will get harder as I climb up the ladder."

Mr. Cain, my new consultant, was the newest addition to three other consultants. I took to him almost immediately. The registrar, Mr. Ibrahim Hussein,
came from Egypt, and he smoked a pipe. They were extremely happy to have
me because I took pleasure in investigating and treating the aged patients
before and after surgery. Neither of them were interested in any subject or
problem outside orthopaedics. They taught me to do simple and complicated

procedures. It was a productive six months with them. They were both generous with their advice to me of "how to pass the primary examination."

Bernadette and I had resolved to pass our primaries in our respective field of medicine and surgery. I was finding it rather easier to study for the postgraduate degree than the undergraduate courses. During my surgical internship, I got hold of the latest editions of Ganong's *Medical Physiology*, *Last's Human Anatomy* and Walter Israel's *General Pathology*. So far, I have resisted buying extra books rather than those three. I will continue working on them.

Chapter 29

1982 in England

Hull City and Freetown become twin cities. The folks from Trinidad and Canada descended on us. We owned our home in Harrogate, North Yorkshire.

The New Year started on Friday and we planned to spend it with the Golledges, Robert and Rahaneh. We have always enjoyed their company. Robert is British and Rahaneh a Trinidadian. "Robert and Rahaneh were quite interesting. They reminded me, in many ways, of us—the male partners are more open and outgoing." The fun day ended and was followed by a busy weekend. We were both on call for our respective hospitals. "At 8 A.M. I was called to see my first patient with chest pain. This was her third post-operative day. I made a diagnosis of myocardial infarction supported on the ECG. Although it was the best thing for her, I was disappointed that she had to be moved. I wanted to manage her myself."

On getting home one evening, we discovered that somebody broke into our house and stole food, jewels, the television, and cash. Three days later the police called me to identify some stolen goods. We recovered my tennis bag, which was used to empty the freezer. The police visited the thief's home when the neighbours reported them for quarreling. "Berns was on call today and so I left for home alone. It was a cold house made worse by the absence of Berns. After dinner I settled down to read."

I am now coming to the end of my six-month training in orthopaedics with Mr. Terry Cain. I applied for an SHO post in urology based at Sutton. The competition was stiff; three of the five candidates had already passed their

Primary Fellowship examinations. The interview, dominated by the senior surgeon, went all my way.

My next six months was with Mr. Richard Heslop and Mr. Don Newling in urology. The job was situated at the Princess Royal Hospital. The present registrar from Nigeria due to leave soon. He was not a particularly likeable man. The two consultants were completely contrasting people. Mr. Richard Heslop was a fine clinician while Mr. Don Newling was involved in many drug trials. The new registrar was from Ghana, very much liked by Mr. Heslop. This meant that he was allowed to do open and endoscopic work under supervision. For my part and being patient, I watched and assisted on many occasions.

"At the end of my six-month training in urology, we had a conference." Between Berns, George, and I, we agreed that I went down to London and study for the "Primary." I joined a "crash course in the city." This evening course had nothing new to offer, but it had the advantage of being able to compare oneself with other candidates. The students came from all over the world.

To cover my time during the day, I registered at the Hammersmith Hospital with two aims in mind. Firstly, I wanted to spend time in the post-mortem room. Secondly, to attend Grand Ward Rounds. "The course ended yesterday but I do not think things went according to plan. The motorbike had a knock and it was still suffering from the aftereffect. Prof. Weinbren had nothing to offer in basic pathology. The ward rounds were not helpful and there were no demonstrations at the course. In short, I had to push myself. Fortunately I have Berns and George on my side.

"I got up early and set out the tapes for the day. It was a wonderful idea tapping my own voice, the exercise is now paying off". So from now on, I shall take my recorder on all trips. It worked out well this morning as I rode slowly into town while listening to them.

"Yesterday, I assisted at an autopsy. It was helpful in cheering me up immensely. Indeed I have become very fond of Berns. This is probably because absence makes the heart fonder. The reality is that I appreciate her support for me. I have always loved her but I am probably not so good at showing it.

"George is always finding ways to help me take my mind off these endless examinations. This time we were off to Alicante in Spain for two weeks of tennis. I did my final packing yesterday while he started doing his a week ago. In the group was Elizabeth, the lonely woman, and six men. We had two coaches, Andrew and Douglas. The director, Stonebridge, joined us at the beginning of the second week.

"Mr. Stonebridge took over the coaching. He was fit and an excellent teacher. We played a lot of tennis, but I managed to revise all the topics I took with me to Spain. To crown it all I won the end-of-course tournament and became known as the champion for the rest of our stay." I had no difficulty settling into my studies on getting back to London. I was deeply indebted to George.

On getting back to London, I hit upon an idea, which considered George. I decided to work in the kitchen whenever he went to bed. This way he was not disturbed and I was able to avoid the cigarette smoke. "The exams are two weeks away and I seem to cover everything." However, a trial run at the English version of the Primary did not go my way. I was not disappointed because from experience, it was a temporary hold-up.

A week later I was back home in Hull. I have always been amazed by the craving of friends and relatives to visit England, the motherland. Bernadette's relatives from Trinidad and Canada were no exception.

We rented a van and drove down to London to collect our guests from Canada and Trinidad. They arrived in time but we lost time getting out of London. They were not particularly impressed with what they had seen so far of England. They slept all the way, once we hit the motorway. Cec had already prepared the meal on our arrival, which was considerate of her. There were now nine of us in a three-bedroom house. My sermon to everybody was that clean and tidy up after you and we will make it. The guests included Mom, Dad, Chalet and her mom, Jean, Christopher and his mom, Marjorie, and June.

We took them around Hull, including William Wilberforce Museum, the Humber Bridge, and the Beverley Races. Using the North Sea ferry, they left for a tour of the continent. They came back two weeks later, tired and haggard but cheerful. Cec went back to Dublin, Mom and Dad to Trinidad, and the rest to Canada. Berns and I settled into our routines.

My routine, of course, meant studying for the Primary in between my hospital work—clinics, theatres, and ward rounds. After the viva examination, I took the first available train out of Glasgow. I got home to a tidied home and picked a note that read:

Dear Francis:

WELCOME HOME. By now, you would have known the result of your exams; congrats if you have passed, if not, remember we still have each other and you have my support to try again; each time you get closer and more confident. I have left some potatoes in a freezer bag, the mincemeat in a plastic container, and the baked beans in a cup in the fridge. Sorry the kitchen is in such a mess, but the meal is very nice, so please help yourself.
  Well, bye for now.

Love
B

As usual, life (studying) just went on as if nothing happened. I failed physiology and hence the whole Primary. I was not unduly disappointed. One day I stayed home alone to study. "I know I am supposed to be reading harder than ever, but somehow, I have lost confidence in myself, which is unusual. It is a passing thing. I will make it. I am sure as day follows night."

Cec spent the weekend of October that ran into November with us. She came over from Dublin to collect my motorbike. Like her sister, she was determined to be independent transport-wise. It was a wet morning but she managed to go for a ride. She was a good student. She was cheerful for the whole weekend.

I was on call for the whole of today with Mr. Newling. I thought I managed to do everything for my patients but Mr. Heslop, the senior urologist, managed to find fault with me. I have sometimes wondered what he wanted to instill in me. It was a rough day. In addition to the surgical problems, there were patients with medical problems. One patient had pleuritic chest pain that was due to pulmonary embolism strongly supported by the ECG (echocardiogram). They transferred him to the Infirmary.

Bernadette was now in public health training proper. The decision was a wise one. She went into public health full time and before I could get my next training post SHO, they promoted her to a registrar position. Berns' new job brought us to Harrogate.

We lived in a hospital accommodation similar to the one at Kingston General Hospital—large, spacious, and difficult to heat. The hospital authorities had already made plans to get rid of the buildings. They wanted us to move as soon as possible. This prompted us to look for our own house. We thought that renting was money down the drain.

I got a job as SHO in the Casualty Department at Queen Elizabeth Hospital, Gateshead. I was to start at the beginning of next year. I had never failed any exam after a year's attempt and the FRCS Primary was no exception. The year 1983 was the year to unlock the Primary code.

On December 17, 1982, we signed on the dotted line to own a three-bedroom semi-detached house situated north of Harrogate. It sounded easy until the lawyers became involved. Abbey Building Society, the mortgage company, was satisfied to give us a loan. We identified the house of our choice located at a quiet end of the town. Now, at least from our point of view, the problems started. "The lawyers dragged it on to infinity." However, when we received the keys, all was forgotten.

Chapter 30

1983 in England

The Queen Elizabeth Hospital employed me as SHO. I passed the Primary Fellowship Examination. I enrolled for the DTM&H course at Liverpool.

At the Primary examination, one met many different people—old and new. "At the table during breakfast was Mathew Frazer. He had attempted the exam many times but no luck. He was pleasant and extremely hardworking. We became friends and revised together. The next candidate was a year my junior and hailed from Trinidad. It was his first attempt and he was very confident that he would sail through. He was a ceaseless talker and most of the talking was centred on his brilliance as a budding surgeon. While seated in the waiting room two Nigerian doctors went into blows. They were previously arguing over the course of the radial nerve as asked in the MCQ section of the exam. Those waiting rooms seem to bring the worse out of people; the atmosphere was tense and potentially explosive."

When I attended the interview for the present job, it was only the consultant and an administrator on the panel. It did not attract a high caliber of candidates. The department was well staffed, headed by Mr. Michael Reece. Mr. Reece was a general surgeon but branched into emergency medicine because he could not be promoted into a consultant position. The doctors were all, except me, in training to becoming *general* practitioners. There were very little teaching activities in the hospital. Dr. King, the tutor, made an attempt to encourage consultants and junior doctors to attend the weekly meetings but were poorly attended.

The hospital had little to offer in the way of entertainment. I tried going for long drives to kill the boredom. Gateshead and Newcastle were the same cities separated from each other by the Tyne River. It was a hilly city. To commute was not a problem; the Metro was clean and extremely user-friendly. Besides, I had my own transport in the form of my Honda 50. Yet I was not able to make use of these facilities to exploit Tyneside fully. Many reasons would have contributed to this.

Firstly, my job took precedent. For a typical month, I worked as follows. As first officer, I worked for one week between 9 A.M. and 5 P.M. In the second week, I worked on the wards and did minor surgery. During the third week, I worked as the sole officer on night duties. Finally, the fourth week, I was off. I spent my week off down in Harrogate doing things around our house. When not on duty I studied for my Primary. All these contributed to my not enjoying Tyneside.

However, accommodations were excellent. My flat was spacious—a large bedroom, a sitting area with a study table and a bathroom to be shared with another doctor. This meant that the occasional weekend visits by Berns were spent relaxing in the flat and eating our own cooked food.

Prior to my working in the department, I had learned many ways to manage an ingrown toenail. However, I learned from Mr. Reece a simple technique to treat the condition. He called the technique the "Phenolization of Nail Matrix." I researched and wrote a paper on *The Treatment of Ingrown Toe Nail by Wedge Resection Using Phenolization.*

It had a success rate of over 75 percent with minimal complications, mainly burns from undiluted phenol. It was exciting doing the research because I spent hours in the library at Newcastle University.

Three weeks to go, I ran into an SHO orthopaedics. He was preparing for the Primary examination. Dr. Ahmed Sadhu had made a few attempts already. We arranged to study together but often he was very poorly prepared.

Ahmed invited me home one evening for supper. At home was his wife, mother-in-law, and a three-year-old daughter. It was now obvious to understand why he had poor concentration. Each time the telephone rang, the little girl responded with a four-letter word. The child picked it up from her father, who was frustrated by the frequent calls to attend to patients.

Finally, the days had arrived. Ahmed and I boarded an evening train to Glasgow. The MCQs, the practical anatomy, and viva went well. However, I was not confident enough to wait for the result. I took the first available train back to Gateshead.

I had decided to forget about the Primary (pass or fail). I started reading the recommended books for my next course, *Diploma in Tropical Medicine* and *Hygiene at Liverpool.* In less than two weeks, the Royal College of Physicians and Surgeons of Glasgow sent me a note to say I passed the Primary.

Chapter 31

1984 in England

I enrolled in the Tropical School of Medicine and Hygiene, Liverpool. I passed the Primary Fellowship Examination. Frank Bruno, for the first time, lost his boxing crown.

Cec and her boyfriend, Kenneth Chai Hong, spent Christmas with us. All four of us celebrated the New Year with a glass of champagne each. Berns and I took pride in looking after our house while I took special interest in the abandoned garden at the back. I drove Berns into town to buy curtains for the house but came back home emptyhanded.

The overnight gale force blew off some of the roof tiles. One of the windows leaked water. We could not contact the contractors. Instead, we drove to Leeds to pay for the road tax for my bike and for Berns' to have her hair done. I was not surprised to find the salon closed. Our sisters, for whom time was not so important, ran it. Traveling back to Harrogate was hazardous because it was snowing.

Berns left midweek for Sheffield to attend a seminar aimed at her training. She left only a few hours ago and I was missing her already. However, I had a lot to preoccupy myself. I transferred all our belongings from the hospital accommodation to our new house. As I emptied the last load from the car, I met with our new neighbours, Mark and Catherine. They were friendly and offered to assist in whatever way they could. Allowing for the twinges in the low back (most likely due to the use of muscles not used for a long time), the day was successful.

The builders arrived and successfully replaced the tiles while I worked inside cleaning the floor. Cec dropped us a note to say thank you for looking after them over the Christmas break. I collected Berns from the train station. She looked tired but surprisingly, she was irritable and easily annoyed. After a meal of curried trout, which I prepared earlier in the day, we settled down to watch television. Bernie was still not in a talking mood and I let things go by.

On the following Saturday, we drove into Leeds to shop for the house. We (or Berns) succeeded in buying something for the bedrooms. Berns accused me of not making decisions. To me it was a thought-provoking statement. In ten out of a hundred decisions I made, Berns would agree with me. My response to her decisions was the exact opposite. A man who is non-confrontational had been my weakness, which she had picked up early in our relationship.

I accepted a place at the School of Tropical Medicine and Hygiene, Liverpool, for the Diploma Course. Berns drove me to the train station bound for Liverpool to view my new accommodations.

"During the course at Sheffield, one of my senior male colleagues kissed me." She finally broke her silence.

"For some men, this is natural regardless of your wedding ring," I responded. "Besides, you are attractive and bright. Men like beautiful women around them."

She made no verbal response but internally, she must have been saying, *This is Francis all over.*

Two weeks later, I was back in Liverpool with my motorbike. My room was too big for me. The size made it expensive for heating up. My first breakfast downstairs was a bowl of cereal, fried eggs and bacon on toast, and a cup of tea. I felt good. The ride to school was pleasant, enhanced by the fine weather. The drive took me through the Mersey Tunnel, into the City Centre, along the train station and library and then up a gentle incline to school. The whole journey took me under twenty minutes.

I had read some of the books for the course while on night duty at Gateshead, and so I sounded impressive in the eyes of my colleagues and lecturer. My landlady was a divorcé of a Jewish background. She became excited when I told her that one of my best friends in college was from Israel. She had her two children living with her, a lodger from Zimbabwe and myself. Unfortunately, at least from my point of view, the garden to this lovely semi-detached house was lost to an ugly garage. The three rooms were quite spacious. I was allowed to cook. However, I brought my already prepared food from home to last for the week. At the end of each day, I had many optional locations to study—school library, city library, and town library at Wellesley. Unfortunately, I could find no nearby park to exercise. This to me was a big negative because I was unable to do my chest physiotherapy. One or twice a week I babysat for my lady, which allowed her to go out and play cards with her friends. These evenings brought the worst out of the seven-year-old boy. The older girl, ten years of age, insisted I did her homework with her. I happily helped but somehow, I thought it would misfire in the near future, particularly when I decided to concentrate on my final examinations. I have always enjoyed the company of children, probably because I never remembered childhood days.

The school, as part of the University of Liverpool, was just one building. There were no spaces to pack a car and none for bicycles and motorbikes. I left the bike by the side of the building and luckily, it was never tampered with while in class. I left it at the back of my new residence when I went home on weekends.

Our house was really becoming a home. We did something to it every weekend. Berns was no longer worried but relaxed. She enjoyed her training and earning money to keep us going. The Leeds' hairdressers were unpredictable but when they did turn up, they did an excellent job. Today was one such Saturday. She looked radiant. The edge of her hair was lengthened with matching artificial hairs.

George accepted our invitation and arrived early Saturday morning from Buckden. He enjoyed shopping and was good with his hands. Like me, he did not tolerate window-shopping. It was snowing outside and naturally cold. George continued with his chain-smoking. The living room became stuffy; breathing became difficult for me and my coughing worsened. On the following Monday, we went our separate ways: George down to Buckden, Berns to work, and I to college.

I took my usual train to Leeds after the last lecture on Friday. On Saturday, we drove into town after a shaky start. The car would not start but we got it going when Berns emptied a whole can of WD40 onto everything accessible underneath the burnet. The car got going but smoked like a chimney. Berns and I were friends up to a point while in Leeds. She insisted on going to yet another shop to compare prices. Our aim, as always, was to stay within our budget but not at the expense of convenience. On getting home, she went upstairs to study, and I stayed downstairs to do the same.

It was snowing on arrival in Liverpool. The atmosphere, or should I say the ground, was covered white. It was slippery, wet, and unhealthy. At the end of the day's lectures, I walked down into the city centre to get a bus that never came. I opted for the underground, which stole precious and necessary time off my studies. Everybody in the house was sneezing and the seven-year-old blamed me for it. He was innocently passing on what his mother may have told him. After eating, I studied until 12 A.M., when I started writing the day's events.

Like clockwork, I dropped into the lab to view what was for demonstration before each lecture. At the end of the day, I was depressed. I could not convince myself that I recognized any of the parasites. I must realize that the only diagnostic tool in the tropics is the microscope. Therefore, for the rest of the week, I was going to do something about it. On getting back to #47 in Wallassey, I studied until 12 midnight.

Sitting directly behind me in the lab was Michael Ross, a general practitioner, in Liverpool. I never liked him because he was always talking during lectures. I was therefore hesitant to go home with him when he invited me for a cup of tea. He was pleasant and looked scruffy. He graduated from the University College Hospital, London, completed his MRCP examination, and had an M.Sc. degree in community medicine. He also spent two years in Jamaica as a general physician. The house was built in the seventeenth century, bearing various holes and scars. Indoor, there was nothing in order.

Another lodger in the house was a student from Malawi. He was an undergraduate in economics at the University. He was an extremely hard worker but disorganized. All the same, the landlady tolerated him quite well. We walked together to the train station every Friday morning. This gave us the opportunity to talk about our respective countries and people. He shared his freshly prepared meals with me. I too shared my pre-prepared supper with him brought with me from Harrogate. This give-and-take made life bearable during our studies.

News from Sa Leone was never encouraging. I was worried about my sister. She wanted to be independent but I did not think she had the brains to do so. She did not live with her husband but she became pregnant for him. I vowed to write to him every month until he responded. She was indeed in a mess but sending her more money was not the answer. Berns, on the other hand, received a telephone call from Cec to say that she had fallen out with her boyfriend. The poor girl must be having a terrible time in her private life. It really must have been very difficult for her because the problem kept cropping up. It was probably easy for us to say to her to learn to live with it. But what about the men she would become involved with in the future, wishing to have children?

"As the course approaches its end, I am beginning to irritate my landlady. I am spending less time with her children and the little time at the house is spent locked up in my room. I no longer offer her spot diagnosis of the neighbours', friends', and family problems. I no longer play with the cat because he is not looking well. It will not be long when either of us crack up," I commented to Berns one weekend.

Things back home in Harrogate were looking good. The furniture was in and we now had a new efficient fire heater. We could proudly call #18 as our own. At the same time I secured an SHO job in general surgery at the Huddersfield Royal Infirmary to coincide with the end of my course. I am becoming more comfortable with the microscope and my test results are above 70 percent on average.

When I came downstairs this morning for breakfast, my landlady and family, for the first time, were nowhere to be seen. Instead, there were two letters on the dining room table, respectively addressed to Felix and myself. Mine read: "Dear Francis, would you be kind enough to tidy your room? Moreover, it would be helpful if you could put your dishes away. Thanks a lot. Mrs. D." I did not know what to make of this letter. I only used the kitchen to heat up my cooked food. I used my room to study and sleep in my bed. It must be a gentle way of telling me to move on.

I got home on Friday. The train drive was comfortable. Berns and I tidied the living area and kitchen and went our separate ways. The rest of the day was spent at each other's throats. I was angry with her because she had the house in an upside-down state and I accused her of watching too much television. She was annoyed with me because I did not help her to look for her misplaced timetable. Berns never stopped amazing me. She now had all the comfort of accommodation because of her hard work but seemed to have stopped functioning. She had become disorganized and worse than ever before.

Finally, Mrs. D released the missile. In the middle of my unmade bed (religiously made by her as part of the contract) was a note addressed to me. "Dear Francis, I am giving you a notice to vacate my house in a week's time." I predicted this. I packed my belongings before going to bed. The following morning, I handed Mrs. D her key and set off to school. At the luncheon break, I told Mike my eviction notice and we both just laughed about it. He would not allow me to look for new accommodations and I moved in with his family.

Studying and revising with Mike were wonderful. We both knew our stuff. The exams came quietly and ended abruptly. Mike topped the class and I was close by. I would have loved to explore Liverpool but I took off to Harrogate immediately after receiving my DTM&H certificate. I tried to keep in touch with Mike and family but he stopped responding.

I resumed work in Huddersfield Royal Infirmary (HRI) as SHO in general surgery and urology on call. The unit also composed of a registrar and an intern. It was a true general surgical unit and the team soon realized that I was willing to learn. I was also going to enjoy myself. Cec was settled in Dublin, Berns deeply involved in her training, and George happily retired in Buckden. This situation gave me the opportunity to spend twenty-four hours a day in hospital.

Slowly, the consultant invited me to assist him in his private practice (without pay) and at two NHS cottage hospitals. My ultimate aim was to return to Sierra Leone to practice and this place was ideal to learn. Whenever possible I became involved in gynaecology, urology, paediatric surgery, ENT surgery, etc.

My consultant was trained in New Zealand. Being a left-handed surgeon, he was forced to be ambidextrous and well trained. He quickly appreciated my deficiencies but willing to let me do everything within my capabilities. I personally enjoyed working with the registrar as well, who was generous in everything, including food, drinks, and small/big talks. My intern was engaged to another intern, both allowing each other the laxity to concentrate on their work. She picked me up from my room each morning to do an hour's ward round. After six months of my attachment, I became the pivotal centre of managing the patients. I knew all our patients.

Berns' parents arrived from Trinidad. They were staying with us. Dad was experiencing difficulties with his sinuses. As usual, I jumped into action and arranged an interview with one of our physicians. He was cleared.

I wrote to Dan to congratulate him and his girlfriend on the arrival of their baby girl last month. If they loved each other, I suggested he married Edna. They accepted our invitation to spend Christmas with us. I wrote to the SamForays, apologizing for not reciprocating them with our photographs. The truth was that Berns and I were hardly together. Our jobs took a lot out of us.

Chapter 32
1985 in England

I was offered the post of registrar in the surgical training rotation in Bradford. Bernadette was accepted for the MPH training course in Leeds. Cecilia graduated from medical school in Dublin. The Bradford fire disaster occurred at the football stadium.

Daniel and his family had been with us since Christmas. Cec too came over from Dublin, and so we had a full house at the start of the year. We celebrated the coming of the New Year with glasses of water. We received calls from Barry and Andrea on behalf of everyone in Trinidad and Tobago and George from Buckden.

N'Gundia (four months old) managed to wake everybody up at 5 A.M. It did not bother us but I was concerned about the possibility of disturbing the neighbours' sleep. They came with me to Huddersfield to board the train for London. In my extra concern for their safety, the train rolled off the platform while I was still on board. The twenty minutes allowed free parking had expired and the car ticketed. After my hospital work, I wrote an apologetic letter to the Kirklees Metropolitan Council for parking my car in excess of the allotted time. I enclosed a cheque worth the fine.

The dust had settled after everyone had gone back to their respective tasks. In order to maintain our upkeep and pay our mortgage, we decided that we must work and study for our respective postgraduate degrees. I applied for a correspondence course. My tutor sent me material to study followed by essay questions. Under exam conditions lasting for three hours, I was to answer the questions. I was excited about my first installment.

As usual, I did my mini ward round with the intern after which I assembled the team members for the consultant's arrival. He joined us an hour later. He was pleased to see the registrar, SHO, HO, and medical students. Like a little god, he made no apologies for being late. I led the team around the wards.

Last night I covered for urology. We had an Iocum consultant. A forthree-year-old gentleman, admitted from the Emergency Department, had priapism (sustained painful erection). The registrar started the surgery to decompress the penis and made excellent progress. The consultant, however, insisted on taking over. Soon we all realized that he had not done the procedure before. This episode once again emphasized to me that I must pass my FRCS examination in the next year.

After a satisfactory ward round with Mr. Graham and team, I attended the radiology conference, after which I drove to Harrogate. Berns had left the house in an immaculate state and I felt welcome. I missed her a lot but it was a sacrifice we had to make to achieve our aim—get the appropriate certificates. She had gone down to Birmingham to attend a seminar.

The week had started and as usual, I completed my mini ward round with my intern. After lunch, I joined Mr. Graham in the operating theatre (OT). He was in a hurry, resulting in finding faults with his assistances. Actually, the scrub nurse was incompetent. It was later rumoured to me that she was Mr. Graham's private patient. According to Berns, this was again another reason why I had to pass my FRCS examination.

I ran into a doctor today in the anaesthetic room. He was from Egypt trained in ENT surgery. I estimated his age at forty-five. He was training to be a general practitioner. He realized there was no chance for him to go beyond his present grade of registrar. He anticipated that he would eventually work for a consultant who would be younger and inexperienced than himself. I was aware of this myself already.

My day came and I took it. Mr. G allowed me to do the list today to be supervised by the registrar. It was difficult but I was determined to do well. The theatre, in the presence of Mr. G, was normally quiet and workers business-like. The turnaround time became prolonged and a lot of movement and talking. All the same, it was a successful Friday.

As I wrote today's event, something kept crossing my mind. From my undergraduate days to the present, I have seen or heard doctors fighting for patients. However, looking at it critically, it was only a tiny minority who genuinely believed and practiced it. The majority were excellent fighters for self-preservation. Many a time consultants did not meet eye to eye. The unfortunate aspect of this was the dragging of the junior doctors into the web of fighting.

We spent this weekend preparing for the coming spring. Berns promised herself to plant flowers while I opted to plant for food. I spent most evenings reading Bailey and Love's *Textbook of Surgery,* opened on my laps before the television. Berns was in an annoying mood this Sunday afternoon by shouting, screaming, and not being at ease.

Dr. Monica Shackleton was with Berns when I got home. Monica was Berns' colleague at the course. They became friends at the start. She had spent some years in Canada before coming back to England in 1976. It took her many years to readjust. Berns prepared an excellent meal. Despite the horrible weather, she was not willing to stay away from York. Fortunately, the snow eased its grip before she set off.

It was a hectic day for me. It started with my usual mini ward round. I joined Mr. G to assist him at gastro-oesophagectomy on one of his private patients. It took us over six hours. The last one to two hours brought the worst out of him. On going back to my room, I telephoned Berns, who told me that she had bad news from TnT. Andrea and her son, Glen, sustained injuries in a road traffic accident. Thieves broke into the parents' home but got away with little.

Never had I experienced so much snowfall in Yorkshire. I spent the whole day in theatre today. On emerging, I was faced by the rainy snow. It occurred to me then that the best place to be is Sa Leone. I had to withdraw this wish when Dominic telephoned me to tell me about the death of his brother, Mark. He may have been only a couple of years older than I and had a great future. He died from the complications of high blood pressure, a subarachnoid haemorrhage. The medications may not have been available or he did not comply or poor management.

My six-month contract was coming to an end. Mr. G wanted me to "stay on" but I wanted to "move on." Was I that good that Mr. G did not want me to go, or did he have other tricks up his sleeve? I may not go beyond the grade of registrar in UK, and therefore I had to prepare myself for Sa Leone or TnT. I was therefore going to leave, although not to a job. I laid my priorities before him. Foremost, I had to pass my FRCS exam, secondly to be a registrar and thirdly as SHO in other specialist units (plastic, gynaecology, anaesthesia). He made no concrete promise. The other reason why I had wanted to move on was the lack of research despite the high patient turnover; the weekly audit meeting was poorly supported.

I completed the mini ward round with my intern and went to theatre. "The list is yours," declared Mr. G. While assisting me from the other side of the table, I successfully completed a cholecystectomy, appendicectomy, and three haemorrhoidectomies. He promised to push me through the registrar post in Bradford. It was all smiles when I got home. But so far in my life, I have learned not to say, "Tight until it is in the hand." It was a matter of sitting, waiting, and seeing.

After two hours of reading for my correspondence course, I sorted out my young seedlings. Most of the transplants had died. I was probably too optimistic to transfer them when they were only one week old after germination. This was what I called learning by mistakes. We got news from Cec that she passed her final MBBS examination. I was not particularly surprised because she was focused and bright. George, Berns, and I were very happy for her. She opted to go back to Trinidad to do her internship.

I attended an interview for a registrar post in Bradford. Of all days, my car refused to move an inch this morning. It was snowing, wet, and cold. My intern was too happy to give me a loan of her car. In fact, she offered to drive me to the interview. Of the four candidates invited, I thought I was the most ideal. I had more basic knowledge but was least experienced. Two of the three consultants opted for experience and so I lost. However, at the end of the interview, one of the consultants approached me and told me that they all thought highly of me. He gave me encouraging words. This was a confidence booster. Besides, I was not perturbed.

On getting home, I got on with my gardening and then the correspondence course. I seemed to underestimate the role played by sludge in British gardens. According to Mrs. F, they were devils. Two weeks later, I received a letter from the Bradford District Administrator offering me a job as registrar. I was over the moon. Berns was excited on hearing the news. She reminded me of the two main advantages—I would be closer to home and since it was a teaching institution, it was good on the CV.

The contract was for two years, which started in orthopaedics. My unit shared a senior registrar with another unit. This meant that I was under the direct supervision of the consultant most of the time. Unlike Hull, the majority of the work was cold rather than trauma. My predecessor won the verbal presentation price at the Yorkshire Surgical Society. He described a technique to repair a ruptured Achilles' tendon. This meant that the hospital was actively involved in research and clinico-pathological conferences. The drive between home and work was easy.

Harrogate was a tourist city. It had many excellent hotels with conference rooms. It attracted shoppers and visitors, mainly on weekends. The authorities carefully maintained flower gardens and spas. In order to increase the value of the house, I agreed with Berns to take half of my garden to build a garage. The land space left for me was about 18 by 10 feet. I used half of this to grow Irish potatoes and the other half with strawberries. Berns planted her flowers along the driveway. In the front, I tried my hands at planting different varieties of roses.

The weekend beginning Friday, May 10, was assigned to my unit for emergency cover. There was nothing special about this weekend. For the whole Friday, I had only three emergencies to warrant operation—two fractures and the removal of foreign body in the foot. Then Saturday afternoon came.

I was in my room with my operative surgical book opened on my lap while watching television. I was watching a soccer game between Bradford and Lincoln Cities. The first forty minutes of play produced no goal. But a few minutes before halftime, a glowing light appeared from the back row of one of the blocks. The roof caught fire and within minutes, the whole stand became engulfed in fire. Panic broke. I saw children being thrown over the wall to escape and most people spilled onto the pitch. I assumed correctly that the dead and injured would be brought to our hospital, the Accident and Emergency Department.

At the start, we sent the minor cases home. There was no shortage of staff. As the casualties arrived, we directed the dead to the mortuary room and those with respiratory distress from smoke inhalation were admitted straight to the wards. The bulk of the injured people had some degree of burning. The superficial burns were dressed and sent home to come back for review in a day's time. Moderate- to severe-burn patients were further prioritised. Following stabilization, those with deep burns went straight to the operating theatre for removal of dead tissue. Those patients with mild to moderate burns were often restless and cried with pain; they were admitted onto the wards for wound dressing, control of pain, and rehydration. I had no course to take any patient to theatre for broken bones.

On reflection, when I got home two days later, I was impressed with the enthusiasm of the staff members and the pride with which they did their job. It was probably disasters like these that brought out the best of the human race. The staff in the Department of Plastic and Reconstructive Surgery further managed these patients. Before moving on to my next attachment, we learned that 56 people lost their lives and more than 265 others sustained some degree of injury.

Chapter 33

1986 in England

Dominic and family spent New Year's Day with us in Harrogate. Sir, your car is now ready for its final rest in the scrap yard. I became a Fellow of the Royal College of Surgeons of Edinburgh by examination.

Dominic and family—Gloria, Sahr, and Tamba—joined us in the last two days of last year. A day after celebrating the New Year, DY left for London to do some errands for the High Commission. Berns and Gloria went shopping in Leeds. The boys and I went for a walk in the gardens. Sahr cried the whole way back because of pain in his toes. As for Tamba, it was all fun and smiles.

I took my car for its annual service. The mechanic did a wonderful job but he was blunt with me. "Without too much strain on it, this car will only last you for another year," he declared to me.

Berns had decided to take things into her own hands. Whenever possible she assisted me with my chest exercises. She gave weekly tutorials based on revisions and articles in the *Surgery Journal*. The contents of the magazine were aimed at surgeons revising for the FRCS examination. We set this year aside to pass the fellowship, having now completed training.

Two letters came to hand today. Alfred wrote to tell me that Pa Harry was being evicted from his rented house in New England. This boosted our resolve to own our own house. The lesson is that we must own our house whether it was made of grass or mud or concrete. The other letter was from Joseph Tamba. The letter was essentially a book list. I sent him three of the six books.

Well, my first attempt at the FRCS was a failure. I was, however, encouraged that the clinical components of the exam were excellent. The result seemed to suggest that I had the general knowledge but needed to be more detailed and specific. This should not be a problem to resolve.

As usual, I started my ward round on K1 Ward. I found the outgoing SHO most unhelpful. He was not around to hand over the patients to his colleagues. The day went smoothly and NA's clinic was less boring than other days. He was now opening up to me. NA was the most senior surgeon in Bradford and had a lot of power. He was an excellent surgeon who had written books in surgery and was a member of the Board of Examiners of the Royal College of Surgeons. He kept to himself most of the time.

Berns came to spend the weekend with me. To be on call at St. Luke was not always exciting. She was coughing, which was complicated by chest pains and a sore throat. She was in a terrible state; she had red and swollen eyes, and she was anorexic. I managed to acquire a bottle of codeine linctus. It was just as well because the take was light and I was able to nurse her.

MW was the other consultant for whom I worked. I took him and the rest of the team for the ward round. At the end of the round, he was generous in his praise. He responded to my complaints—not enough teaching. In theatre, he taught me a few surgical techniques. MW was the youngest of my three consultants, although he was in his fifties. He loved Indian foods and cinemas. He spoke to some of his patients in Urdu. He was an uncomplicated surgeon. He trained me to do paediatric surgery and I was able to teach our senior registrars from Leeds. He also gave me the opportunity to assist him in his private practice.

Today, I spent my spare time reading SamForay's book, *No Lasting Fear.* It was an absorbing novel with excellent dialogue. I read it into the small hours of the morning. At the end of it, I had many suggestions to make but the FRCS examinations were all over me.

Berns' tutorial classes on weekends continued with success. GV telephoned to wish us well. He invited us down to London, but I told him that the FRCS took priority now. During the week, I made my usual ward round with my junior doctors before going to the clinic or theatre. Mr. MW had to abandon the list to me because he was unwell. It went well. However, I noted an incident as given below in my diary.

I had done many procedures now on my own and grown in confidence. Over-confidence combined with carelessness always spelled disaster. One of my patients was a thirty-year-old lady with an incisional hernia following two Caesarian operations. "Her urinary bladder formed part of the hernia sac, which I accidentally entered. This became obvious only when the patient returned to the ward. With the help of my senior registrar, we repaired it. I allowed my senior to speak to our consultant. I contacted the lady's husband and apologized after full explanation. I looked after the patient every day until she left for home in a satisfactory condition. Understandably, the patient sued for damages. Following my written statement, the Health Authority took full responsibility."

May had arrived and I was better equipped for the FRCS exams. I enjoyed the written papers. I almost missed my clinical examination because of trying to save a few pounds on transport. It was pouring rain but I insisted on taking a bus, which never came. I walked part of the way and then boarded a taxi. All went my way. I answered every question thrown at me. I was the first candidate and did not have to wait long. As I turned the corner, I heard one of the examiners say, "He knows his stuff." On going back to the hospital a day later, colleagues were curious to know the outcome. "I am hopeful," was all I could say to them.

On May 24, 1986, at 1 P.M., I received a call from Berns, who addressed me as Mr. Francis Saa-Gandi. She had the strength to call the college about the result. I had passed the FRCS of Edinburgh. I had won a bottle of wine in the last course for FRCS at the Royal Infirmary, Leeds. Appropriately, Berns and I opened it and had it with our meals over the weekend.

"On weekends, between our various tasks, we prepared and ate our meals together. We watched television together. Examination pressure, at least for the moment, is off and so I can start performing my role as a loving husband."

A month had gone since passing the exam and Mr. MW's clinics were no longer over-subscribed. I did my first mastectomy today after which I went to the clinic. I saw patients until 5 P.M. I found myself doing more work beyond the call of duty.

I did my side of the bargain. I passed the FRCS exam and the consultants were teaching and allowing me to carry out many operative procedures. I assisted in repairing a ruptured abdominal aortic aneurysm and successfully did one on my own (something like "monkey see, monkey do").

There were no entries in the diary between July and October.

Just as the mechanic had forecasted, my car had finally arrived at its final resting place. Therefore, I had been without a car for the past three months. Berns took me to work whenever possible or otherwise she dropped me at the bus station. One morning, probably the coldest this winter, I boarded a bus into town. A lady walked in looking all flushed, cheaply and badly dressed. "They are taking over. They do what they like. This Paki bus driver went past us," she announced as she tried to find a seat. A little Asian girl tried to assist but she was rough with, and rude, to the poor girl. In Bradford, for sure, distrust between the Asian and White communities is here to stay for a foreseeable future.

It was my turn. I woke up this morning, extremely cold, with a high fever, sweating, musculoskeletal pains, and painful coughing. I lost my appetite, resulting in an empty stomach with severe hunger pains. Like most other days for whatever reason, on getting to work, I felt better. I managed to get through the day. I had to find a way to exercise regularly.

For Christmas, I got a pair of pyjamas, which Berns wanted me to try on. When I did put it on, I spent the day watching television, that addictive grey screen. Mom telephoned to wish us a happy Christmas and kept us abreast with things in Trinidad and Tobago.

A year ago, Berns and I applied to work in the Ministry of Health in Trinidad and Tobago. Yesterday, we received a letter from the Chief Medical Officer, Dr. Elizabeth Quamina, offering us jobs but on the proviso that we passed our examinations.

My next posting was with Mr. Alan Mearns (AJM) and Mr. Nigel Saunders in thoracic surgery.

Chapter 34
1987 in England

Appointed as registrar at Maidstone General Hospital. The lowest temperatures recorded in Britain. Bernadette successfully completed the DTM&H course.

The alarm clock woke us up this morning in my on-call room. This first day of the year was wet. After my ward round, we drove off to Leeds to shop for food. Berns went to the office to work on a paper for publication while I stayed home to cook.

To me, the authorities organized the training rotation quite well. I was now in thoracic surgery (thoracic), the last six months of my two-year contract with the Authority. When on call, I covered for General Surgery. This made the task less boring and tedious. This way, I kept abreast with my general surgical skills.

Today was my second meeting with AJM and I thought I was going to learn a lot from him. He was a wonderful man—quite intelligent and blunt but crude and bragged. Within a week, he taught me to do oesophagoscopies and bronchoscopies safely. My SHO spent yesterday a lot of time with a patient who had perforated oesophagus (a hole in the gullet). I asked him to take the rest of the day off. AJM and I took the patient to theatre for a formal thoracotomy (to repair the defect).

AJM, over the years, took his children to Devon in a camp to look after handicapped people. These few days in the New Year were no exceptions. The day-to-day running of the unit went well. However, I admitted a new patient in whom I diagnosed a perforated oesophagus. Fortunately, an locum consultant from the other unit was willing to help. We saved the patient.

Back to work after a relaxing weekend, I received a telephone call from Mr. Addison, Head of the Surgical Department. "I will like to extend your contract for another six months at least. The department does not like to lose their good registrars before they secure a new job somewhere."

"Thank you for the offer. I am grateful and I am flattered," I replied. "However, I will like to move on to do more general and urological surgery."

"That is a reasonable response, but the offer remains for a month."

I was unable to go home today. The snow was terrible and it was extremely cold for the past two days. Temperatures similar to these occurred twenty-five years ago according to records. In three days' time, I was to attend an interview in Manchester and I hoped the weather would have improved by then. I did attend the interview but the job went to another candidate who looked capable. I had resigned myself to more disappointments.

Back at work, I carried out my days' work with fun. However, every day was different. At about 12 midnight, I was about to record the day's events as being fruitful. The nurse in charge of my ward telephoned me to administer morphine to a patient who was dying. I flatly refused. I am not a god. They trained me to save lives and not deliberately take them away—at least not at this stage of my training. In my ward round the following morning, I found that the patient had died. In his note, the night nurse recorded that "the patient died at 12:05 A.M. and the doctor contacted." I found this malicious. She did not contact me after the patient's death.

Now that the major exams were over, I had to turn my attention to research and/or publication. It was not long coming. AJM asked me to prepare a paper on lung tumours for presentation at Field House, Postgraduate Centre. The presentation went well judged by the questions raised from the floor. AJM was proud of himself because the other consultants complimented him for the coaching. I undertook a retrospective study of computerized axial tomography scan guided biopsy of lung tumours.

Some evenings were relaxing in the canteen. The diners were few and were not often under undue stress. This evening I sat at a table with one of the SHOs in General Medicine. She graduated from Leeds; she was originally from Kenya of Asian parents. She invited me to play tennis at her club. The following weekend when on call, I accepted the invitation. The club was beautiful on the surface but somehow I did not feel welcome. As it was my customary practice, I did not return. So far in my life, I have never given any organization cause to throw me out.

"Over the years I have come to recognize two types of surgeons: anatomist or physiologist. AJM is a physiologist. By this, I mean he manages his patient in terms of their physiological and biochemical abnormalities. It makes sense because the change in the condition of chest patient can change very rapidly. Their demise is often due to an imbalance between the oxygen and carbon dioxide concentrations. Mr. Addison is an example of an anatomist. He is slow and meticulous. He is capable of creating bloodless field. I am developing into being a bit of both."

AJM joined me later after my ward round with my two junior doctors. I took him around to see all the patients. After the end of ward round refreshments, he invited me home. Their house was large and spacious. It was located in a high-class area of Leeds. They maintained the gardens well. Mrs. Mary Mearns was a hospital administrator. She was bright, generous, and gentle. Sarah, the oldest daughter, was outgoing, resembling her father in many ways. She was a law student and seemed to have no problem with the course. Catherine, the second daughter, was reserved and less into academia. Elizabeth, the youngest girl, wished to be a journalist. She studied hard and seemed more organized than the rest of the family members. "I only bring home my best and this man from Sa Leone is one of them," he declared to his family.

Like my previous projects, once I got my teeth in there was no letting go. I had anticipated some resistance collecting the data. The technicians in the pathology department were more than generous with their time. They taught me how to make slides for cytology and to determine the presence of cells in aspirate. The radiologists were just as helpful. The consultant identified the lung lesions and showed me how to obtain tissue specimens. Within three months, data collection was complete.

I found myself lumbered with another project. This time we wanted to find out the accuracy of history to determine the nature of an oesophageal stricture. We also wanted to find out the reliability of x-ray findings in determining the nature of a stricture, whether cancerous or benign.

About the diseases of the gullet, I had enough information to present in a scientific meeting. Indeed, my paper was accepted for verbal presentation at the Yorkshire Surgical Society meeting in Grimsby. It generated some questions. We used the principle written in *The Interpretation of Diagnostic Data,* applied in Clinical Epidemiology. We were able to determine the sensitivity and specificity of the tests (history, stricture length). A registrar from Leeds won the overall best presenter award. His topic was on pancreatitis. It was an excellent paper, crisp and to the point.

It was Bern's turn to go to school while I had to work to support both of us and pay the mortgage. I went for an interview for a registrar's post in General and Urological Surgery in Maidstone General Hospital, Kent. I pulled it off. This meant that Berns could attend the London School of Hygiene and we could meet on weekends in London.

Apart from the surgical training in the hospitals, Bradford had little to offer. There were few theatres and hardly any large sporting facilities. I had visited the park on a few occasions but it did not lend itself for frequent visits. The main attraction, however, was the Photographic Museum. I always enjoyed the history of camera development through the huge 3-D screen. Asians owned most of the stores, and I was always uneasy when shopping in those stores. The proprietor followed me around the store. Therefore, Bradford was not my hunting ground for shopping, either for food or for home.

By the time I left Bradford, the Mearns and my family had become friends. I spent a lot of time with AJM. During one of our meetings, we decided to do more work on the lung tumours and gullet narrowing with the aim of publication. By virtue of their respective jobs, Berns and Mary ran into each other in meetings. Berns thought highly of Mary as being a bright and hard \working person. We remained friends until their passing at the time of writing. He was truly one of my mentors.

I started my new appointment on July 2 with Mr. Peter Jones (PJ). There were two other surgical units headed by Mr. Michael Fern and Miss Mary South. In addition to their general surgical work, they all did urology. The contract was for two years. Mr. Jones was dynamic both technically and academically. Like the other unit, ours composed of a consultant, the registrar, and an intern. The catchment area was relatively small and one was not overwhelmed by emergency work. It was an excellent job in that I was in charge but in direct contact with the consultant.

Kent fit the name as being the Garden of England. Maidstone itself was a hilly city but the countryside was relatively flat. It was wonderful feeling as I rode on my bicycle with fresh air in the nostrils and green farmland. Then one evening, I discovered a recreational centre composing of a tennis club (four grass courts and one hard court), a bowling lawn, a football pitch and a clubhouse encompassing a bar, restaurant, and billiard table.

This to me was a Godsend. By coincidence, Sadie Curtis, one of my theatre sisters, was a member of the tennis club. Within days, I applied for membership and was accepted. After a month in the club, I was invited to join the first team.

There was never a boring time in Maidstone. I enjoyed working with PJ and he allowed me to do a lot of work on my own. I had my own list working next door to him. Soon after, Susan, his wife, joined the unit to do some day surgery. I took an instant liking to her. She was pleasant, uncomplicated, and willing to learn.

"I love my flat. It was one of many in the doctors' quarters. My only window overlooked an open field. The field was separated from the buildings by a drain one side of which was protected by a barbed-wire fence. Both were to prevent the cattle and sheep from wandering into our compound. However, they forgot to cater for at least two families of rabbits. They lived and made more babies on our side of the fence but fed from the other side." Unfortunately, the gale force a few days ago blew over two of the five oak trees, making the field unsightly. Bernadette completed the DTM&H course in London and successfully passed the examination. She was now back in Harrogate.

The winter weather had definitely set in. Apparently, this year was recorded as the coldest winter in Britain since 1922. George left this first Monday morning of the New Year for Buckden. All three of us had a wonderful Christmas break in Harrogate. Back in Maidstone I managed to exercise by going for my bicycle rides. This hospital would have been perfect if we had a post-graduate centre and student attachments. However, there was pressure on the clinicians to at least start clinico-pathological weekly meetings.

The dreaded winter was almost gone and there was spring in the air. The authorities designated June as health month. Sadie and I entered the tennis tournament as mixed double. We came against PJ and his partner. We won against them and then went on to win the whole tournament. Thereafter, PJ invited me home to play tennis with some of his friends, mainly from the hospital.

Just like the Mearns, the Jones have become my mentor, family friends and, in a way, my other parents.

I was in the recovery room today checking on one of my patients who had colon surgery. The nurse in charge was Mrs. Georgina Turner-Pelling. She was originally from the Greek side of Cyprus. I found her knowledgeable and friendly. In Dublin my friends were from Turkey and so I never got the Greek's side of the Cyprus story. She invited me some time later to meet with her family. Richard was the husband who loved motorcycles and two daughters, Maria and Helena. It was a relaxing afternoon and I thoroughly enjoyed myself.

It was time to move on again. I applied and was offered a registrar post in urology based in Hull. I went back to Yorkshire. However, as I write we visited the Jones' and Georgina's families annually in Kent. We remained permanent friends.

Chapter 35

1988 in England

Adrian had a successful treatment of his pituitary tumor. We revisited Trinidad and Tobago.

I started the New Year in a new job in Hull as urological registrar. I recognized most of the workers who were still here during my stint as an SHO. Adrian, Berns' dad, had his pituitary tumour removed through the nose. I assisted. Berns, as usual, continued with her caring for all of us. "Each day I admire the woman; she is gentle, loving, and generous."

On finishing my hospital work, I went to see Dad, whose neurosurgeon was happy with his progress. He suggested we take him home in two days' time, but the old boy showed little enthusiasm. Coming back to Hull had created two opportunities for me. My newfound park offered the opportunity to jog, walk, or play tennis every evening. I was also now able to start relearning my French.

Dad had a rough night because of a blocked nose. When I saw him this morning, he was blowing his nose dangerously hard. At about 6 P.M. the women arrived from Harrogate and I took them to see him. They pounced and reminded him about his undoing of all the good work done by the surgeon. In addition, they could not understand why he did not want to come home. We left about an hour later, and I was sure he was too happy to see the back of us.

I qualified to play table tennis for the Hull Health Authority team. We lost all our doubles but won one single. Interestingly we enjoyed ourselves more in this than when we won a week ago. The following day, I had a lengthy clinic with Mr. H.

Berns was becoming less and less tolerant of the cold. Each time I turned off the heater, she woke up instantly from her sleep. She hated staying with me in hospital when I was on call. "Dad arrived home this week and has made a steady recovery. He now breathes on most occasions through his nose rather than through his mouth. Sunday morning was quiet and so I took Dad for a walk. It was slow going but we both enjoyed it."

The third SHO joined us before the ward round. The young doctor was from Germany. She was over-weight almost straight from the medical school. Since graduation, she had only worked in a blood transfusion unit. It was therefore a hectic day for me. We however managed to complete our tasks on time.

Today's list was short but the high tension created by the senior consultant made it very long. He did not approve of drug trials on surgical patients. The younger consultant was one of the teams selected to carry a drug trial on patients with prostate cancer. The company involved was Imperial Commercial Industries (ICI). Being the registrar, I collected the data but was not paid for my troubles. Rightly or wrongly, I believed that I was learning to do research. I felt the same when not paid when I assisted him in his private practice. However, on occasions I felt it was a daylight robbery.

A CT (computerized tomography) scan of Dad's brain showed residual tumor. The option was to re-explore or go for radiotherapy. The girls decided against surgery. The treatment was delayed because of the breakdown of the x-ray machine. Things were not so bad, however, because the flat I got for them at the hospital was clean, spacious, and warm. This way we saved a lot of money and it removed the inconvenience of transporting him every day from Harrogate to Hull and back. After tennis, I resumed my French lessons.

My sister wrote me today, narrating the hard times at home. Not unexpectedly, she blamed me for her troubles. Over the years, I have learned that "it is virtually impossible to lose a relative in Sa Leone. They always find you."

According to the European Economic Community rules, citizens of member countries had to be employed first before all others. My present two German doctors fell into this category. Marion spoke little English and was very inexperienced. I was up most of the night managing patients with her. I was tired when I got into theatre and Mr. H was not to know that. I did let him know. I told him that unnecessary time was being spent on the new doctors.

One of my German doctors gave me a lift today to the outpatient clinic. She admitted to me that she was in a dilemma because she had limited experience and spoke little English. I reassured her that she would make it. "She was white and that the authorities are desperate for junior doctors. It was the wish of everybody, patients and health providers, to make NHS a white organization. However, what happens to the non-white? They go back home but this is only possible for the newcomers who knew where they came from."

Dad seemed to be more confused today, the end of a week's treatment, than usual. I did not think it was due to the treatment but rather ageing. Mom, who was four years younger, was not much help. Berns had told me before that it was a relationship that had existed for over thirty years—Mom commanded and Dad executed. We spent the cold days indoors. There was always a lot of food to eat. Berns was wonderful in fulfilling all her Mom's demands. This meant that she went to sleep instantly on getting into bed because of exhaustion.

I had an unexpected visitor today from ICI. Mr. Hobson was the coordinator of the prostate cancer trial drug. We went through the work I had done thus far. He was satisfied with my progress.

Before jumping into bed to write down the day's events, I watched a documentary on television. It was on the latter days of Dr. Martin Luther King's life. It seemed to suggest that injustices in the life of the modern black man continued. "Unfortunately, most of the troubles are due to the black man himself. I did not think this would change during my lifetime."

I received a letter today (March 16) from Port of Spain General Hospital (POSGH), Trinidad, offering me a summer attachment with Mr. Jorsling, a general surgeon. This was wonderful news. I would take the opportunity to get to know more people in the hospital.

The Catholics never stop amazing me. I narrated a story to Mom that I read from the newspaper. It was about the death of two British soldiers. A Catholic priest attempted to give mouth-to-mouth resuscitation to one of the dying men. They pushed the priest aside and shot the man in the head. "The priest should not have been there because the man was not Catholic," Mom remarked to me.

For the first time in Hull, I got held up by the bridges on my way from Harrogate. Numerous canals traversed Hull, which were still functional in transporting goods. The canals had overlying bridges, which swung, revolved, or rose. Each bridge took its time. They must be exciting to watch them as they went through their respective motions when one was not in a hurry.

I vented my feelings to Mr. H a few weeks ago, and the exercise may have paid off. He allowed me to do most of the procedures, including a nephrectomy. It was a successful day.

I had seen many changes in Dad. "He hates coming out of the house, probably because it is cold for him. He eats a lot and makes no effort to burn off the weight he had gained." I therefore made no resistance when one Sunday Berns suggested we went to the Lake District for the day. It was one of the remarkable places where man had utilized nature to its fullest. The landscape was breathtaking and it got you into the mood of relaxation. It was crowded with all sorts of people all up to something—just admiring nature's beauty, indulgence in water sports, walking, mountain climbing, and some like me, to find out what prompted Wordsworth to write his poetry. I hated poems in school. I learned them to pass exams without understanding their contents. Therefore, the outing achieved two things. Firstly, Dad changed and was out in the garden, often watering my plants. Secondly, I started reading Wordsworth poems again. They are now better appreciated having now understood his countryside.

I received a telephone call from AJM reminding me about the next Yorkshire Surgical Society meeting. It was being held in Leeds and my paper had been accepted for oral presentation. I gladly accepted the invitation because it could at least improve the volume or weight of my CV. In the meantime, Dad had his last cycle of radiotherapy.

Mr. N became ill, meaning that I was now in charge of his unit. Suddenly I was no longer under the control of Mr. H. Unfortunately they called me from all angles. Mr. N got himself involved with many things, like drug trials for malignant and benign prostatic diseases and bladder cancers. To keep me going, I went to the park every day at about 5:30 pm for some exercise. At the end of the day, writing my diary was difficult; I was tired. Indeed, I am now in total agreement with Wordsworth when he said that writing should be by inspiration rather than by demand.

George telephoned me today to say that Home Office had requested references from him on our behalf. We were being considered as British citizens by naturalization.

Dad had fully recovered and so they had gone back home. Cec had already left and was hard at work. We left London for Trinidad (TnT) on May 1 to evaluate job prospects for both Berns and myself. We set off late but arrived on time in Port of Spain. Cec, Mom, Andrea, and her three children were all there to receive us. The dry season was here as suggested by smoke, burning bush, and brown lawns. My first impression was that most of the fires were due to reckless cigarette smokers.

The following day I met with Mr. Jorsling and his registrar. I spent a lot of time with Mr. Pooran, both in and out of hospital. Berns had made the rounds in the Ministry of Health and the Caribbean Epidemiology Centre. Today marked the beginning of our third week in TnT. It had been a wonderful experience. Health for all by the year 2000 seemed an impossible dream for TnT. Life seemed to be cheap. The junior doctors worked under the most outrageous conditions. Except for interns, there were no on-call rooms. The nurses seemed to have no reason to kill themselves. There was little or no reward. The wards and departments were poorly equipped. It looked, therefore, that hospitals under the control of the ministry offered hardship to both the patients and health providers. "I did not think we should be in a hurry to come back. We must first improve our bank accounts and acquire more diplomas," I hinted to George on our return.

We spent the rest of our holiday driving around Trinidad. One of our drives took us down to Mayaro. It was the biggest beach I had visited so far. Glen and Siobhan came with us for the drive. It was a nice drive. En route, we bought fresh watermelons, mangoes, and seafood. In 1942, when Dad was a bachelor, his father advised him to invest in land close to the beach. He bought six acres of land. His papers were all in order but he could not locate the land physically.

Today was one of many public holidays in TnT. The many holidays resulted from the mixed community, each with its religious beliefs. Auntie Esther, the youngest of Mom's four sisters, developed bowel obstruction, which was due to colon cancer. I was able to contribute in the early diagnosis and treatment. The prognosis was bad, as the cancer had already spread to other parts of her abdominal cavity.

Few days later, she returned home. She was not short of support. She had two grown-up children and husband, all willing to support.

After a game of tennis, I went to see Andrea and her family. Barry was home, attending to his plants and the lawns. Also home were Glens, Shivy, and Gabby. I found Shivy quite a bright little girl. She helped her older brother to read. She offered me something to drink and properly tied my shoelaces. She was all smiles and never spoke out of turn. She was pretty.

We had a few more days to go back to England. My next task for these days was to clear the two empty lots next to the main building. Shrubs and elephant (razor) grass mainly covered both lands. There were some mature trees, including two mangoes, two coconuts, bananas, West Indian plum, and guava. We did well on the first day. After breakfast, we resumed from where we left off. I clipped the hedges while Dad put the final changes to what we did yesterday. We did another successful day's work but at the expense of my fingers, which had now become covered with blisters. I could hardly write afterwards. In mid-afternoon, we bought some citrus plants from one of the government farms to plant.

We were now back in Hull and I had three more months of the first one year to go. I had to decide whether to renew the contract or move on. I had to move on for two main reasons. I did not think I was getting to do many surgical procedures. No doubt, I saw a lot. Secondly, Bradford University accepted my proposal to do an M.Phil. degree on the same subject I presented at the last Yorkshire meeting. In the meantime, the *British Journal of Urology* accepted one of my two papers for publication.

Christmas was just around the corner with its attendant cold. Three children were staying with George in Buckden. Their father was once George's friend while he was in Nigeria. We invited all four of them to come for Christmas. The girl and one of the boys played tennis. We had fun at my newly discovered tennis court, abandoned behind one of the administrative buildings. Harrogate as stated before was a tourist city and a place where people retire. It was known for its shops, tea, and coffee bars and conference rooms, but not for sports.

Chapter 36

1989 in England

Berns appointed as District Medical Director. Offered the position of Senior Registrar in General Surgery in Port of Spain.

I had a year of my contract to go in Hull, but I wanted to move on. The New Year had arrived but there was nothing substantial in the pipeline. I had attended a few interviews but failed to secure any of them. One of the interviews stood out. I attended an interview in Mecclesfields for the position of post-fellowship training rotation that went through a professorial unit. They offered the job to a better-qualified surgeon. However, they asked me to stay behind for "a second interview." They gave me two reasons why I failed in the interview. Firstly, three of the candidates have nearly completed their master's thesis and I was far from mine. Secondly, one of my referees had not been fair to me.

Berns in the meantime had always been one step ahead of me. She was presently a consultant with a health district. She applied for the post of Director of Public Health in Airedale. Cec got through with her MRCP with little sweat. My next task was to get a job close to Bradford (to collect data for my study), Leeds (to work with AJM), and home to travel every day. Such a job arrived one month before the end of the first year of my contract.

The interview at Rochdale District Hospital in Lancashire went well. They wanted a registrar with experience in both general and urological surgeries. They assigned me to Mr. Mann (urology) and Mr. Humphreys (general) for the first six months. Also attached to each unit was a rotating senior registrar from Manchester, one SHO, and an intern. I started work in February. My previous experience made work here very easy. I had my own list but worked often with each consultant. To fill my time, I took on two more projects (in addition to my Bradford research). One study was on a case report and literature review, and the second involved a retrospective study of ruptured mycotic aneurysms in the district over ten years.

It took me just under two and a half hours to Bradford on M62 motorway and one hour to Harrogate. I had to be fit to maintain this workload successfully. My room overlooked two tennis courts. I took the opportunity to play with anybody who turned up on the courts. At other times, I wandered into town. At home, I worked in the garden to grow vegetables. This hectic schedule meant that I did not make full use of the social life in the hospital. They had a lively social club with a bar, table tennis, and a pool table. I guessed one could not have them all.

As the days went by, I continued to gain respect from my senior and junior colleagues. I had no difficulty with any of the staff members. I had always maintained that people go to work to make a living. Some honestly work hard for their earning while others do little or nothing for theirs. I normally put this latter group at arm's lengths. They blamed everyone else except themselves for not performing.

It was not too long when I had trouble in the data collection for the abdominal aneurysm. Records for the latter years were complete but not so for the earlier years. They kept the earlier ones on microfilms, which were poorly preserved. I had to befriend a lady from the medical records to help me retrieve the appropriate information. We worked hard once a week, followed by lunch. We made it in three months.

Back at home in Harrogate, we had to catch up with the spring. One of the attractions in Harrogate is flower gardens. Public lawns had different colourful flowers but exactly similar plant heights. We the residents attempted to bring the colours to our respective homes. Berns liked growing sweet peas but they were difficult to get rid of. They were like my Irish potatoes because they too reappeared the following year.

The end of my first six months in Rochdale was already on me. I had, however, analyzed the data I collected. It generated a lot of interest among the consultants and colleagues. The consultants were full of praise and encouraged other surgeons in training to do research. I was thankful and grateful. To me it was a trial run for the M.Phil. degree project.

For the degree course in Bradford, Dr. Valerie Randall was to be my internal supervisor and Mr. Alan Mearns as my external supervisor. In the first instance, I had to learn more about the computer. Berns and AJM came to my aid. My first investment was in a Sinclair Word Processor. The accompanying printer was just as heavy and cumbersome. Mrs. Elaine Beldone, the ever-helpful secretary at the Thoracic Department, kept all new x-rays and records for me. At the end of each weekend, I discussed my written work to both supervisors at their respective homes.

Wednesday was my on-call day. At 9 P.M., I sat down to write the operative findings of a three-hour surgery I had just completed. At the same time, I received a call from Berns. "Guess what?" she asked. After a few guesses I gave up. The Pan American Health Organization had offered her a position of medical epidemiologist, which would be based in Trinidad. She had applied for the post a year earlier and forgot about it. This was good news. This meant I had to renew my application to the Ministry of Health in Trinidad.

I had set myself to finish collecting the data for my thesis and was writing it up in the next three months. I turned down the renewal of my present contract for another year. It was a shame because I had my own operating list, which composed of general and urological procedures. I was confident that at least one of my three papers would be accepted for publication. Berns was settling down nicely in her new job as medical director of Airedale District Health Authority.

The summer was not too hot and the days were therefore ideal to work outdoors. This weekend Berns was away in a conference in New Castle upon Tyne. As I sat in my dearth chair in our back garden, I went into my occasional daydreaming, which went like this. "Suddenly we now have three options in our future lives. We could live and work in the UK. That will be unfair to our respective countries. We are not really wanted here anyway. Our second option is go to Sa Leone. The authorities have a job for me as clinician but not for Berns, who is a public health consultant. The position with our third option is now clearer. Somebody at the Ministry of Health in Port of Spain did not seem to appreciate the qualification of Berns (MB; MPH, DTMH, and MFCM). They offered her the position of District Medical Officer, equivalent to a General Practitioner (with MB)."

One month later, October 20, I received a telegraph from Port of Spain offering a post of senior registrar in Surgery at the Port of Spain General Hospital. Both of our jobs were due to start on February 3, 1990. "To finish writing my thesis, sell Berns' car, and get our house on the rent market meant working against the clock. Late-night visits to my supervisors became more frequent. Of course, our respective tasks in hospital went on as usual," noted in my diary.

Our departure date was set for January 15, 1990. Pickford, the removal company, came and packed our belongings within days. The men were professionals and I enjoyed making tea for them almost on the hour. Berns joined me, as we did for her theses, to print out the pages at the University printing room. Other panic-stricken students were around but orderly.

My supervisors had no time to have a final look at the work. I met my deadline and was relieved when finally submitted. All involved in the work were supportive and wished me the best.

Part Five
Trinidad

Chapter 37

1990 in Trinidad

July 27, 1990, marked the coup attempt in Trinidad and Tobago. My thesis for the M.Phil. degree accepted. We bought our own house.

I telephoned from the airport and apologized profusely to our tenants for leaving empty cardboard boxes on the lawn at the back. Although I asked him, Mr. Austin, to use part of the rent to pay for the clearance, he was not happy. We must have given them a bad impression. Unfortunately, we had run out of time. I promised myself to write as soon as we arrived in Trinidad.

The flight from Gatwick Airport to Washington was comfortable and enjoyable. We spent two weeks in Washington—the time used to get Berns orientated to her new job. The accommodation was spacious and had facilities for self-catering. On each day, I went on a conducted tour of the city or just took off and went for walks. I was enjoying myself for the both of us. The city was made of history and easy to get around. In many ways, it contrasted with London.

The next leg of our journey to Trinidad took us to Barbados. The accommodation was not comfortable and it was twice as expensive as in Washington. There were other doctors from the various islands. They were here for a one-week conference centred on the Montserrat volcanic eruption. I found myself extremely uneasy at the hotel because the proprietor followed me around with her eyes. When mentioned to other doctors, they all had something to say.

We finally made it to Trinidad. We arrived in the middle of the dry season as indicated by smoke and fire on the hillsides. The grass on my parents-in-laws' lawns were brown but alive. Accommodation was no problem; we stayed with Mom and Dad. We used Cec's car to move around and to travel to work and back.

On my first day at work, I reported to Dr. Winston Ince, who was the medical chief of staff. I was very impressed with him. He wanted to know how much tennis I played and urological work I had done before. The answers were all in the affirmative. The surgical department was made of four general surgical and one urological unit, each headed by a consultant.

I was anxious to do well in the job and willing to share my knowledge. However, at the end of three months, I did not feel welcome. There was a Society of Surgeons but I was never invited to join, although one of my colleagues was the secretary. When on call I spent most evenings in the common room. This made me available to assist all my junior doctors.

While in the common room one evening, I overhead that one of the junior doctors was in trouble managing a patient with a kidney abscess, a life-threatening condition. I volunteered to assist the doctor. The next day I was approached by the consultant of the unit, who told me, "My unit is not under your jurisdiction." I told him that all my post-graduate trainings had involved general and urological surgery. He asked me to furnish him with my CV and two references from my previous consultants. Within three weeks, three references from my previous consultants addressed to him arrived. I happily took my CV and the three letters to him but he directed me to the Ministry of Health on Sackville Street, Port of Spain, without even touching the envelopes.

I made a vegetable garden from a corner of Dad's plot. I had a good harvest of peanuts and sweet corn. Cassava, mainly for its leaves, was planted along the wall. The sweet potatoes were not as successful as the cassavas. I was more interested in their leaves to cook but they were devoured by hungry caterpillars. Dad and I planted various types of bananas and more citrus plants. I played tennis three times a week and once a month, I went out to sea with my tennis pal, Carlyle, to fish. My first outing was terrible. I took a lot of food and fluid while on board. When motion sickness got me, I brought up everything. I stuffed myself with anti-emetics during the subsequent trips.

The external examiners of my thesis requested I appear before them to defend my work. This was a good start because it was not rejected outright. The interview was due in two weeks, which I attended. I was to resubmit after some alterations and corrections. I challenged myself to finishing it by the end of the year.

During our acute emergency cover, I noticed that many of the hospital admissions had no justification to be there. However, there was no published work to support this. I decided to test the hypothesis. Having written the protocol, I discussed it with my wife, an epidemiologist, and Mr. Michael Spinks, a statistician. They agreed to join in. Over the following three months, I saw all patients admitted to the wards during our twenty-four-hour on-call berth. The study showed that over 60 percent of hospital admissions were avoidable. We presented our findings in a paper entitled "Avoidable Hospital Admissions" at the first TnT Research Council meeting. The Ministry of Health showed interest in the paper some five years later through the late Dr. Angela Boyd-Patrick. The majority of our hospital admissions now came through the District Health Centres. This was a wonderful move in the right direction.

On June 5, my wife's birthday, I received a note from AJM to tell me that our paper, "CT Guided Biopsy of Lung Tumour," had been accepted for publication in the *Journal of the Royal College of Surgeons* of Edinburgh.

Berns had to do many duty travels over the Caribbean Islands and I stayed on to work in hospital and look for a home. For six months of hunting, I finally discovered one north of POS. The land space was about half an –acre— ideal for producing my own foods (vegetables, fruits, fish, and eggs). I collected Berns from the airport at 9 P.M. and she would not go home until she looked at the location of our new home. She fell in love with the spot almost instantly.

All was going fine until one Friday afternoon, July 27, 1990. A group of men staged a coup d'etat at the Red House, the House of Parliament. I wrote an article ("It Helps to Remember Faces," Br Med J 1990; 301: 1468 - 9) about the episode. "It was a raining season but the day was dry, sunny, bright, and there was not a cloud in the sky." At about 6 P.M. the weather in Port of Spain changed suddenly into "Black Friday." My SHO and I had just completed amputating a non-salvageable right forearm of a twenty-five-year-old woman. "While we were dressing the stump the theatre sister walked into the operating theatre and in her usual joking manner announced that the television and radio stations had been seized by the Jamaat Al Muslimeen (group of Moslems) people." All of us present burst out laughing but she just smiled and left the theatre. However, within an hour she was proven right over the national radio and television stations.

I went home immediately to get ready for a possible influx of casualties based on my Bradford experience. "At 11:30 P.M. I had a telephone call from my senior house officer requiring my help in hospital, as many injured people had been brought in from the station." An ambulance collected me. "The driver took us through an unmanned barricade with a 'NO ENTRY' sign. I did not protest and wrongly assumed that he had previous arrangements with the appropriate authorities. Suddenly, a man appeared from the dark and flagged the van to stop, and within minutes we were surrounded by about twenty men in plain clothes with guns and knives. There was no leader and everybody gave orders. The driver and his mate had identification cards with them but I had none, only my stethoscope. My captors immediately assumed that I had kidnapped the other two men." I was ordered out of the van and to lie down with my hands behind my head at gunpoint.

"As my life flashed before me, I recognized one of the policemen, who had been a patient in one of our wards. I seized the opportunity and said to him, 'You're the man we treated with gunshot wounds about two months ago on Ward 14. Don't you remember your surgeon?' Indeed the man recognized my face and apologized for the rough handling. I was helped to my feet and allowed to get back into the ambulance. Remembering a face had helped to save my life.

"On Wednesday, five days into the siege, news came through that the hostages had all been released unconditionally." The effects that this coup attempt had on the already overstretched medical services have yet to be calculated. The nation remained in the dark because no official enquiry had been established to investigate the reason(s) for the coup attempt.

I refer to this coup because it reminded me of the Bradford fire disaster. In both situations, it was remarkable to see the willingness of the community to work together in the time of suffering.

It was after this event that my diary writing became erratic and inconsistent.